No Power Without an Image

No Power Without an Image

Icons Between Photography and Film

Libby Saxton

EDINBURGH
University Press

Edinburgh University Press is one of the leading university presses in
the UK. We publish academic books and journals in our selected subject
areas across the humanities and social sciences, combining cutting-
edge scholarship with high editorial and production values to produce
academic works of lasting importance. For more information visit our
website: edinburghuniversitypress.com

Edinburgh University Press Ltd
The Tun – Holyrood Road
12(2f) Jackson's Entry
Edinburgh EH8 8PJ

First published in ardback by Edinburgh University Press 2020

Typeset in 11/13 Adobe Garamond Pro
IDSUK (DataConnection) Ltd, and
printed and bound by CPI Group (UK) Ltd,
Croydon, CR0 4YY

A CIP record for this book is available from the British Library

ISBN 978 1 4744 6315 7 (hardback)
ISBN 978 1 4744 6316 4 (paperback)
ISBN 978 1 4744 6317 1 (webready PDF)
ISBN 978 1 4744 6318 8 (epub)

Contents

Figures

Acknowledgements

This book emerged out of a collaborative research project with Guy Westwell and Jeremy Hicks on iconic images of political violence. My first debt is to them, for coming up with the idea of exploring the relation between the iconic, the photographic and the filmic, and for the illuminating conversations which, along with their articles on the subject, sparked many of the thoughts in the following pages. The project began with a symposium at Queen Mary University of London on 15 June 2013 and led to the co-authored dossier 'Rising Flags, Falling Soldiers: Film, Icons and Political Violence', *Screen*, 57: 3 (2016). I am grateful to the fascinating speakers at the symposium, to the anonymous readers of the dossier, for their insightful feedback, and to *Screen* for allowing me to include here a revised and expanded version of my essay ('The Falling Soldier and Film', pp. 353–61).

My next debt is to Gillian Leslie, the Senior Commissioning Editor for Film Studies at Edinburgh University Press, for her positive and encouraging feedback and generous assistance and advice. I am deeply grateful to the editors of the series 'Edinburgh Studies in Film and Intermediality', Martine Beugnet and Kriss Ravetto, for their attentive reading of and detailed comments on the manuscript, which have enriched it. Similarly, the two anonymous readers commissioned by the Press made astute suggestions and alerted me to several discussions of icons in photography theory that I had overlooked; I owe them a huge debt of thanks too. I would also like to acknowledge Ian Brooke's careful copy-editing of the manuscript.

Aude Raimbault, Head of Collections at the Fondation Henri Cartier-Bresson in Paris, kindly sent me a dossier of archival material relating to his film *Le Retour* (*The Return*, 1945). Toby Haggith, Senior Curator in the Second World War team at the Imperial War Museum London, also generously provided a rich set of resources and reflections. I thank Queen Mary for awarding me the two periods of sabbatical leave in which much of the research for this book was completed. I am grateful to my colleagues in the Department of Film Studies, particularly Janet Harbord and Sue Harris for their help and encouragement with the project over several years in their roles as departmental Research Leads and mentors. Conversations with Lucy

Bolton, Jenny Chamarette, Lisa Downing, Anat Pick and Kiera Vaclavik about photographs, film stars and icons sacred and secular have helped to shape the project and keep me going; their writing has been a source of inspiration and Lucy also thoughtfully gave me relevant books. I am grateful to Emily Watson, Katie Watson, Paul Stubbings and Colleen Cotter for advice on the eclectic subjects of icon theology, military terminology, Andy Warhol and iconic photographs from the United States respectively. For helping in a variety of important ways, I also thank Claire Boyle, Alice Hall, Oliver Kenny, Susannah Miller, Isabel Rocamora, Viki Walden, my sister Ruth Saxton and my parents, Pat and Owen Saxton. My biggest debt is to my partner, Chris Darke, for alerting me to all sorts of relevant films and literature, discussing the book's ideas, reading the manuscript carefully and providing practical and emotional support.

Introduction

By the early 1980s, discussion of the 'icon' was flourishing within photography theory. The Greek term *eikôn* from which this word derives 'comes from the verb *eikô*, which [. . .] properly means: "I am similar"', clarified the Christian patriarch and philosopher Nikephoros at the height of the Byzantine controversy over the legitimacy of images.[1] At stake in this eighth- and ninth-century philosophical and political crisis was the relation of images to each other and the power they confer on their controller. While the icon became 'a sacred painting or sculpture', wrote the photography critic Vicki Goldberg in 1991, 'today the word extends to secular images [. . .]. I take secular icons to be representations that inspire some degree of awe – perhaps mixed with dread, compassion, or aspiration – and that stand for an epoch or a system of beliefs.' Photographs make particularly good icons, Goldberg went on, because they both 'specifically represent their subjects and easily acquire symbolic significance'.[2] As well as 'symbol' I use the related term 'emblem' because it can mean a kind of image: a picture of an object 'representing symbolically an abstract quality, an action, a class of persons, *et cetera*'.[3] Since Goldberg's intervention, 'icon' has continued to refer to a handful of photographs which through frequent reproduction have come to sum up a significant event, such as a war, disaster or revolt, and related ideas, and arouse powerful emotions. Replacing labels such as 'historical stereotype', the designation 'icon' quickly caught on in popular discourse on images and now regularly adds an accent to the titles of collections of photographs in books or online archives.[4] Sometimes, the adjective 'iconic' applies not only to a selection of pictures but also – further stretching the word's meaning – to the photographers who took them.[5] In the same era, a growing pile of scholarly monographs dedicated to an individual photograph have at once investigated and reinforced their cultural status as icons. For example, the photograph of the small boy under armed guard in the Warsaw Ghetto (1943), Hocine Zaourar's image of the grieving Oum Saâd, who European newspapers misleadingly nicknamed the 'Madonna of Bentalha' (1997), and most recently Robert Capa's so-called 'Falling Soldier' (1936) have all had their iconic credentials confirmed in this way.[6] A slew of essays and occasional book-length studies have meanwhile attempted to define the shared properties of photographs picked out as either national or universal icons. The concept has also provided a curatorial rationale for photography exhibitions, such as Audrey Leblanc and Dominique Versavel's display of 'Icônes de mai 68' (Icons of May 68), which marked the fiftieth anniversary of the uprising (Bibliothèque nationale de France, 17 April–26 August 2018), and an editorial criterion for books and catalogues appended to them.

Photographs have also played a crucial role in the creation of another, overlapping kind of icon. As well as a small class of celebrated stills and occasionally their creators, the term has broadened to denote renowned figures who encapsulate widely shared ideals. The icons considered by global media studies scholar Bishnupriya Ghosh, for example, in her inspiring study of popular visual culture, are Mother Teresa, Arundhati Roy and Phoolan Devi: 'highly visible public figures whose symbolically dense images and lives circulate at high speeds [. . .]'.[7] Ghosh coins the term 'bio-icon' to emphasise the way in which the icon's '"life story", the formalized *bios*' shapes the 'powerful sign' that she constitutes.[8] The icons discussed in Ghosh's book and other recent reconsiderations of the phenomenon, then, consist of flesh and blood, but reinforce the etymology of the word by manifesting as images. Even in accounts such as Ghosh's which track the passage of icons through 'transnational (televisual, cinematic, print, oral and digital) media networks' and insist on their intermediality, photographs, as we shall see, occupy a central place.[9]

That photographs are 'instantly convertible into a symbol' and possess a distinctive capacity to 'contain' and 'compress [. . .] events or ideologies', as Goldberg suggested, is not the only reason why they receive special attention in many recent reappraisals of icons.[10] They are also more likely to linger in our minds and physical environs than moving images. Pictures of the Vietnam War brought this difference home to viewers in Europe and the United States. Although documentary footage from the war zone regularly flooded television screens, it was often photographs, encountered in newspapers, magazines, cinema newsreels or TV news broadcasts, that people remembered. The photographer and sociologist Gisèle Freund singled out one of these images in the conclusion to the history of the medium she published in 1974. *Life* had already selected the photograph of the young Phan Thi Kim Phúc (Nick Ut, 1972) screaming in fear and pain after having ripped off her napalm-drenched clothes as one of its 'pictures of the year', exemplifying the power of magazine editors in the middle decades of the twentieth century to determine which images would become icons.[11] Freund validated this choice by noting simply that this image, which 'painfully symbolises war', 'will remain forever engraved in the memories of those who have seen it'.[12] Perhaps she was thinking of this photograph, which depicts a scene also recorded by a television crew, when she observed, as reported by the filmmaker Teri Wehn-Damisch, that 'it's always the still image and not the one in motion that stays etched in our minds, becoming ever after part of our collective memory'.[13]

The quality of indelibility that Freund and other writers including Susan Sontag attributed to a handful of photographs of Vietnam in the early 1970s derived not only from their traumatic subject matter but also from the way they physically hung around in spaces that people lived in or routinely passed through. Since the late 1920s, which witnessed the emergence of a new breed of abundantly illustrated magazine in Europe that *Life* would go on to emulate, the still photojournalistic image had lingered on tables in homes and waiting rooms.[14] This paper artefact provided a material connection to memory with which the fugitive images of cinema newsreels and, from the 1950s, television news could not compete. The rise of what we now call the photo-icon during the twentieth century depended on its repetition in newspapers and particularly magazines, which let readers grasp hold of, pore over and revisit images they favoured or which haunted them.[15] The publication that at the end of 1972 lent institutional backing to the iconisation of the photograph of Kim Phúc, the last of *Life*'s 1,864 issues, also marked the end of this era.

Yet the very same magazines that had a key part in creating the iconic photograph and gave it a durable form modelled themselves in crucial ways, especially in the 1930s, on cinema. One of the most important was the French weekly *Vu*, the first title to publish Capa's 'Falling Soldier', in an issue which also contained, tucked away on a later page, a diminutive copy of another future icon, Dorothea Lange's 'Migrant Mother' (1936).[16] *Vu* and other illustrated magazines that sprang up in interwar France imitated the motion pictures by seeking out dynamic images, such as those photojournalists were producing with the new, lightweight Leica, and arranging them in stories that dramatised movement. Publications such as *Vu* and *Life* also juxtaposed photojournalistic icons in the making with film stills, that is, photographs taken on sets during film production, and occasionally film frames, also known as photogrammes (the separate images that make up a piece of film). Memorable news photos mixed in these magazines with still pictures that, as the film theorist Laura Mulvey has discussed, enabled film fans to remember and physically hold onto 'precious moments, images and, most particularly, [. . .] idols' in spite of the ephemerality of the cinematic experience.[17] Mulvey intervenes here in the debate about stillness and movement that has persisted in cinema studies since the 1970s and which has fuelled interest in the circulation of film still photography.

Taking its cue from this culture of what has been called 'paper cinema', this book aims to contribute to the debate about iconic images by exploring what the filmic can tell us about photographs in this genre. What does cinema's replacement of painting in the 1930s as photography's principal 'interlocutor', in Dominique Baqué's terms, have to do with the emergence of the photo-journalistic icon?[18] What insights do magazines inspired by cinema provide into this category of image? What role has the photojournalistic icon played in film publicity and how does it relate to the iconic status of the film star? How did developments in documentary filmmaking and cinema newsreels and the rise of television news, which competed at once with its filmic equivalent and with illustrated magazines, affect the production and circulation of the iconic image? What can we learn about the iconic from the double lives of some of the twentieth century's defining photographs as sequences filmed in motion for cinema or TV? Why did fiction, historical and essay films and videos incorporate and rework iconic photographs and film footage with particular frequency from the 1960s to the 1980s? Why have such photographs and the concept of the icon intrigued film critics and theorists since the late 1960s? And how can cinema elucidate the relation between the photojournalistic icon, political violence and popular movements for social change? This book attempts to answer these questions by re-examining seven iconic photographs associated with mid-twentieth-century instances of war and political contestation, sometimes in the light of related documentary footage, most of which has had less scholarly attention: the 'Falling Soldier'; the 'Gestapo Informer' and the film *Le Retour* (*The Return*; both by Henri Cartier-Bresson, 1945); stills of Thich Quang Duc's self-immolation (Malcolm Browne, 1963) and newsreel of Ho Dinh Van and other Vietnamese Buddhists protesting in the same way; two pictures of Ernesto (Che) Guevara (by Alberto Korda, 1960 and Freddy Alborta, 1967) and television images of his corpse; and the 'Marianne of '68' (Jean-Pierre Rey, 1968). The rest of this introduction explains further the scholarly and theoretical debates to which these historical case studies aim to contribute, and then sets out my rationale for choosing to focus on these images.

Icons Between Photography and Film

This section explores in more detail why icons have attracted fresh attention in recent decades and why the single fixed image, rather than the moving image sequence, has been – explicitly and implicitly – central to this debate. The remarks by Goldberg cited above echoed the philosopher Patrick Maynard's claim, in a fuller discussion of the topic, that the photograph 'often functions as [the West's] secular "icon"'.[19] In an article published in 1983, Maynard proposes that religious icons can illuminate the particular 'historical *functions*' of photography.[20] He stages his inquiry as an 'heuristic dialogue' between three female interlocutors. One of them, Veronica, argues that photographs and icons both belong to a broader class of image 'whose *function* is largely that of manifesting [as opposed to merely describing or illustrating] what it depicts'.[21] The 'manifestation image' provides a 'sense of presence' and 'contact'.[22] This category encompasses both the Western relic and the Eastern icon: the seeming manifestation of presence by holy images painted by human hand 'is made possible by' icons that are 'allegedly acheiropoietic, appearing either by emanation or by direct printing from the original', such as the Turin Shroud.[23] This is why, suggests Veronica (whose significant name derives from 'vera icona', meaning 'true image', and also refers to a cloth on which Christ is supposed to have left an impression of his face), 'the Byzantines should have invented photography; they would have understood it better!'[24] Maynard's text extends a strand of scholarship that draws analogies with icons in order to offer deeper insights into photography.

The Shroud affords a material link between Maynard's dialogue and another philosophical account of images published just over a decade later, which provides one of the most significant recent reassessments of the icon. Marie-José Mondzain's *Image, icône, économie* (*Image, Icon, Economy*, 1996) traces the source of our 'contemporary imaginary' in the West to the distinction between the invisible image and the visible icon proposed by Christian philosophers to defend the Church against the charge of idolatry during the 'iconoclastic crises' that rocked eighth- and ninth-century Byzantium. Like W. J. T. Mitchell's *Iconology: Image, Text, Ideology* (1986), another vital and more often cited resource for icon studies, Mondzain's book tracks the struggle between detractors and defenders of images.[25] While Mitchell concentrates on image theory since the late eighteenth century, Mondzain's primary sources are manuscripts from the era of the Byzantine disputes. Nevertheless, one of her chapters turns out to be about photography. The controversy over the Shroud, which photographs enflamed, illustrates the persistent modern implications of the early polemics. In contrast to Maynard, Mondzain stresses the link between images and institutional power. The Church's celebration of photographs of the surviving relic reminds her of the rehabilitation of the icon which, over a millennium before, had paved the way for the same imperially ambitious institution to exploit the symbolic power of images.[26] In the words of the title of my book, which I have borrowed from *Image, icône, économie*, 'no power without an image'.[27] Mondzain explains: 'to attempt to rule over the whole world by organizing an empire that derived its power and authority by linking together the visual and the imaginal was Christianity's true genius'.[28] The ecclesiastical establishment, she argues, recruited photography to this project. In 1898, when two long exposures revealed on the Shroud a human outline invisible to the naked eye, believers began to attribute the miraculous nature of the acheiropoietic icon to the camera image.

As one such commentator quoted by Mondzain puts it, 'a photograph is not a portrait made by human hand'.[29] While Maynard construes the photograph and the acheiropoietic icon as separate examples of the same kind of image, then, Mondzain recounts the emergence of 'the fantasy of an acheiropoietic photography'.[30]

The analogies drawn by Maynard and Mondzain between photographs and Christian effigies not only foreshadow my discussions (in Chapters 1, 3 and 4) of journalistic images of a Spanish militiaman, Vietnamese self-immolators and an Argentinian revolutionary that revive the religious connotations of the word 'icon'. Mondzain's claim that 'we are today the heirs and propagators' of the 'iconic empire' envisaged by early Christian thinkers who first licensed 'the process of globalizing the image' also resonates with my consideration of the relationship between these globetrotting pictures and twentieth-century varieties of imperialism.[31] While Mondzain incorporates photography into an analysis of 'iconocracy', her term for 'the question of the empire of the gaze and vision', Robert Hariman and John Louis Lucaites, scholars of rhetoric and public culture, are drawn to the same medium by its affinity with democracy.[32] Their intricate landmark study (2007) frames the iconic photograph as the 'signature work' of photojournalism, 'a characteristically democratic art'.[33] Icons, they explain, 'are doing more than reproducing a structure of power'. Challenging the 'iconoclasm' of influential approaches to the media, such as ideology critique, Hariman and Lucaites argue that iconic photographs 'demonstrate how photojournalism underwrites democratic polity', while warning that those of US public culture 'increasingly underwrite liberalism more than they do democracy'.[34] My book draws inspiration from Hariman and Lucaites's attention to 'common resources for political action on behalf of the common good' while tracking the circulation of iconic images beyond liberal democracies.[35]

Rather than the capacity of icons to endorse democracy, Ghosh concentrates on their 'potentialities as a catalyst for social change'.[36] Like Mondzain, one of her interlocutors, Ghosh underlines the relevance of the Byzantine contexts when 'icons came to be extraordinarily powerful instruments of ecclesiastical politics' to contemporary 'iconoclashes'.[37] As illustrated by the early ninth-century text *Antirrhetics* by Patriarch Nikephoros (which Mondzain translated into French), the icon has a 'dangerous potential to bind affect to hegemonic political projects'.[38] But Ghosh distinguishes her approach from the iconoclasm that Mitchell's *Iconology*, another of her sources, has influentially tracked by highlighting 'the social transformations made possible through collective acts of icon adoration or desecration'.[39] Like American studies scholar and art historian Nicole R. Fleetwood's 'racial icons', who include Trayvon Martin, Diana Ross and Serena Williams, the *Global Icons* (2011) whose worship and vilification Ghosh investigates are public figures, as noted earlier, rather than camera images.[40] Nevertheless, her study accords a prominent place to photographs. For example, it opens by evoking the capture in 1983 of Phoolan Devi, 'India's most famous bandit queen', an event immortalised in a photo that 'found iteration everywhere: in news stories, on television, and in posters for [Shekhar] Kapur's film [about her life]'.[41] In this respect, there is some overlap between Ghosh's global icon and historian Jeremy Prestholdt's 'icon of dissent' (2019), a concept which unites the archaic sense of 'image' with the meaning of 'celebrity' that 'icon' began to acquire in the nineteenth century. The iconic figures discussed by Prestholdt – Che Guevara, Bob Marley, Tupac Shakur and Osama bin Laden – '[are] thus a synthesis of person, image, and mythos'.[42]

Just as germane to the approach I develop in this book is the critical role that Ghosh's research grants to movement. When she characterises the icon as a 'moving technology', she is not suggesting that it appears to move in the manner of a film or video image.[43] Rather, she is alluding to the often apparently magical force that it exerts on its devotee, which a semiotic approach to the icon as a sign cannot adequately explain.[44] 'The force of icons', she writes, 'lies in the hydraulic "pull" of an embodied encounter [. . .].'[45] Scholars in different fields, Ghosh points out, have divergent understandings of what icons 'pull' us towards. 'For some, icons move us toward a greater truth or divinity, while for others, the icon plunges us into nature. But the icon always opens to an elsewhere – to the chaos of vibrant matter.'[46] In Ghosh's account, which is influenced by feminist theories of matter and corporeal dynamism, icons 'can mobilize the affective transfers necessary for moving subjects towards a larger social network'.[47] Her model of the icon as a 'technology', rather than sign, capable of mobilising people to work together for social change particularly informs my discussion, in Chapter 4, of cinematic explorations of Guevara's historical capacity to set crowds in motion.

As Ghosh reminds us through her engagement with star theory, on which my chapters on Guevara and the 'Marianne of '68' draw too, cinema studies has also discussed iconicity. But the story of an anonymous figure, rather than a star, provides a more fitting place to conclude this brief survey of some of the most incisive recent accounts of icons and directly anticipates my concern with the relationship between photography and cinema. In *La Voie des images* (*The Way of Images*, 2013), film historian Sylvie Lindeperg chronicles the elevation to iconic status of an image of a young girl in a headscarf.[48] This is not a photograph. The picture comes from rushes for an unfinished film shot from March to May 1944 in a transit camp at Westerbork in the occupied Netherlands, and directed by the Jewish prisoner Rudolf Breslauer on the orders of the camp's commander, a member of the SS. A rare close-up frames the girl in the doorway to a cattle wagon which would deport her to Auschwitz-Birkenau. Lindeperg movingly describes the exceptional qualities that made this shot susceptible to iconisation: it 'contains the historical event, gathers it all up in a facial expression, seizes it in the singular, unique and non-interchangeable moment when the gaze of the child encounters that of the camera operator'.[49] Established as a symbol of the Shoah by the early 1960s, the image mutated into an emblem of the genocide carried out against the Roma and Sinti communities after a journalist discovered her identity in 1994.[50] In a passage that cites photography criticism and provides an important precedent for my project, Lindeperg explores the iconicity of Settela Steinbach in terms of stillness and movement. It is not just that her picture has circulated as much in fixed as in animated form.[51] Lindeperg also draws attention to Steinbach's stillness in the moving image: 'in this unique shot, the filmmaker meets the photographer'. Breslauer creates 'a perfect *cine-photograph* (*ciné-photographie*), a pure moment of eternity'.[52]

No Power Without an Image

This book builds on Lindeperg's writing on the iconic 'cine-photograph' of Steinbach.[53] As well as engaging with icon theory, it draws on a range of philosophical and theoretical reconsiderations since the 1970s of the relationship between photography and cinema, and of the confluence of still and moving images.[54] I seek to show how icons yield a novel way of thinking about stasis and motion and, in so doing, to develop a methodology that readers can use to consider other iconic images and the moments they render historical. In the era of the digital, as Laurent Guido and Olivier Lugon point out, 'it is as though still images have become but a subcategory of animation, a transitional situation whose inevitable transformation is a click away'.[55] The notions of the icon and the index developed by the philosopher and mathematician Charles Sanders Peirce in the late nineteenth century have resurfaced, as Annette Kuhn and Guy Westwell note, 'in the recent revival of debates, in the wake of the digital revolution in cinema, around the sign-referent relation'.[56] However, this is not a book about digital images. It contributes instead to the growing body of literature that looks back to past interactions between photography and film.[57] I turn now to the interplay between these media and the intertwined histories of writing on the still/moving relation, icon study, and political struggle as I continue to sketch out the contexts in which the book places its primary corpus of images.

Each of my chapters centres on one or two iconic photographs and pieces of film that resemble them. The order in which I address these images broadly corresponds to the chronology of their elevation into icons. The seven stills discussed in detail span an era that began with photojournalism's incorporation of fine-grain 35mm film stock and the emergence and proliferation of dynamically illustrated magazines, and ran until the late 1960s, when photo-icons increasingly coexisted as pieces of film recorded for cinema or television. For example, whereas the 'Gestapo Informer', like the 'Falling Soldier', typically illustrates the power to capture the 'decisive instant' that distinguishes photography from cinema and Alborta's iconic picture of Guevara's corpse is often compared to paintings, I focus on the double lives led by these stills as moving images.

Like Cartier-Bresson's photograph, which was first used to illustrate film reviews, Capa's began its public life shortly after its creation in a form of the 'paper cinema' pioneered by French magazines. By the 1960s, however, it had evolved into a fixed tableau whose reappropriation began to disrupt filmic motion. The apparent reference in *La Jetée* (*The Pier*; Chris Marker, 1962) to the 'Falling Soldier' coincided with the multiplication of photographic 'forms' that Raymond Bellour identifies in cinema at the start of this decade.[58] Scholars including Bellour, Garrett Stewart and Amy Rust have explored the evocation by the photographs, freeze-frames and other kinds of stasis that penetrated films during the 1960s and early 1970s of the fatal and the apocalyptic.[59] These accounts provide useful frameworks, I suggest, for thinking about the cinematic afterlives not only of Capa's snapshot, but also of still and moving images of Quang Duc's and Dinh Van's protests by immolation and of Guevara's corpse.

In the early 1960s, pop art also began to use news pictures to 'create its own iconography of disaster', as Georges Didi-Huberman reminds us in a recent exploration of the paintings, sculptures and filmic moments echoed in another iconic photograph.[60] The convergence of tendencies in advertising, revolutionary iconography and popular fashion during the 1960s also plays a vital role in Prestholdt's history of the iconic resonance of figures of dissent.[61] According to the art and photography historian André Gunthert, it was under the influence of pop culture (including posters of film and music stars), as well as news coverage of the war in Vietnam and the revolt of students and workers in France in 1968, that photographs began to acquire iconic distinction.[62] Referring to the framing of images in *Life*'s issue of 26 December 1969, Gunthert underlines the significance of this 'veritable mutation in the cultural status of photojournalistic images, where the perception of a change in historical regime, the memory of the defeat of Vietnam and the horizon of pop culture were superimposed'.[63] My first three chapters argue that the 'Falling Soldier', the 'Gestapo Informer' and images of Quang Duc and Dinh Van foreshadow this shift by attaining iconic stature in earlier eras. However, several of the images on which this book concentrates emblematise the moment Gunthert identifies as pivotal: not only the 'Marianne', photographed during a demonstration in Paris in May 1968, but also the pictures of Guevara dead that travelled around the world at the end of 1967, and Korda's portrait of the 'Heroic Guerrilla', which gained prominence in the wake of the revolutionary's death and became an international symbol in the following year's protest movements.

At the same time, photography theory was becoming increasingly interested in the concept of the icon, though this term did not yet designate a special class of historical images. For example, in a critique in 1970 of the view that images naturally resemble the reality they represent, as encapsulated in Peirce's notion of the iconic sign, Umberto Eco emphasises the cultural or conventional dimension of photographs: 'we know that sensory phenomena are *transcribed*, in the photographic emulsion, in such a way that even if there is a causal link with the real phenomena, the graphic images formed can be considered as wholly arbitrary with respect to these phenomena'.[64] Nevertheless, Frank Webster insists on the 'special relevance' of the iconic mode of signification in his analysis of the 'new photography' that emerged in the wake of the uprisings of 1968 'as symptomatic of a polemic against anachronistic conservatism'.[65] The 'backbone' of this movement was 'student rebellion', the subject of the photo-icon examined in the final chapter of this book, the whole of which shares Webster's concern with the political consequences of the creation and transmission of images.[66] It is to 'the iconic quality' not of exceptional images, however, but of photographs in general, especially those encountered in the news, that Webster attributes their capacity to 'signify at least initially with a particular power', even though they can quickly turn into symbols.[67] In the immediate aftermath of 1968, Eco's essay appeared in the film journal *Cinemantics*, alongside notes by Peter Wollen, who was applying the tools of semiotics to cinema. In an influential text published in 1969, Wollen suggests that film theory has neglected the iconic aspect of signs. André Bazin's and Christian Metz's discussions of film aesthetics, read by Wollen as prioritising the index and symbol respectively, do not account for the full range of film language.[68] Just as pertinent to cinema is the 'most labile' sign in Peirce's second trichotomy, which pulls depiction 'towards the antinomic poles of photography and emblematics'; 'both these undercurrents are co-present in the iconic sign'.[69] Wollen associates this sign with the pictorial and painterly dimensions of cinema. The philosopher Gilles Deleuze, also drawing on Peirce, would redefine it in the 1980s, with reference to cinematic close-ups, as 'the set [. . .] of the affect and the face', as I will discuss in Chapter 3.[70] As we have seen, however, the photographic 'undercurrent' would also receive sustained attention in this decade's debates about the icon.

In the period between Wollen's and Deleuze's interventions, cinema studies began to think in detail about stillness, as film and media theorist Eivind Røssaak has charted, including that of photojournalistic images.[71] Before 'icons', era-defining pictures of this kind were sometimes denounced as 'stereotypes', as mentioned earlier, or 'clichés', aptly in view of the damaging assumptions they often promote about gender and race. (More recently, in a similar vein, the artist Pascal Convert has described them suggestively as 'déjà vu imagery'.[72]) They are censured in these terms in at least one of the cluster of essays on photography that *Cahiers du cinéma* published in 1976. The cover of the journal's July–August issue announces this theme by magnifying the central figure of the later of the two iconic photographs of Quang Duc enshrouded by flames. This magazine reproduces and castigates as commodities several of the photo-icons mentioned in this book. Others on which I focus, including several iterations of the 'Heroic Guerrilla', recur in a television programme broadcast the same summer, in which Jean-Luc Godard and Anne-Marie Miéville deploy the tools of semiotics and video to attack photojournalism's economy. Several of my chapters engage with these early commentaries on the genre of the iconic photograph, as well as Wehn-Damisch's and Freund's photo-cinematic dialogue about this class of image in the documentary *Photographie et société: d'après Gisèle Freund* (*Photography and Society: According to Gisèle Freund*, 1983).

While the book engages in particular detail with French debates about images, it traces the journeys of its primary corpus of icons through space as well as time. It tracks them from their origins in Spain, Germany, Vietnam, Cuba, Bolivia and France into magazines, cinemas, television news broadcasts, art exhibitions and museums in France, Sweden, the UK, Australia, the US, Canada, Cuba and Argentina where they also gained iconic resonance. Chapter 4 and the Epilogue also discuss the global reach of icons, drawing on Ghosh's research into this phenomenon. The book does not aim to construct comprehensive accounts of the travels of the images on which it focuses or of their roles in film history but to explore in depth some of their most revealing recurrences.

The remainder of this introduction summarises each chapter's contribution to my filmic reassessment of the photo-icon. Commentators have often considered Capa's snapshot of a Loyalist militiaman collapsing on a Spanish battlefield on 5 September 1936 to epitomise the photograph's distinctive capacity to capture exceptional instants that in recent decades have been called 'iconic'. Chapter 1 explores instead how this image transitioned between photography and cinema for the first half-century of its life. The chapter examines its depiction of motion and time and traces appropriations of it by the 'paper cinema' of magazine 'picture stories' and, from the 1960s to the 1980s, by films from the sci-fi, war and documentary genres and scholars who usually write about moving images. These remediations of the 'Falling Soldier' in France, the US, the UK and Australia reveal shifts in form and meaning that conventional accounts of it, centred on photography, have overlooked. I argue that it evolved from a moving image into a frozen one and from an emblem of meaningful sacrifice into a template for meditations on intense violence and apocalyptic destruction. The cinematic career of the 'Falling Soldier' has also problematically affirmed maleness and whiteness as somatic norms in conflating heroic gestures with cruciform poses.

Chapter 2 builds on recent research into Cartier-Bresson's parallel work in photography and cinema. The relationship between his photos of interrogations of alleged collaborators in a camp for displaced persons in Dessau, Germany, in June 1945, and moving pictures of these scenes in his documentary *Le Retour*, warrants reconsideration from the perspective of iconic image studies. One of these snapshots, which portrays a former deportee exploding with rage at a woman she accuses of informing on her, recurs in collections of photo-icons and has come to epitomise the 'decisive moment'. Drawing on Didi-Huberman's analysis of another iconic photograph, the chapter seeks precedents for Cartier-Bresson's, which pulsates with the anger of liberated deportees, in depictions of gesturing female bodies in Renaissance art.[73] I then examine how *Le Retour*'s animated crowds elide differences between forced labourers, prisoners of war and survivors of the concentration and death camps, helping us situate the photograph in the context of efforts to reunify France after the war. Finally, the chapter considers the post-war circulation of the celebrated photograph in the guise of a film still.

The third chapter opens by evoking two photographs of Quang Duc self-immolating on 11 June 1963 in protest against the government of the Catholic Ngo Dinh Diem, which quickly spread around the world. While the story of these iconic images has been told in detail, film of monks and nuns who followed their compatriot Quang Duc's example has remained in the margins of scholarship. The pieces of footage remain a footnote in histories of the iconic figure of the peace activist in flames. But moving images of the wave of self-burnings also reached global audiences, through newsreels shown in cinemas and especially through television. This chapter presents the first detailed study of pieces of film of male and female Vietnamese Buddhists who emulated Quang Duc in protests by self-immolation witnessed by large numbers of viewers in the 1960s. I explore how developments in cinema and television news reporting helped to reinforce the iconicity of photographs of the burnings as well as making films of them iconic. I unsettle the conventional opposition of the iconic photograph to the forgotten moving image by tracking these pictures of non-violent activism through the first generation of European and North American newsreels, art films and installations that used them to incarnate – and often depoliticise – violence on the other side of the world.

Chapter 4 adds to the extensive academic writing on Che Guevara as icon by offering the first sustained discussion of how he elucidates connections between photography and film between the late 1960s and the early 1980s.

We know him best as a bereted face derived from Korda's semi-telephoto shot of 5 March 1960, which circulated widely in the years following Guevara's murder, along with photos of his corpse taken on 10 October 1967, including Alborta's celebrated multifigure tableau. I pursue reproductions and reworkings of Korda's and Alborta's photo-icons and Bolivian television footage of Guevara dead across newsreel, documentary and essay films from Cuba, France and Argentina. I suggest that these appropriations revitalise the notion of *photogénie* and the metaphor of the mass face that became popular between the two world wars in European writing on photography and cinema as both distinct media and new interlocutors. While accounts of Guevara's iconicity have typically tracked the evolution of Korda's picture into a globally recognised facial outline, I argue that cinema has challenged iconic photography's tendency to separate individuals from crowds.

The fiftieth anniversary of May '68 occasioned the publication of new research into photographs that have come to define the French uprising, which also mobilised Guevara's image.[74] Study of photojournalistic coverage of these events has remained largely separate from analysis of cinema's involvement in them. Chapter 5 links these two image repertoires. One still of a flag-waving woman rising above a crowd on 13 May became a symbol of the protests; I discuss how it fits into film history. That this woman, Caroline de Bendern, had modelled in fashion magazines reinforces the link between iconicity and photography. But I also compare and contrast her performances in a *ciné-tract* (1968), a short composed of stills, and the film *Détruisez-vous* (*Destroy Yourselves*, Serge Bard, 1968) with the photomontages in France and abroad that turned her into the 'Marianne of '68'.

The Epilogue summarises the book's arguments and explores why de Bendern has reappeared in the last few years alongside other fearless young female protestors. The viral spread of digital photographic and video images of women confronting heavily armoured police and neo-fascists in contemporary Macedonia, Chile, America and the UK has disturbed the exclusionary norms of beauty that de Bendern's 'Marianne' perpetuates and that underpin what Fleetwood critically theorises as 'iconic whiteness'.[75] In a different way from the (screen) star images of Guevara and de Bendern, two other symbols of popular political movements, these recent pictures also reinvigorate the interwar concept of the face of the crowd.

Notes

1. Nikephoros, 'Extracts from the *Antirrhetics*', trans. Vassiliki Dimitropoulou, in Marie-José Mondzain, *Image, Icon, Economy: The Byzantine Origins of the Contemporary Imaginary*, trans. Rico Franses (Stanford, CA; Stanford University Press, [1996] 2005), pp. 233–45 (p. 238).

2. Goldberg, Vicki, *The Power of Photography: How Photographs Changed Our Lives* (New York, NY: Abbeville Press, 1991), p. 135.

3. *The Shorter Oxford English Dictionary*, vol. 1 (Oxford: Oxford University Press, 1973), p. 644.

4. Bergala, Alain, 'Le pendule (la photo historique stéréotypée)', *Cahiers du cinéma*, 268–9 (1976), 40–6 (translations from this text are mine). See, for example, *Steve McCurry: The Iconic Photographs* (London: Phaidon Press, 2012).

5. See, for example, *Always Audrey: Six Iconic Photographers. One Legendary Star* (Woodbridge: ACC Art Books, 2019).

6. See Raskin, Richard, *A Child at Gunpoint: A Case Study in the Life of a Photo* (Aarhus: Aarhus University Press, 2004), Hanrot, Juliette, *La Madone de Bentalha: histoire d'une photographie* (Paris: Armand Colin, 2012) and Lavoie, Vincent, *L'Affaire Capa: le procès d'une icône* (Paris: Textuel, 2017). Jean-David Morvan, Séverine Tréfouël and Sylvain Savoia's graphic novel *Cartier-Bresson, Allemagne 1945* (Charleroi: Dupuis, 2016) and Georges Didi-Huberman's *Ninfa dolorosa: essai sur la mémoire d'un geste* (Paris: Gallimard, 2019) also revolve around iconic photographs, but only occasionally use the term 'icon'.

7. Ghosh, Bishnupriya, *Global Icons: Apertures to the Popular* (Durham, NC: Duke University Press, 2011), p. 4.

8. Ibid., p. 12.

9. Ibid., p. 4.

10. Goldberg, *The Power of Photography*, p. 135. Similarly, David D. Perlmutter identifies a '"summing up" quality' as 'a special value of the news picture' (*Photojournalism and Foreign Policy: Icons of Outrage in International Crises* (Westport, CT, London: Praeger, 1998), p. 17).

11. *Life*, 'The Year in Pictures', 73: 25 (29 December 1972), 54.

12. Freund, Gisèle, *Photographie et société* (Paris: Points [1974] 2017), pp. 203, 204 (translations from this text are mine).

13. Teri Wehn-Damisch, cited in Krauss, Rosalind, '". . .And Then Turn Away?": An Essay on James Coleman', *October*, 81 (Summer 1997), 5–33 (10).

14. On a significant French example of this developing magazine culture, see especially Frizot, Michel and Cedric de Veigy, *Vu: The Story of a Magazine*, trans. Ruth Sharman (London: Thames and Hudson, 2009) and Leenaerts, Danielle, *Petite histoire du magazine 'Vu' (1928–1940): entre photographie d'information et photographie d'art* (Brussels, New York: Peter Lang, 2010).

15. On the role of magazines in the emergence of the iconic photograph, see, for example, Gunthert, André, 'Les icônes du photojournalisme: de l'information à la pop culture', in Audrey Leblanc and Dominique Versavel (eds), *Les Icônes de mai 68: les images ont une histoire* (Bibliothèque nationale de France, 2018), pp. 19–31.

16. *Vu*, 445 (23 September 1936), 1106, 1115.

17. Mulvey, Laura, *Death 24x a Second: Stillness and the Moving Image* (London: Reaktion, 2006), p. 161.

18. Baqué, Dominique (ed.), *Les Documents de la modernité: anthologie de textes sur la photographie de 1919 à 1939* (Nîmes: Jacqueline Chambon, 1993), p. 84.

19. Maynard, Patrick, 'The Secular Icon: Photography and the Functions of Images', *The Journal of Aesthetics and Art Criticism*, 42: 2 (Winter 1983), 155–69 (164). I am grateful to Damian Sutton for drawing my attention to this article.

20. Maynard, 'The Secular Icon', 167.

21. Ibid., 165.

22. Ibid., 165.

23. Ibid., 165.

24. Ibid., 164. See Mondzain, *Image, Icon, Economy*, p. 195 for clarification of the historical role of acheiropoietic images in Eastern and Western Christianity and comments on the legend of the 'veronica'.

25. Mitchell, W. J. T., *Iconology: Image, Text, Ideology* (Chicago, London: University of Chicago Press, 1986).

26. Mondzain, *Image, Icon, Economy*, pp. 200–2.

27. Ibid., p. 158.

28. Ibid., p. 151.

29. Ibid., p. 199.

30. Ibid., p. 193.

31. Ibid., pp. 151, 162.

32. Ibid., p. 152. For illuminating comments on iconic photographs and photographs of iconic figures in the light of Mondzain's concept of 'iconocracy', see the political philosopher Susan Buck-Morss's 'Visual Empire', *diacritics*, 37: 2–3 (2007), 171–98 (182, 194).

33. Hariman, Robert and John Louis Lucaites, *No Caption Needed: Iconic Photographs, Public Culture and Liberal Democracy* (Chicago, London: University of Chicago Press, 2007), p. 3.

34. Ibid., pp. 13, 19, 20.

35. Ibid., p. 20.

36. Ghosh, *Global Icons*, p. 4.

37. Ibid., pp. 4, 73.

38. Ibid., p. 79. Mondzain translated, presented and annotated Nikephoros's writings in *Discours contre les iconoclastes* (Paris: Klincksieck, 1990).

39. Ghosh, *Global Icons*, pp. 4, 71–2.

40. Fleetwood, Nicole R., *On Racial Icons: Blackness and the Public Imagination* (New Brunswick, New Jersey, London: Rutgers University Press, 2015). I discuss Fleetwood's approach in the conclusion to this book.

41. Ghosh, *Global Icons*, p. 1.

42. Prestholdt, Jeremy, *Icons of Dissent: The Global Resonance of Che, Marley, Tupac and Bin Laden* (London: C. Hurst & Co., 2019), p. 9.

43. Ghosh, *Global Icons*, for example pp. 8, 9.

44. For a thorough analysis of semiotic approaches to the icon, including the influential frameworks developed by Charles Sanders Peirce and Roland Barthes, see the first chapter of Ghosh's *Global Icons*, 'Moving Technologies', pp. 37–67.

45. Ibid., p. 3.

46. Ibid., pp. 8–9.

47. Ibid., p. 4.

48. Lindeperg, Sylvie, 'Fabrication et destin d'une icône', in *La Voie des images: quatre histoires de tournage au printemps-été 1944* (Paris: Verdier, 2013), pp. 83–93.

49. Ibid., p. 186 (translations from this text are mine).

50. Wagenaar, Aad, *Settela*, trans. Janna Eliot (Nottingham: Five Leaves, 2005). Wagenaar's research informs Harun Farocki's exploration of this iconic image in his essay film *Aufschub* (*Respite*, 2007). For discussion of Holocaust photographs as icons, see Brink, Cornelia, 'Secular Icons: Looking at Photographs from the Nazi Concentration Camps', *History and Memory*, 12: 1 (2000), 135–50 and Wollaston, Isabel, 'The Absent, the Partial and the Iconic in Archival Photographs of the Holocaust', *Jewish Culture and History*, 12: 3 (Winter 2010), 439–62.

51. Lindeperg, *La Voie des images*, p. 187.

52. Ibid., p. 187.

53. Another important precursor is Guy Westwell's consideration of convergences between photography and cinema in 'One Image Begets Another: A Comparative Analysis of Flag-Raising on Iwo Jima and Ground Zero Spirit', *Journal of War and Culture Studies*, 1: 3 (2008), 325–40.

54. See, for example, Metz, Christian, 'Photography and Fetish', *October*, 34 (1985), 81–90; Deleuze, Gilles, *Cinema 1: The Movement Image*, trans. Hugh Tomlinson and Barbara Habberjam (London: Athlone Press, [1983] 1986); Bellour, Raymond, *Between-the-Images*, trans. Allyn Hardyck (Zürich/Dijon: JRP/Ringier/Les Presses du réel, [1990] 2012); Stewart, Garrett, *Between Film and Screen: Modernism's Photo Synthesis* (Chicago, London: University of Chicago Press, 1999); Mulvey, *Death 24x a Second*; Sutton, Damian, *Photography, Cinema, Memory: The Crystal Image of Time* (Minneapolis, MN; London: University of Minnesota Press, 2009); and Farinotti, Luisella, Barbara Grespi and Barbara Le Maître (eds), 'Overlapping Images: Between Cinema and Photography', *Cinéma&cie*, xv: 25 (Fall 2015).

55. Guido, Laurent and Olivier Lugon, 'Introduction', in Guido and Lugon (eds), *Between Still and Moving Images* (Eastleigh: John Libbey, 2012), pp. 1–5 (p. 1).

56. Kuhn, Annette and Guy Westwell, *Oxford Dictionary of Film Studies* (Oxford: Oxford University Press, 2012), p. 367.

57. For a helpful overview of this 'turn toward history' within scholarship on still and moving images, see Røssaak, Eivind, 'The Still/Moving Field: An Introduction', in Eivind Røssaak (ed.), *Between Stillness and Motion: Film, Photography, Algorithms* (Amsterdam: Amsterdam University Press, 2011), pp. 11–24 (pp. 15–16).

58. Bellour, *Between-the-Images*, p. 16.

59. Stewart, *Between Film and Screen*, pp. 75–109; Rust, Amy, 'Hitting the "Vérité Jackpot": The Ecstatic Profits of Freeze-Framed Violence', *Cinema Journal*, 50: 4 (Summer 2011), 48–72.

60. Didi-Huberman, *Ninfa dolorosa*, pp. 34–5.

61. Prestholdt, *Icons of Dissent*, for example pp. 21–3.

62. Gunthert, 'Les icônes du photojournalisme'.

63. Ibid., p. 19 (translations from this essay are mine).

64. Eco, Umberto, 'Critique of the Image' (1970), in Burgin, Victor (ed.), *Thinking Photography* (London, Basingstoke: Macmillan, 1982), pp. 32–8 (p. 33). Important precursors include Roland Barthes's 'Rhetoric of the Image' (1964), which briefly alludes to the 'coded' and 'non-coded iconic message[s]' of a photograph (in *Image Music Text*, essays selected and trans. by Stephen Heath (London: Fontana Press, 1977), pp. 32–51 (p. 36)).

65. Webster, Frank, *The New Photography: Responsibility in Visual Communication* (London: John Calder, 1980), pp. 4, 172.

66. Ibid., p. 4.

67. Ibid., p. 173.

68. Wollen, Peter, *Signs and Meaning in the Cinema* (Bloomington, IN: Indiana University Press, [1969] 1972), p. 136.

69. Wollen, *Signs and Meaning*, p. 152. For an early example of Charles Sanders Peirce's writing on icons, indices and tokens or symbols, see 'On the Algebra of Logic: A Contribution to the Philosophy of Notation' [1885], in Houser, Nathan and Christian Kloesel (eds), *The Essential Peirce: Selected Philosophical Writings*, vol. 1 (1867–1893) (Bloomington, IN: Indiana University Press, 1992), pp. 225–8.

70. Deleuze, *The Movement Image*, p. 108.

71. Røssaak, 'The Still/Moving Field', p. 11.

72. Convert, Pascal, 'Images passages', http://www.pascalconvert.fr/histoire/lamento/lamento.html (last accessed 1 April 2020), revised version of an article in *Art Press*, 'Images et religions du livre', 25 (2004), 90–5.

73. Didi-Huberman, *Ninfa dolorosa*.

74. Leblanc and Versavel (eds), *Les Icônes de mai 68*.

75. Fleetwood, *On Racial Icons*, p. 63.

CHAPTER ONE

Paper, Water, Ice: The Falling Soldier

Something has knocked the man backwards, made him lose his footing and grip on his gun. The image is still but captures movement; he couldn't pose off-balance like this. It pulsates with energy, the force of an impact close to the camera. Taken near Córdoba in Spain, probably by Robert Capa on 5 September 1936, during the early stages of a civil war between defenders of the Republic and insurgent fascist generals, the photograph is often described in captions as depicting a Loyalist militiaman felled by a Rebel bullet. Whether or not this is what it actually shows has been debated for nearly half a century. As Vincent Lavoie points out, 'the Capa affair' has become the 'matrix' for questioning the authenticity of iconic photojournalism.[1] Regardless of its relationship to accompanying texts, the photograph rapidly turned into an exemplary image of a human being in war, as implied by the generic name given to it by the magazine *Life*, which has stuck in commentary in English: the 'Falling Soldier'.[2] For many commentators it also exemplifies photography's unique capacity to create icons, exceptional, idealised pictures that incarnate historical events, in contrast to film's more ephemeral and elusive images. But the history of Capa's most celebrated photograph is inextricable from that of cinema. In some ways resembling a film frame, it has provoked both tribute and critique by filmmakers and film theorists. Its public life demonstrates that we need to pay attention to film in order to understand iconic camera images.

In folding the 'Falling Soldier' into cinema, I draw inspiration from the debate about still and moving images which has gone on in film studies for at least half a century and was revived by the emergence of electronic and digital media. The violence of the war in Vietnam led European and American commentators to distinguish television's transitory images from the lingering of photographs on the page, in homes and other everyday spaces, and in the mind. For instance, in 1973 Susan Sontag contrasted the former medium's 'stream of under-selected images, each of which cancels its predecessor' with the latter's material form as 'a slim object that one can keep and look at again'.[3] Her example is Nick Ut's immediately ubiquitous still of Phan Thi Kim Phúc, the Vietnamese girl who had been burned by American napalm, which Sontag argues 'was certainly more memorable than a hundred hours of televised barbarities'.[4] Three decades later, in digital environs, Sontag reiterated this point, this time citing as evidence the enduring profile of the 'Falling Soldier': 'non-stop imagery [. . .] is our surround, but when it comes to remembering, the photograph has the deeper bite'.[5] Sontag's suggestion that fixed images are more memorable than moving ones supports the conception of photography as uniquely capable of encapsulating historical events that has gained popularity, as André Gunthert argues, since the late 1960s.[6] During its early life, Capa's still didn't compete with moving images for prominence and influence to the same degree as Ut's. There is no known film of the scene on the hillside near Córdoba. Although images flowed less constantly in the late 1930s than they later began to on television screens, newsreels and documentaries, including *The Spanish Earth* (Joris Ivens, 1937), exported moving pictures of the war overseas, none of which is remembered as widely as the 'Falling Soldier'. Sontag describes every photograph's 'neat slice of time' as 'a "privileged moment"', distinct from the current of moving images.[7] Capa's picture owes its longevity and iconicity to its rare portrayal, according to magazine layout designers and other editors and commentators, of the instant of death.

Yet other accounts of still and moving images have drawn attention to the interconnected histories of photography and film, turning towards what Eivind Røssaak labels 'the in-between'.[8] Similarly, I suggest that Capa's image was continually in transition between the two media from its creation in 1936 until the mid-1980s, when digital technology was about to provoke reconsideration of the still/moving divide. I examine the photograph through a filmic lens, discussing its shaping of movement and time and its afterlives in magazines that emulate or analyse cinema and on the movie screen. These publications and films come from Europe, the US and Australia, where Capa's picture is particularly well known. Most of them perpetuate the Eurocentric and patriarchal assumption that heroes who die in war are white and male, even when they recognise the photo as a 'stereotype'.[9] Not only has the 'Falling Soldier' long epitomised photography's capacity to capture the exceptional instant. It also evolved, I suggest, from a moving image of a noble sacrifice in the 'paper cinema' where it first came to life into a frozen template for filmic evocations of apocalyptic destruction and senseless death.

A Privileged Instant or Any Instant Whatever?

The 'Falling Soldier' symbolises a pivotal moment in the entwined histories of photography, cinema and war journalism. Before Capa's pictures of Republican troops, rarely had the public seen soldiers close-up in combat. Some of the most haunting photographs of the Crimean War and the American Civil War portray the aftermath of battles: landscapes strewn with cannonballs and dead bodies, sometimes rearranged for the camera, and a burial party striking poses.[10] To ensure a sharp image, their creators had to focus on stationary people and objects away from the thick of fighting because they were using collodion wet plates, which needed exposing for several seconds and immediate treating with chemicals and water in a mobile darkroom.[11] Corpses abound in civil war photography since, as H. Bruce Franklin notes, 'among all human subjects, those who stayed most perfectly still for the camera were the dead'.[12] Although photographs of the First World War often took shape instantaneously on flexible strips of film, those of soldiers under fire remained unusual. A much-reproduced still of a French grenadier arching his body as a bullet arrests his advance through a sea of mud turns out to be a frame from a filmic reconstruction, *Verdun, visions d'histoire* (*Verdun, Visions of History*; Léon Poirier, 1928), rather than a documentary image of 'death in the making', to borrow the title of a collection of Capa and Gerda Taro's photographs of the violence in Spain.[13] The phrase highlights the spontaneity and immediacy of the picture of the Republican militiaman, who appeared on the book's cover. The Spanish war was the first reported on in what Sontag calls 'the modern sense' – by close-up action shots that sped into the printed press.[14] The 'Falling Soldier' owes its energy and apparent proximity to bodies in mortal danger (both the militiaman's and Capa's) to the small, light, easy to manoeuvre Leica, which increased its user's freedom of movement. Developed in the 1920s, this camera accommodated a lens with a large maximum aperture, enabling fast shutter speeds, and recorded stills on 36-exposure rolls of the same fine-grain 35mm stock used to make cinema. It made possible the sharp delineation of moving bodies in action that continued across several images.[15] In recording dynamic gesture, Capa's image troubles the distinction between photograph and film frame. It illustrates what Dominique Baqué calls the role of photography's 'interlocutor' that cinema inherited in the 1930s from painting.[16]

Iconic photographs are more often compared to paintings than to films.[17] The narrator of Susana Fortes's novel *Waiting for Robert Capa* (2012) likens the 'Falling Soldier', for example, to Francisco Goya's 'Third of May, 1808' (1814), another legendary dramatic image of a Spanish patriot with raised arms facing enemy rifles during a war. The canvas foretells this man's death by depicting what Gotthold Ephraim Lessing calls a 'fruitful' or 'pregnant' (*fruchtbar*) moment: 'Painting can only make use of a single instant of an action, and must therefore choose the one, which is most pregnant, and from which what has already taken place, and what is about to follow, can most easily be gathered.'[18] Capa's picture provides scant information that frames the soldier's fall within a larger narrative compared to Goya's, where some prisoners lie in a bloody pile and others wait in line to meet the firing squad. But Lessing's comments on painting time resonate with David Bathrick's remark, in a discussion of photos and film of the Nazis' concentration and death camps, that icons 'claim implicitly to tell the whole story'.[19] Although pregnant moments created with a brush only sometimes 'come to represent large swaths of historical experience', as photo-icons do, both these kinds of painting and photograph use a single instant to evoke a longer duration.[20]

However, the pregnant instant of painting was replaced in photography, scholars have suggested, by the transitory or fugitive one.[21] The Kodak camera, which went on sale in 1888, popularised the taking of instantaneous (later called snapshot) photographs.[22] These images appeared to their first generation of viewers 'at antipodes to the carefully chosen emblematic moment in the evolution of an action that Lessing saw as the goal of the visual arts'. Compared to paintings and sculptures, they looked 'incomplete'.[23] Whereas the pregnant moment is a fictional representation, the photograph 'is always by the force of circumstance a "decisive instant" torn from reality'.[24] In contrast to the incompleteness originally attributed to snapshots, pictures of 'decisive' instants appear whole and finished. In 1952, Henri Cartier-Bresson called 'decisive' the moment at which the moving elements of 'continually vanishing' phenomena, such as a facial expression, are 'in balance': 'photography must seize on this moment and hold immobile the equilibrium of it'.[25] The 'Falling Soldier' happens to show someone losing his balance but appears decisive because it arrests motion and invests it with drama. While Cartier-Bresson was seeking to define what photography alone could do, the invention of the decisive moment is inconceivable without that of cinema. As David Campany puts it, 'while photography may have begat cinema, cinema begat the "decisive moment"' not only by providing the film on which the Leica recorded but also by requiring the older medium 'to make a virtue of its own stillness'.[26] This was in spite of Cartier-Bresson's insistence that photographers 'work in unison with movement'.[27]

A different view of the snapshot emerges in the opening pages of Gilles Deleuze's first book on cinema, published in 1983, three decades after Cartier-Bresson's remarks. In contrast to the photographer, Deleuze is interested in the snapshot not as a unique form of expression, but as a 'determining condition' of cinema.[28] This is because cinema shares what Deleuze, following Henri Bergson, presents as the modern scientific conception of movement in terms of a 'mechanical succession of instants'.[29] Whereas the long-exposure photograph (*la photo de pose*) belongs instead to an ancient tradition that understands motion as transition between poses or privileged instants, cinema's procession of equidistant snapshots 'reproduces movement as a function of any-instant-whatever [*en fonction du moment quelconque*]'.[30] There are echoes here of Sontag's description of television a decade earlier (also cited above) as a 'stream of [. . .] images, each of which cancels its predecessor'.[31] Unlike Sontag's essay, this passage of *The Movement Image* risks reducing the photograph to a static piece of cinema, as Damian Sutton points out, but its distinction between two kinds of moment helps explain further how Capa's picture shapes time.[32] While it resembles a decisive moment, the qualities it shares with a film frame – an 'instant which is equidistant from another' – fit into the lineage of the any-instant-whatever.[33] Capa's account of taking the picture also distances it from the privileged instant or pose and equally from the exact composition sought after by Cartier-Bresson: 'I just kind of put my camera above my head and even didn't look and clicked a picture when [the *milicianos*] moved over the trench'.[34] This recollection implies that the power of an image caught on the fly, as if by accident, derives from a mechanical process and luck, rather than posing and composing. Régis Debray deems this snapshot 'too shaky for an icon', reinforcing the association in photography studies of iconicity with the fixed image.[35] The picture's supposed flaws – the cropped feet and rifle butt and the slightly blurred shoe – appear to authenticate Capa's description as traces of the movement of the soldier and photographer at the any-instant-whatever of their encounter.[36] Yet photography's privileged instants are also often unposed, as some of Cartier-Bresson's images demonstrate. As different ways of depicting time and movement, the any-instant-whatever and the decisive moment are useful ideas for understanding not only the creation but also the publication history and cinematic appropriation of the 'Falling Soldier' and other iconic photographs.

PAPER CINEMA

The public first encountered the 'Falling Soldier' in *Vu*, one of several weekly magazines published in France between the world wars that drew inspiration from motion pictures. Borrowing a phrase coined in 1937 by Jean Selz, Thierry Gervais has likened the dynamically illustrated pages of *Vu* and *Regards*, which also printed Capa's photo, to a 'little paper cinema'.[37] A case in point is a 'picture story' about the Spanish Civil War in *Vu*'s issue of 23 September 1936, where the collapsing militiaman appears alongside other photos attributed to Capa. Two subheadings, 'how they [soldiers] fell' and 'how they [refugees] fled', draw attention to traces of movement in the stills arranged beneath.[38] A caption further specifies that the two largest pictures show soldiers who 'were hurtling down the slope' when 'suddenly, their flight [was] ended' by a 'fratricidal bullet'. The imaginative verbal descriptions of the photos are like filmic intertitles. What Ludovic Cortade, discussing the American magazine *Life*'s response to TV and to developments in cinema technology in the 1950s and 1960s, calls the 'cinematisation' of the fixed image is foreshadowed by *Vu*'s sequencing of photographs of similar actions and gestures, which is reminiscent of the way in which films create the illusion of movement.[39] There is a particularly close resemblance between the two falling soldier pictures, which appear adjacently and look like different phases of the same movement, as if they had been borrowed from one of Eadweard Muybridge's motion studies, or a photographic version of a double take, even though the Leica operator needed time to advance the film stock manually. The illusion that they chronicle the same death is reinforced by their abrupter captions – 'Hit!' (*Touché!!!*) and 'He falls!' (*Il tombe!!!*) – on the front page of the 28 June 1937 issue of *Paris-soir*, where they complement the drama of Antoine de Saint-Exupéry's adjacent account of a night embedded with Republican troops on the Carabancel front.[40] This later presentation distracts from the unlikeliness of Capa catching two soldiers as they took bullets in what cloud formations and prominent grass stalks reveal is the same place and (almost) the same moment. The two photos have often appeared together, supporting Robert Hariman and John Louis Lucaites's claim that icons 'become composite images: of the several versions of themselves, of the other photos surrounding the event, of the other images of the historical era, and so on'.[41] What is more, the falling soldiers suggest that the cinematic principle of montage plays a role in icon composition. The imaginary movement created by the selection, cropping and layout of images in *Vu*'s feature also reinforces what is often called the humanism that links Capa's photos of people caught up in the violence in Spain and of supporters of the French Front Populaire (Popular Front) in the same period.[42] The formal energy of this photomontage renders more real and compelling the bravery and suffering of ordinary people: men who have given their lives and women and children who have lost everything except for each other. As Baqué notes when discussing interwar 'committed photography' (*photographie engagée*), dynamism is an ethical quality.[43] *Vu*'s story brings tragedies of the war to life to elicit support for the Republican side, evidencing and justifying the magazine's antifascist and pacifist editorial line in this period, rather than singling out any image as exceptional.[44] At the same time, however, it perpetuates a clichéd narrative of male military sacrifice, in contrast, for example, to Taro's belatedly celebrated portrait of a Republican militiawoman aiming her pistol during training the previous month.

A fortnight after *Vu*, the American magazine *Time* again highlighted the dynamism of the snapshot that would become iconic by pairing it with another to construct the illusion of motion continuing between frames.[45] The accompanying article explains that one of the Loyalist soldiers leaping over a trench in the first image is immediately 'clipped' by a bullet that 'bowled him to the ground' in the second, which is cropped into a close-up of his toppling body. The militiamen in both pictures face the same direction, as if the photographs were film shots edited in the continuity style. *Vu* and *Time* animate Capa's stills – creating what Cortade dubs the 'photogramme effect' – for different purposes.[46] *Time* reproduces the photos not as a tribute to the courage of Republican soldiers (who were on the side of what it denounces as the 'proletarian Terror' ruling Madrid) but as authentic pictures taken in 'the thick of recent fighting' (in contrast to the fakes it alleges were flooding out of Spain).[47] As the caption states: 'Capa and the Whites [Rebels] were shooting simultaneously'.

Even when the 'Falling Soldier' had lost its value as a news photograph, which Siân Reynolds defines as 'the capture of a dramatic event on film printed on the front page within hours', it reappeared in the printed press.[48] So began the process of iconisation – with its maturing from a photojournalistic image into a historical, decontextualised and enlarged one. Whereas *Vu* and *Time* placed it next to equally significant instants, other publications singled it out as a decisive and synecdochic one. It occupies over half of a page without other images in the 12 July 1937 issue of *Life*, where the unnamed soldier stands in for the half a million who, according to the accompanying text's title, lost their lives in the first year of the war.[49] The caption, which mentions that Capa took the picture and that it shows the instant of the militiaman's death, also validates it, in Gunthert's words, as an example of 'a photographic feat', unlike *Vu*'s verbal narration which focuses only on the scene unfolding in the image.[50] In fact, *Life*'s feature on Spain leaves the reader wondering whether photography or cinema makes the best pictures. Capa's photo prefaces the announcement of Ivens's new film. We turn the page to find the first of two double spreads of film frames from *The Spanish Earth*. A short introduction presents the documentary as 'practically the first worthwhile picture coverage' of a war that 'has few good pictures', which turns out to mean few 'action shots'.[51] The photogrammes that follow transport us to recently shelled streets, a gun-site in a battle-damaged building and fields strafed with bullets. 'The close ones have a zipping whisper and the really close ones crack', remarks one of Ernest Hemingway's captions. Another line of his voice-over (not transcribed in *Life*), 'this is the true face of men going into action. [. . .] Men cannot act before the camera in the presence of death', tries to allay the concern about fakery that *Time* had raised next to the 'Falling Soldier', but also draws attention to the confinement of Ivens's camera in this sequence to the periphery of battle, in contrast to the photographer's apparent position in the middle of it.[52] Capa's 'action shot', then, continued to invite comparison with film frames, just as it had in *Vu* and *Time*, when, a year into the war, it was beginning to accrue iconic power.

To understand how filmmakers and film theorists have approached the 'Falling Soldier', it is necessary to say a few more words about the wider travels of this incipient icon. The same week as *Life* selected it as a singular image of the moment of death by a notable photojournalist, which could symbolise the masses of people killed in the war, a special issue of *Regards* devoted to Spain also signalled its growing importance. The image dominates the page in question. Around the militiaman fits a letter by André Wurmser warning a 'non-interventionist Pyrrhus' that underneath his 'militant pacifism' he is 'the real bellicist'.[53] This text turns the soldier who undergirds it into a personification of Spain abandoned to fascist bullets and bombs by democratic France and Britain, and an emblem of what Baqué, discussing Capa's photos of Madrid in an earlier issue of *Regards*, describes as 'the ethics of just combat'.[54] As Françoise Denoyelle observes, from this moment on the photo incarnated 'Spain and its Republic sacrificed' by their allies. Its symbolism, Denoyelle points out, is 'premonitory and polysemous'; as the threat of fascism grew, it began to refer beyond Spain to Europe, becoming 'an emblem of the defeat of democracies'.[55] So the image started to stand for both a seismic event and a belief system three decades before 'the process of iconisation of news photographs' that Gunthert argues got properly underway after 1968; it was prophetic in this sense too.[56] The picture's meanings continued to broaden as it travelled internationally, returning, for example, on the front of Capa and Taro's *Death in the Making*, published in New York in 1938, as an action photo by an auteur. On the one hand, as Barbie Zelizer has shown, it confirmed to American viewers that the sacrifices of the Loyalists in Spain were meaningful and noble and became 'emblematic of what a generalised heroic death in war might look like'.[57] On the other hand, anticipating Gunthert's analysis of *Life*'s reproduction, Zelizer suggests that the image simultaneously 'celebrated photographic form' – the picture-taker's skill and the medium's ability to represent 'death as action'.[58] She cites Raymond Demoulin's remark that Capa 'practically invented the photojournalistic idea of the decisive moment'.[59] Typical is the banal reference in a book of Capa's photos published in London in 1964 to his 'great picture of man and war – the Spanish Loyalist at the instant of death', which expands further to cover a full double spread.[60] I turn now to the incorporation of this emblem of photography's – and a particular photographer's – special capacities around the same time by cinema, which further modified its form and meaning.

FROZEN FIRE

The militiaman's most discussed cinematic cameo fittingly concludes a land-mark film in the history of photography and cinema's mutual enrichment. A conscious or unconscious citation of Capa's picture ends a story told almost entirely in stills. The unnamed protagonist (played by Davos Hanich) of *La Jetée* (Chris Marker, 1962), whose combat necklace from the Third World War identifies him as a soldier, fixates on a mental image from his childhood that – when he travels back to it through time – turns out to show his death; his resemblance in this final moment to the Republican fighter has become part of the film's mythology. Both combatants fall backwards with open chests and reach one arm out towards the left side of black-and-white images backdropped by huge skies and low horizons. This section of the chapter discusses how the sense of *déjà vu* we feel when watching the film's denoue-ment has informed commentary on the relationship between still and mov-ing images, and adds to the debate by resituating the scene in the history of appropriations of Capa's iconic image. I suggest that *La Jetée* sheds light on the evolution of the formerly dynamic 'Falling Soldier' into a fixed tableau and complicates the picture's association with meaningful death.

The demise of Marker's protagonist extends across several images; the decisive instant that Capa skilfully captured in close-up has no single equiv-alent in the film. We first glimpse a toppling body (crucially, we don't see whose) in the foreground on the left of a mysterious image in the prologue. Although only its lower parts appear, its position in the scene resembles that of the Republican soldier in the iconic photo and its blurred-ness recalls his movement. When the memory returns at the end of the film, this fall is pro-longed across three photographs. These versions, where the main character has moved into focus and the centre of the frame, look more constructed than Capa's, which (as mentioned above) he claimed was snapped spontane-ously. The first brings us even closer to its subject than the historical photo; in the second and third he moves further away. The hero's collapse decom-poses into an image sequence that reminds Philippe Dubois of Muybridge's experiments, the results of which I earlier likened to the falling soldiers placed next to each other by *Vu*.[61] As Dubois points out, the effect is to make the protagonist seem to collapse in 'majestic' slow motion, just like one of the war film heroes discussed in the next section of this chapter.[62] The serial shots of his death replace the one 'exceptional, enduring' image or 'ideal iconographic form' around which the debate about iconic photographs has revolved and of which Capa's picture has become an emblem.[63] In spite of Marker's use of cinematic techniques to animate photographs, commentar-ies on his evocation of the 'Falling Soldier' have dwelt on its stasis.

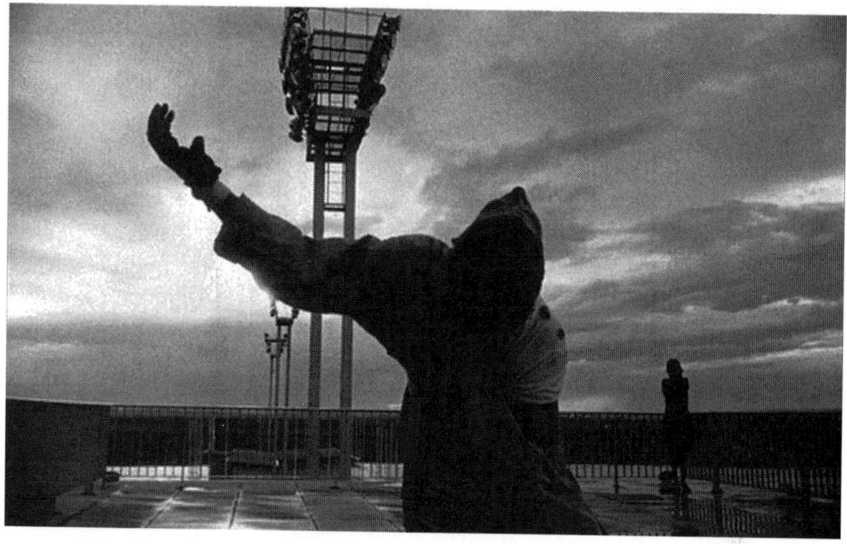

Figure 1.1 *La Jetée* (*The Pier*; dir. Chris Marker, France, 1962).

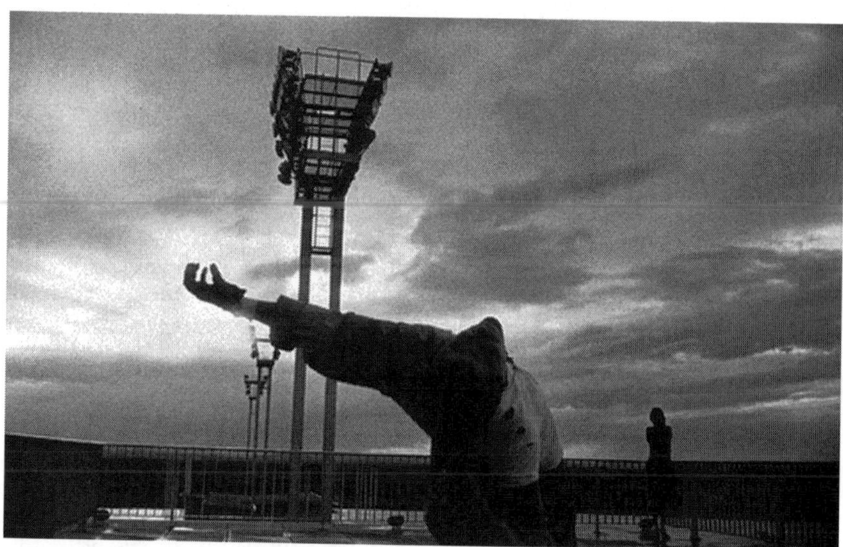

Figure 1.2 *La Jetée.*

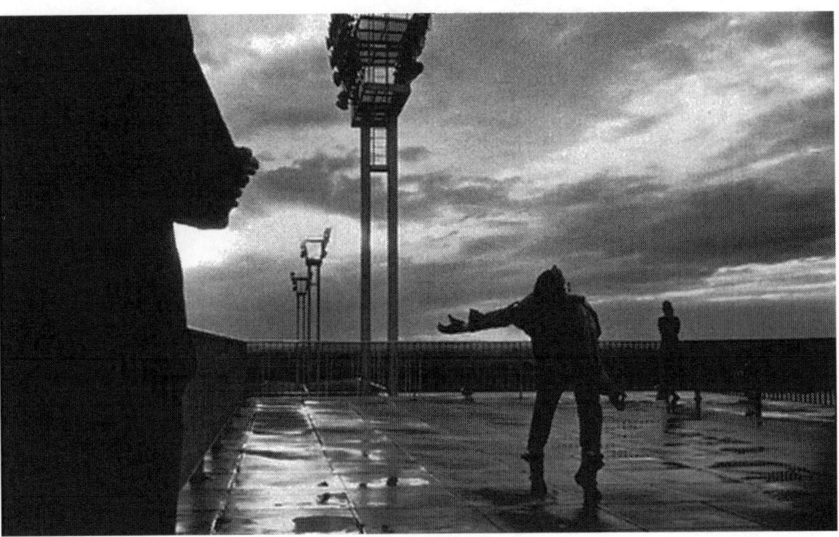

Figure 1.3 *La Jetée.*

The 'pivotal image' that *La Jetée* 'models' on Capa's picture occupies a privileged place in a short essay by Peter Wollen that reconsiders the relation between photography and cinema.[64] Originally published in 1984, this piece does not mention the concept of the icon, which had played a crucial role in Wollen's reappraisal of cinematic signs at the end of the 1960s using the three categories outlined by Charles Sanders Peirce.[65] Nevertheless, it appeared in an era when there was widespread discussion in photography theory, as explained in the Introduction, of both Peirce's iconic sign and the religious understanding of the icon as a sacred image.[66] Wollen's remarks on the 'Falling Soldier' also followed in the wake of reassessments of iconic photojournalism in *Cahiers du cinéma* and in films for television by Jean-Luc Godard, Anne-Marie Miéville and Teri Wehn-Damisch (which I discuss later in this chapter and in the following ones). But Wollen's explicit interlocutor is Roland Barthes, who had recently proposed that 'the very essence, the *noeme* of Photography', which he names '"That-has-been"', 'deteriorates when [the] Photograph is animated and becomes cinema'.[67]

To counter what he construes as Barthes's 'absorption in the still' and presentation of photography 'as a spatial rather than temporal art', Wollen turns to research on 'aspect', 'a dimension of the semantics of time common to both the still and the moving picture'.[68] From this field he borrows distinctions between state, process and event; a process is ongoing and seen from inside, while an event is complete and seen from outside. Photography's stasis complements the depiction of states, as Barthes implies in remarking that 'what founds the nature of Photography is the pose'.[69] But Wollen is also interested in 'the photograph which signifies an event', in which 'we sense something paradoxical', 'like a frozen tongue of fire'.[70] We tend to perceive news photographs as belonging to this category, Wollen observes. He refers, for example, to Capa's photojournalistic image as the '*locus classicus*' for depicting death as an event.[71] The iconic photographs of the denunciation of an alleged collaborator and a self-immolation discussed later in this book also 'freeze fire' in this sense; of course, the flames in the latter image are no metaphor. As we shall see, the other photo-icons on which I focus show states (the images of Che Guevara) that incarnate processes and a process (the picture of a demonstration in May 1968) that symbolises an event. In an observation that underlines the emblematic status of Capa's photo, Wollen likens its tense to 'the habitual narrative present in Russian' where one sequence of events represents a repeated sequence (one death stands for many).[72] The images *La Jetée* bases on the 'Falling Soldier' turn death back into a one-off event. While the protagonist's other memories appear as states or processes, his fatal shooting 'is seen from the outside as a complete action'.[73] Although Wollen clarifies that, unlike Barthes, he is 'not always longing for a way of bringing the flow [of narrative, of images] to a stop', his comparison of film to fire and photography to ice frames Capa's image of the event of death as frozen.[74]

Stillness becomes the main theme of another interpretation of *La Jetée*, written three years later, that mentions its restaging of the 'Falling Soldier'. The film exemplifies what Raymond Bellour calls the 'forms of the "photographic" that invaded cinema at the beginning of the 1960s'.[75] Moreover, its reconstruction of the iconic photograph illustrates how images and bodies 'come to a stop' in cinema at 'exceptional or fundamental moments'.[76] Bellour refers to the re-enactment of the soldier's fall, borrowing a term from photography criticism, as 'a decisive instant'.[77] In the final sequence of fixed images, the main character runs along a viewing platform at Orly airport towards the woman he loves until the bullet halts him. The photographs that copy Capa's – the time-traveller's childhood memory around which all the other images revolve – encapsulate what Bellour sees as the film's 'lesson': that 'the overly still image, the far too visible suspension of time, leads irremediably to loss and death'.[78] Just as Wollen associates the 'Falling Soldier' with ice, so too Bellour's discussion of its remediation foregrounds paralysis, in contrast to *Vu*'s emphasis on its dynamism.

More recent discussions of *La Jetée* have explored its layering of fictional and historical images. Patrick ffrench points out that 'the hero's encounter with his own death is also an encounter with the history which would have marked the childhood of many viewers of the film in 1962 and 1963'.[79] It is apt that the image that haunts the protagonist turns out to copy one that has haunted the public, having 'made [Capa] famous almost overnight', according

to *Life*, reporting on his death in 1954.[80] ffrench approaches Marker's remediation of the icon as an example of 'paradigmatic montage', 'where the image
[. . .] is as if superimposed on a photographic instance of the historical real'.[81]
Images of the fictional world appear laid over (or modelled on) documentary
pictures not only of the Spanish battlefield, notes ffrench, but also of the concentration and death camps and of Hiroshima after the atomic explosion.[82]
The scenes of Paris ruined by the Third World War also recall rapidly and
widely published press photos of Guernica decimated by German and Italian
incendiary bombs in a murderous new development in air warfare.[83] ffrench
reconsiders the film's imagery of destruction in terms of 'annulled' movement
and gesture.[84] In ffrench's reading, which draws on Giorgio Agamben's philosophical exploration of the inherent dynamism of the image as gesture, the
film imagines the 'annihilation' of 'the gestural life inherent to humanity' by
'the rigidity of a politics of totality'.[85] *La Jetée*'s allusions to this 'totalised form
of power' echo the denunciation of fascism by Capa's photos of Spanish victims of Rebel shells and bullets and German and Italian bombs and by *Vu*,
the first magazine to publish them.[86] But the film's devastated cityscapes also
invest the soldier's fall, modelled on the most iconic of these images, with an
apocalyptic connotation that is absent from the 'picture stories' of the 1930s
and reminds us that Marker embarked on *La Jetée* in the shadow of October
1962's Cuban Missile Crisis.

As the man runs for the last time towards the woman he loves, the sound
of a Russian orthodox cathedral choir, familiar from earlier in the film, returns
to suggest a Christian interpretation of this story of destruction. Sarah Cooper identifies this music as a piece composed by Alexandr Kastalsky and Piotr
Gontcharov in honour of 'la Sainte Croix' which therefore imports 'echoes of
the crucifixion'.[87] The movement of the protagonist's limbs when he is gunned
down supports the idea that he is sacrificing himself like Christ. The arm that he
and the Loyalist soldier fling out in what ffrench interprets as either a 'reflex' or
'a last gesture of defiance or resistance' also turns them, with their upright, open
stances, into cruciform figures.[88] Marker's restaging of the militiaman's fall resonates with religious interpretations of the iconic photo, which has been compared to paintings of martyred saints.[89] It is not uncommon for photographs
that become iconic in the West to resemble Christian artworks and thus blur
the boundary between icons secular and sacred. As soon as photographers could
record fast movement in focus, the combatant extending his arms into a cross-
like shape became a popular subject. Other well-known versions include American soldiers in South Vietnam throwing a grenade (Don McCullin, February
1968) or reaching up to guide a helicopter (Art Greenspon, April 1968). The
prominence of this selection of images in European and North American media
and public spaces has distracted from the heroic sacrifices of collectives (rather

than individuals), women and people of colour.[90] As Christic figures, they affirm whiteness as a 'point from which to organise and "know" the world', to cite J. Kameron Carter's discussion of Christian theology's debt to Western imperialist constructions of race.[91] War photojournalism's selective allocation of heroising or ennobling gestures also illustrates Sara Ahmed's argument that bodies are 'raced by how they extend into space'.[92] As we shall see, *La Jetée* is not the only cinematic appropriation of Capa's photograph that similarly affirms whiteness as somatic norm by merging heroic gestures with cruciform poses.

CLOSE-UP ACTION

At the end of the 1960s, when Gunthert argues that photojournalistic images first began to acquire the status of icons, an American director researching a film about a Spanish artist rediscovered Capa's images of the civil war.[93] The 'Falling Soldier' would provide the template for the critical motif of Stuart Cooper's later feature film *Overlord* (1975), while the soldier who falls in his short essay film *A Test of Violence* (1969) is Nguyen Văn Lém, a suspected member of the Vietnamese National Liberation Front whose shooting was captured in another iconic photograph (Eddie Adams, Saigon, 1 February 1968). The remaining sections of this chapter explore how the significance of the Republican militiaman's collapse evolves in an era whose icons also include still and moving images of Văn Lém's execution and other scenes of violence and atrocity in Vietnam. Whereas the image of the Spanish militiaman bolsters the cliché of the soldier as martyr in a sacrificial narrative, that of Văn Lém fits the stereotype of the war victim. *Overlord* pays homage to Capa's photo as both document and icon while questioning its long-standing inference that war-time deaths are meaningful sacrifices.

Commentators have focused on the stream of documentary sequences from the Imperial War Museum's archive that meanders through the fictional story, which likewise unfolds in black and white, but the remediation of iconic combat stills also warrants attention. The film first refers to a photo at the end of its prologue, when the fears of young British infantrymen crouching in a Second World War landing craft heading for Normandy are visualised in a shot of a soldier gunned down as he runs across a beach. Cooper was looking for a dramatic form for the presentiment of death that recurs in the ordinary soldiers' letters and diaries on which the film heavily draws, when he had the idea of 'flash[ing] back' to the first of Capa's war pictures to win international acclaim.[94] It seems fitting that a snapshot that resembles a premonition (of the Spanish Republic's fall) should recur as a flashforward in a strand of modern European cinema (to which both *La Jetée* and *Overlord* belong) that persistently disturbs the chronological unwinding of time. A rifle slips from the right hands of both Capa's and Cooper's soldiers, while the latter flings out both his arms, creating a more obvious cross shape than the former. Both images are full of sky. But Cooper stylises Capa's realist image: *Overlord*'s blurred soldier collapses in slow motion to the sound of a dissonant violin chord composed by Paul Glass. This British film borrows the habit of prolonging and aestheticising the moment of killing that American cinema had been practising at least since *Bonnie and Clyde* (Arthur Penn, 1967). As Vivian Sobchack eloquently surmises in an essay on cinema written the year before *Overlord*'s release: 'the most violent of deaths today is treated with the slow motion lyricism of the old Clairol commercials in which two lovers glide to embrace each other. The once abrupt drop into non-being has become a balletic free fall.'[95] While this ballet reassures viewers that the brutal demises Sobchack discusses are meaningful, *Overlord*'s stylised remake of the 'Falling Soldier', which lacks the gore of its contemporary American equivalents, prefaces a narrative that will question the purpose of military deaths.[96]

The flashforward anticipates *Overlord*'s concentration on one individual soldier and comes into focus, both literally and figuratively, as the film goes on. The indistinct figure in this fatalistic vision is framed identically to the main character, Tom Beddows (Brian Stirner), when he first appears in the next, mirroring shot. Both men run towards the viewer in the centre of the screen, suggesting their equivalence. Like *La Jetée*'s main character, Tom is haunted by a prophetic image that is modelled on the same iconic photo and plays a prominent role in his story. When he accidentally tumbles down a hill during military training, the images revert to slow motion and the foreboding music that accompanied the premonition returns. This aestheticised sequence echoes the earlier imaginary image of the soldier dying on the beach, but Tom's fall is incidental to the story and ungainly. The myth of the 'belle mort' (beautiful death) that the film invokes through its allusion to Capa's picture also jars, a few minutes later, with images of the dead.[97] While Tom explores Dorset on his bike, we follow a plane across the channel into a night-time raid on a German city, depicted in documentary footage that momentarily cuts away from the apocalyptic vision of lethal fireworks and burning ruins to the charred and decomposing bodies of bomb victims. Roger Smithers identifies the corpses as belonging to members of the German army attacked from the air while trapped at Falaise in France.[98] This is not how soldiers or civilians are supposed to die in war, according to the film's iconic model of death, where no blood or bodily harm is visible. For Debray, what removes Capa's photo from the war atrocities genre is 'something solar and oceanic' that surrounds the 'luminous sacrifice, suspended in mid-air'.[99] The figure in *Overlord*'s first re-enactment of this picture also seems to float through space; by contrast, the shots of Tom rolling down the hill and of the corpses exclude the sky.

Compared with these disfigured remains, some of which have no faces left, another dead German soldier who appears moments later in Tom's dream looks idealised; filmed for the fiction by cinematographer John Alcott, his skin is pale and soft, his body intact. Tom finds two photos in the cadaver's wallet: a postcard view of Neuschwanstein, which suggests he shared a love of castles with Tom, who we have just seen at Corfe; and a studio portrait of the deceased in uniform. The figure dodging explosions and machine-gun fire in the extended replay of the death premonition that follows might be Tom or the unnamed German. The unidentified fighter repeats the cruciform fall, which is framed, filmed and paced in the same way as the first: frontally, centrally, out of focus and in slow motion. His fuzzy form and noble gestures as he dies in action contrast with the sharply delineated corpses at Falaise. In the next shot, someone – perhaps Tom's mother – places a photo of him among other objects on a lace-covered bureau. This careful gesture and the similarity of the portrait, which shows Tom standing to attention in military jacket and beret, to that of the young German, suggests that he too has perished. Juxtaposing stiffly posing and dynamically gesturing soldiers, the sequence refers to photography's dual capacity to present, through its homage to Capa, 'death as action', to borrow Zelizer's phrase, which echoes *Life*'s search for 'action shots' of the war in Spain, and to remind us of the dead. The doubled photograph also reinforces the idea that Tom's story is that of other young ordinary soldiers ('Tommies') on both sides, just as the Spanish militiaman came to symbolise a conception of war that transcends individual experience.

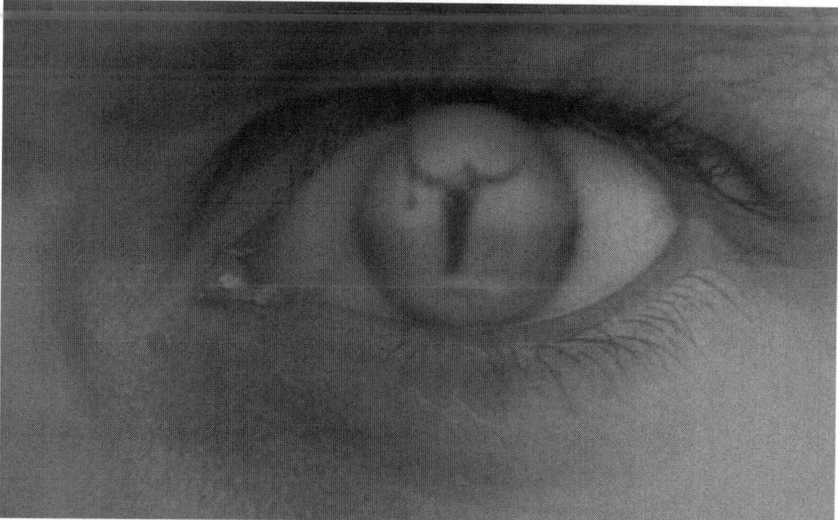

Figure 1.4 *Overlord* (dir. Stuart Cooper, UK, 1975).

The culmination of the narrative in the arrival of Tom's landing force at the French coast on 6 June 1944, now known as D-Day, pays tribute to a wider selection of iconic images. The staged parts of this scene draw inspiration from Capa's surviving snapshots of American troops trying to reach Omaha beach as bullets fill the air, as well as from his memoir of the landing.[100] Like the 'Falling Soldier', these blurred, grainy, chaotic images resemble film frames; in the words of Cooper, who is not the only director who has tried to reproduce them, 'they could be moving pictures' and this is critical to their iconic status.[101] As he waits to disembark, Tom's premonition recurs and he imagines running through the waves and up the beach, as if out of Capa's shots of the assault on Normandy into his picture of the defence of the Spanish Republic. The presentiment plays out within the cinematically magnified frame of Tom's eye, which highlights its status as a kind of foresight. As it repeats in full frame, slow motion and the now familiar violin motif once more give 'meaning and import', in Sobchack's words, to the soldier's 'mortal twitchings'.[102] But this time he collapses in a series of side-on close-ups, not a single frontal shot. The cruciform figure in the iconic refrain fragments into body parts. The film cuts back to the boat, where more close-ups capture Tom's shocked face at the moment he takes a bullet to the head and falls backwards. Both his imagined and actual demise produce dynamic images; while the film incorporates photographs, this climactic sequence departs from the frozenness on which Wollen insists. In contrast to the privileged moment on the beach in Tom's premonition, his accented but abrupt and quick death without leaving the boat and surrounded by a sea of slaughter evokes the any-instant-whatever that mechanically succeeds another. The depiction of his collapse foreshadows the snapshot of another falling soldier taken by Amory Clay, which appears in a recent novel by William Boyd that she narrates; she names this photo after the icon but finds her version 'mundane in the extreme' in comparison.[103] By contrast, 'Capa's soldier, falling back, arms akimbo, would not have looked out of place in a Hollywood B-movie western. The soldier seems to be dying "on stage" as it were.'[104] While this picture had long told viewers, in Zelizer's words, 'that the soldier's death was not in vain but enacted for a cause', Tom's senseless end foregrounds war's chaos and absurdity.[105] In this way *Overlord* joins other films of the Vietnam War era in highlighting what Kent Jones calls the 'misalliance between outsize images of heroism and the harsh realities of survival in combat'.[106]

Overlord adjusts the meaning of the 'Falling Soldier' while highlighting its cinematic quality by restaging it as live action, although the imagined sequences disturb filmic motion by slowing down time. Cooper's earlier film *A Test of Violence* also uses a variety of techniques to animate still images. For example, one sequence cuts back and forth between recent paintings of

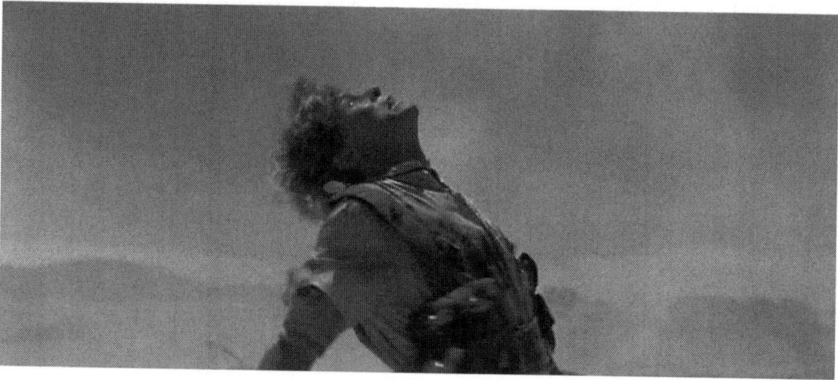

Figure 1.5 *Gallipoli* (dir. Peter Weir, Australia, 1981).

prisoners and executioners by Juan Genovés and iconic documentary footage recorded by Vo Suu, a Vietnamese filmmaker working for an American television network, of Brigadier General Nguyen Ngoc Loan shooting Văn Lém.[107] The cropped detail of Văn Lém's grimace in Adams's photo of the moment of his death also appears but only fleetingly. By paying more attention to the footage, *A Test of Violence* casts doubt on the assumption that film of emblematic historical events merely underlines the importance of photos. Made on the cusp (as noted above) of what Gunthert identifies as the era of photo-icons, Cooper's compilation film presents the iconic image instead as intermedial – composed of pictures that are camera-created and painted, still and moving. Similarly, *Overlord* situates the 'Falling Soldier' between photography and film.

Key features of Capa's picture recurred several years later in another cinematic death scene that questions war's morality. The final image of *Gallipoli* (Peter Weir, 1981) invites this comparison particularly because it is still; David Denby, for example, has read it as a 'remarkable [. . .] freeze-frame replica of [. . .] Capa's immortal photograph'.[108] The film dramatically freezes a fast-moving body. Like the protagonists of Capa's image (as captioned by *Vu*), *La Jetée* and the premonition in *Overlord*, Archy Hamilton (Mark Lee), a talented Australian sprinter who voluntarily joins Anzac troops attacking Ottoman Turkey in 1915, is shot while running and arches his back at the impact. The moment of his death merges Capa's picture, as Campany points out, with an 'athletics photo finish'.[109] Archy had no chance of winning his final race. *Gallipoli*'s last scene depicts wave after wave of terrified Anzacs, armed just with bayonets, pouring out of their trenches as ordered, only to be butchered by machine guns within a few steps. The scale and intensity of this violence recall the apocalyptic destruction which frames the protagonists' deaths in *La Jetée* and *Overlord* and provides a foil to the meaningful individual sacrifice that Capa's photo had long connoted.[110] Whereas Tom's bleak end – and those met by the real troops pictured in *Overlord* – debunk this myth of the worthwhile donation of life, *Gallipoli*'s redemptive reference to the 'Falling Soldier' belies the disenchantment with war that prevailed in Australia as well as the UK after Vietnam. The film exaggerates the way the Spanish soldier appears to hang between heaven and earth and the light that bathes him. It detaches Archy from the ground, framing him against distant mountains and the sky, and his upturned face glows pink and gold in the sunshine. Although his shirt is bloodied, the grace and allure of his death befit his heroism. Like Cartier-Bresson's decisive moment, the image portrays a moving part in balance and draws attention to transience.

What happens to the 'Falling Soldier' when transposed into a freeze-frame and where does the end of *Gallipoli* fit in the history of this device? Over two decades separate Archy's immobilisation from the famous arrest of another running teenage boy at the close of *Les quatre cents coups* (*The 400 Blows*; François Truffaut, 1959). While in Europe the frozen frame became, in Bellour's account, 'the emblem of a modern cinema threatened in its new faculties and intensity', within a decade it evolved from a figure of uncertainty – or in Amy Rust's terms, a 'destabilising force' – into an expressive means for popular American films to make sense of violence.[111] Paradigmatic of this tendency is the paralysing of the outlaw heroes of *Butch Cassidy and the Sundance Kid* (George Roy Hill, 1969) as they launch themselves into their final fight, an image that turns sepia, as Campany notes, 'to convert their violent demise into mythic destiny'.[112] Bellour suggests that the powerful experience of the freeze-frame derives from its play with '*l'arrêt de mort*, the finality of death' (the French term also means 'death sentence').[113] The tragic freeze-frame that concludes *Gallipoli* lacks the ambiguity that characterises the end of *Les quatre cents coups*; it is a fictional equivalent to the class of 'about to die' images that Zelizer defines as depicting 'certain death'.[114] Serge Daney provocatively argues that the frozen film ending had mutated by 1990 into a 'boorish triviality'.[115] Daney likens such final images to posters, that is, promotional pictures; as he puts it, 'the stop on the image [*l'arrêt sur l'image*] is the very essence of advertising'.[116] The instant of Archy's death appeared in publicity material for *Gallipoli* (an image that originated in a photograph of Lee in a similar pose taken for a brochure designed to attract financing for the film). However, the poster enables fans to hold on to the climactic moment in a film which participates in a wider discourse of remembrance. The prolonging of Archy's charge across no man's land by camera shots from several angles and of his inevitable fall by a freeze-frame that euphemistically fades to black may soften the violence of his demise. Yet the accompanying silence is shocking.[117]

As much as the freeze-frame and the fade, it is the image that endures on the poster which sears into memory. This painterly image of heroism and the waste of young life exemplifies cinema's tendency to still, in Campany's words, 'the idealized instant – the pinnacle of the action' and, as Daney points out, 'the résumé, the emblem [. . .] of the whole film'.[118] Campany similarly suggests that 'the way that the image [of Archy's recoiling face and torso] was held made for a kind of summary of the entire situation'.[119] An idealised picture that sums up a historical event or era: these characteristics also define the icon. Exploring *Gallipoli*'s re-enactment of the 'Falling Soldier' illustrates how freeze-frames and iconic images can enrich understanding of each other, beyond the conventional account of iconicity in exclusively photographic terms.

STOP ON THE IMAGE

At the same time as after-images of Capa's emblem of meaningful sacrifice were recurring in on-screen depictions of senseless mass slaughter, films and film journals began to examine it as part of a special class of photos. During and in the aftermath of the war in Vietnam, it was not only the editors of magazines such as *Life*, as existing accounts of iconic images have discussed, but also filmmakers and cinema critics who started to collect and comment on photographs that had come to stand for eruptions of political violence. Why did *Cahiers du cinéma*, for example, devote seven pages to commentary on Capa's picture and other 'stereotyped historical photos' in 1976? In their introduction to the dossier containing the article illustrated by these pictures, Alain Bergala and Jean-Jacques Henry controversially remark that 'photo magazines, today, are the last place for interrogating photos'.[120] Film critic Bergala's essay examines the familiar snapshots not only as favourites of the capitalist news apparatus (as exemplified by *Life*), in spite of the left's historical embrace of the 'Falling Soldier', but also as evocations of a filmic imaginary. His viewing of the photos through a cinematic lens exemplifies the *Cahiers*' concern at this juncture with intermediality – or what Antoine de Baecque dubs 'ciné-télé-photo-vidéo-phagie'.[121] Whereas most accounts of what would later be called the 'iconisation' of photojournalistic pictures marginalise cinema, Bergala's suggests that this process and the cinematisation of the fixed image are intimately linked.

Most of the images reproduced in the margins of his article play significant roles in this book's consideration of transitions between photography and film: they include the 'Falling Soldier', which appears three times, the Jewish boy guarded by German soldiers in Warsaw, one of Capa's snapshots of Omaha beach, Thich Quang Duc's self-immolation, Loan's killing of Văn Lém, and Kim Phúc and other children injured by napalm. Cropped to the same small dimensions, they form rows that bring to mind filmstrips – another version of paper cinema. Bergala's argument that these stills illustrate the routine work of dominant ideology hinges on comparison with moving images. Like the classical Hollywood film, they deny the possibility, he contends, that 'the masses make History'.[122] Rather than depicting an agentic multitude, they tend to isolate an anonymous, innocent, pathetic individual and in so doing 'tirelessly repeat a single proposal: History makes victims, History as fatality, war as absolute evil and as absurdity'.[123] Whereas Capa's militiaman first appeared in the company of other ordinary soldiers and civilians, when he illustrated stories in *Vu* and *Time*, within a year he became a more solitary figure. While for several decades his image supported what Bergala describes as classical cinema's (bourgeois individualist) thesis that 'heroes make History', by the mid-1970s, the *Cahiers* essay implies, he had evolved into one of History's victims.[124] As we have seen, *Overlord*'s and *Gallipoli*'s allusions to the 'Falling Soldier' in meditations on war's tragic waste of young lives register this shift in meaning, although Cooper's use of documentary footage of recruits preparing for the Normandy landings underlines the historical agency of what Bergala calls 'the masses'.[125]

Bergala develops his analogy between dominant cinema and the 'always-already-seen photos' (*photos toujours-déjà-vues*) that border his text by likening them to film frames (*photogrammes*) and freeze-frames – or a 'stop on the image', the literal translation of the French phrase 'l'arrêt sur l'image'.[126] Here his analysis anticipates the remarks by Wollen, Bellour and Daney on the freezing or interruption of movement cited earlier. Bergala argues that the 'freeze-frame effect' (*l'effet d'arrêt sur l'image*) is 'fairly specific to the imaginary of the historical photo' and has the ideological function of producing 'a reality effect, more precisely an effect of instantaneity, of authenticity'.[127] This frozen appearance both signifies that the scene is real and 'appeals to a fictional, narrative imaginary, most often filmic in origin'.[128] According to Bergala, these photos invite us to envision a procession of images modelled on one of cinema's stock dramatic sequences, such as an arrest, execution or battlefield shooting, in the case studied in this chapter which, like most icons, has also inspired filmic re-enactments. More is at stake than in the merely decisive moment; these instants, argues Bergala, are 'paroxystic', since they show fate hanging in the balance.[129]

So in Bergala's account it is those fixed images that evoke cinematic sequences, effects and constructions of history that systems of power ensure that we remember. His discussion of these ideological and formal links between media pre-empts his more recent consideration of cinema's influence on Capa's combat photos that is discernible in the fictional, imaginary quality of these documentary images.[130] Bergala's helpful analysis of iconic photos as stereotypes that – like classical Hollywood – centre on the individual and marginalise the empowered mass needs broadening to take account of gender and race. He denounces the images for portraying 'the human condition' as lonely and painful, but their selection also reinforces inequalities by suggesting that some groups of people are more likely to be victims than others.[131] While criticising the 'whining humanism' often promoted in these pictures by a wide-angle lens that 'isolates' the subject in her 'solitude and [. . .] suffering', he also overlooks humanist photography's tendency to celebrate solidarity, as exemplified in Capa's work.[132] Bergala's focus on the circulation of these photographic 'fetishes' in the mainstream Western media excludes the leftist or popular antifascist or pacifist causes that several of them have galvanised, including the images of the Spanish militiaman and (as explored in Chapter 3) the burning Quang Duc.[133] The capacity of this category of images to resist as well as support dominant ideology has been a central concern of twenty-first-century reconsiderations of the icon.[134]

LIQUID ICON

This chapter has traced the mutation of the 'Falling Soldier' on the page and screen from hero into victim, from emblem of just or necessary violence into icon of war's futility and from an innovative depiction of movement and energy into a petrified cliché. As Guy Westwell observes in another account of an iconic war photograph which pays close attention to its replication in film, 'images accrue a history – certain meanings settle and others are elided: this "history" then provides a weight of signification upon which another image can call'.[135] I have also tracked shifts in the form of Capa's image between photograph and photogramme, memory and premonition, decisive moment and any-instant-whatever. In these ways and by illustrating how iconic image histories connect photography and cinema, I have tried to add to previous accounts of the 'Falling Soldier'. The militiaman's defining appearances in paper and celluloid cinema and filmic re-stagings of his death challenge the prevalent assumption that we should understand secular icons in primarily photographic terms.

I want to conclude this chapter and flag several concerns of the following ones by turning to a documentary essay made by Wehn-Damisch for French television, *Photographie et société: d'après Gisèle Freund* (1983), which features the 'Falling Soldier' prominently. Like Bergala's essay, published seven years earlier in the same country, an eight-minute section of the documentary places Capa's image in a genre designated 'veritable stereotypes', providing my second example of film culture defining the category of photo that would soon be called iconic. Guy Le Querrec and Marc Riboud, members of Magnum Photos, the co-operative whose founders included Capa and Cartier-Bresson, lay out on a table prints of a selection of these icons that overlaps with Bergala's, including the picture of the Spanish battlefield. Wehn-Damisch then juxtaposes several of them – Quang Duc's fiery protest, Jack Ruby assassinating Lee Harvey Oswald, Loan killing Văn Lém and Kim Phúc crying out in pain – with moving footage of another self-immolation, the two shootings and the napalm casualties. For the photographer Gisèle Freund, filmed in conversation with Wehn-Damisch, the montages created on the table we see and on the one we don't on which the film is edited confirm the primacy of the stills: 'the irony is that the more we consume moving images, the more the unique and fixed image prevails over the rest, and becomes the symbol that substitutes for our reality'.[136] Echoing Sontag's comparison of the still and moving pictures of Kim Phúc and other burned children, cited in this chapter's introduction, Freund's comment bolsters the consensus that photography has a singular power, as the female narrator puts it, to 'express and explain the whole of a confusing and complex event'.

However, *Photographie et société* exemplifies how film can make a distinctive contribution to the debate about iconic images. Ostensibly a portrait of Freund and, by extension, a study of photography, the documentary turns out on closer scrutiny to be a dialogue between her and Wehn-Damisch and, by extension, between the different visual media in which they work. For instance, Freund presents the 'Falling Soldier', which 'inaugurated a new style of reportage', as a landmark in the history of photography, whereas Wehn-Damisch also uses it to reflect on cinema's construction of motion from stills. We spot it not only on the table but also in a tray of water or chemical solution. Every so often shots recur of this container filled with multiple prints of Capa's image or with a mixture of the other 'stereotyped' photos, re-enacting the process of developing and washing them. A siphon device keeps the fluid fresh and revolving.

The image whose frozenness has preoccupied film critics since the 1970s thus melted in the mid-1980s into a liquid one. In an essay written at the end of this decade, the photographer Jeff Wall considers the vital role that water has played in the production of still camera pictures (as exemplified by the collodion wet plate mentioned earlier). The liquid chemicals used to make them have come to represent an 'archaism' that 'connects photography to the past, to time, in an important way'.[137] Water, observes Wall, will drain out of the production process now that 'electronic and digital information systems emanating from video and computers' appear set to 'replace photographic film'.[138] It seems fitting that a film that also sits on the cusp of the digital age should liquefy the 'Falling Soldier' and other key historical photos. What is the future of these analogue icons or icons of the analogue? In an important recent reappraisal of photography, Kaja Silverman expands the concept of liquidity to reflect on the movement of images in photography's 'first chapter': 'a continuous stream of evanescent images entered the darkened space of the camera obscura from outside, dynamically analogizing its equally labile source [. . .]'.[139] While the camera obscura became 'a device for arresting [the perceptual world's] image stream', the dynamic analogy would persist in cinema, a medium for which the prints circulating in Wehn-Damisch's tank of fluid offer a striking metaphor.[140] Liquid fixes images but also sequences and animates them. The dynamism accentuated by *Vu* on the first public appearance of the 'Falling Soldier' and lost as the image froze returns as the current of moving images sweeps up the lingering still.

Notes

1. Lavoie, *L'Affaire Capa*, p. 27 (my translation). For details of the controversy, questions raised by different framings of the photograph and how the soldier gained and lost a name, see Lebrun, Bernard and Michel Lefebvre, *Robert Capa: The Paris Years 1933–1954*, trans. Nicholas Elliot (New York, NY: Abrams, 2012), pp. 98–115. It has been established that the picture was taken near the village of Espejo, where there was no battle on 5 September 1936 (ibid., p. 110). Lavoie's book considers in more depth the debate about the authenticity of the 'Falling Soldier' and what it reveals about press photographs.
2. See Leenaerts, *Petite histoire du magazine 'Vu'*, p. 218.
3. Sontag, Susan, 'Photography', *The New York Review of Books*, 20: 16 (18 October 1973), 59–63.
4. Ibid.
5. Sontag, Susan, *Regarding the Pain of Others* (London: Penguin, 2003), p. 19.
6. Gunthert, 'Les icônes du photojournalisme'. On the range of writers who have discussed the affinity between fixed images and memory, see Stallabrass, Julian, 'Memory and Icons: Photography in the War on Terror', *New Left Review*, 105: 1 (May–June 2017), 29–50 (30).
7. Sontag, 'Photography'.
8. Røssaak, 'The Still/Moving Field', pp. 14–15. My remarks on the animation of the 'Falling Soldier' are influenced in particular by Emma Wilson's commentary on Alain Resnais's juxtaposition of still and moving images, in 'Material Remains: *Night and Fog*', *October*, 112 (2005), 89–110.
9. I borrow the term 'stereotype' from Alain Bergala's essay 'Le pendule (la photo historique stéréotypée)'.
10. I am thinking, for example, of Roger Fenton's two versions of 'The Valley of the Shadow of Death' (1854–5 and 1856), Timothy O'Sullivan's 'A Harvest of Death, Gettysburg' (1863) and John Reekie's 'A Burial Party, Cold Harbor, Virginia' (1865).
11. See Silverman, Kaja, *The Miracle of Analogy, or the History of Photography, Part 1* (Stanford, CA: Stanford University Press, 2015), pp. 74–5.

12. Franklin, H. Bruce, *Vietnam and Other American Fantasies* (Amherst, MA: University of Massachusetts Press, 2000), p. 7.

13. Capa, Robert and Gerda Taro, *Death in the Making* (New York: Covici-Friede, 1938).

14. Sontag, *Regarding the Pain of Others*, p. 18.

15. For discussion of these features of the Leica, see Beaumont-Maillet, Laure, 'Robert Capa: une vie de passions', in Beaumont-Maillet (ed.), *Capa connu et inconnu* (Paris: Bibliothèque Nationale de France, 2004), pp. 11–35 (p. 11) and Campany, David, *Photography and Cinema* (London: Reaktion, 2008), p. 27.

16. Baqué (ed.), *Les Documents de la modernité*, p. 84.

17. See Chapter 2 for further discussion and examples of allusions by iconic photographs to the history of Western art.

18. Lessing, Gotthold Ephraim, *Laocoon: An Essay on the Limits of Painting and Poetry*, trans. E. C. Beasley (London: Rugby printed, 1853), p. 102.

19. Bathrick, David, 'Introduction: Seeing Against the Grain: Re-Visualizing the Holocaust', in Bathrick, Brad Prager and Michael D. Richardson (eds), *Visualizing the Holocaust: Documents, Aesthetics, Memory* (Rochester, NY: Camden House, 2008), pp. 1–18 (p. 3).

20. Hariman and Lucaites, *No Caption Needed*, p. 1.

21. See, for example, Vidal, Belén, *Figuring the Past: Period Film and the Mannerist Aesthetic* (Amsterdam: Amsterdam University Press, 2012), p. 116.

22. Silverman, *The Miracle of Analogy*, pp. 82–3.

23. Gunning, Tom, 'The "Arrested" Instant: Between Stillness and Motion', in Guido and Lugon (eds), *Between Still and Moving Images*, pp. 23–31 (pp. 25, 26).

24. Bellour, *Between-the-Images*, pp. 139–40.

25. Cartier-Bresson, Henri, foreword to *The Decisive Moment* (Göttingen: Steidl, 2014), no page numbers (originally published in 1952 as *Images à la sauvette*). Or in Clément Chéroux's terms: 'the decisive moment is a formal equilibrium that reveals the essence of a situation' (in booklet accompanying the 2014 Steidl edition of *The Decisive Moment*, p. 15).

26. Campany, *Photography and Cinema*, p. 27; Campany, David (ed.), *The Cinematic (Documents of Contemporary Arts)* (London: Whitechapel, 2007), p. 1.

27. Cartier-Bresson, foreword to *The Decisive Moment*.

28. Deleuze, *The Movement Image*, p. 5.

29. Ibid., p. 5.

30. Ibid., pp. 4–5.

31. Sontag, 'Photography'.

32. For criticism of this aspect of Deleuze's approach, see Sutton, *Photography, Cinema, Memory*, p. xi.

33. Deleuze, *The Movement Image*, p. 7.

34. Capa, Robert, radio interview in 1947, extract available at 'Robert Capa: "The Best Picture I Ever Took" – A Picture From the Past', *The Guardian*, 29 October 2013, http://www.theguardian.com/artanddesign/audioslideshow/2013/oct/29/robert-capa-spanish-civil-war (last accessed 4 July 2016).

35. Debray, Régis, 'La belle mort', in *L'Œil naïf* (Paris: Seuil, 1994), pp. 146–53 (p. 148) (translations from this text are mine).

36. For assessment of these features of the photograph, see Whelan, Richard, *This Is War! Robert Capa at Work* (New York, NY/Göttingen: International Center of Photography/Steidl, 2007), p. 87.

37. Jean Selz cited in Gervais, Thierry, '"The Little Paper Cinema": The Transformations of Illustration in *Belle Époque* Periodicals', in Guido and Lugon (eds), *Between Still and Moving Images*, pp. 147–64 (p. 162).

38. 'La Guerre Civile en Espagne', *Vu*, 445 (23 September 1936), 1106–8 (translations from this text are mine).

39. Cortade, Ludovic, *Le Cinéma de l'immobilité* (Paris: Publications de la Sorbonne, 2008), pp. 219–20 (translations from this text are mine).

40. De Saint-Exupéry, Antoine, 'Sergent, pourquoi acceptes-tu de mourir?', *Paris-soir*, 5.115 (28 June 1937), 1, 5.

41. Hariman and Lucaites, *No Caption Needed*, p. 300.

42. On the humanist tendency in photography to which Capa contributed, see de Thézy, Marie, *La Photographie humaniste, 1930–1960: histoire d'un mouvement en France* (Paris: Contrejour, 1992).

43. Baqué (ed.), *Les Documents de la modernité*, p. 463.

44. For discussion of *Vu*'s reporting on the Spanish Civil War, including its framing of Capa's photographs of soldiers, see Leenaerts, *Petite histoire du magazine 'Vu'*, pp. 210–20.

45. *Time*, xxviii: 14 (5 October 1936), 20.

46. Cortade, *Le Cinéma de l'immobilité*, p. 219.

47. *Time*, 21.

48. Reynolds, Siân, 'Camera Culture and Gender in Paris in the 1930s: Stills and Movies', *Nottingham French Studies*, 31: 2 (1992), 39–51 (40).

49. 'Death in Spain', *Life*, 3: 2 (12 July 1937), 19–25.

50. Gunthert, 'Les icônes du photojournalisme', p. 25.

51. 'Death in Spain', 20.

52. I am grateful to Jeremy Hicks for drawing my attention to the resonance between this sequence of *The Spanish Earth* and Capa's 'Falling Soldier'.

53. Wurmser, André, 'Lettre ouverte à Pyrrhus non-interventionniste', *Regards*, 183 (14 July 1937), 21 (translations from this text are mine).

54. Baqué (ed.), *Les Documents de la modernité*, p. 322.

55. Denoyelle, Françoise, 'De l'errance à l'épopée lyrique: naissance d'un mythe', in Beaumont-Maillet (ed.), *Capa connu et inconnu*, pp. 49–65 (pp. 60, 65) (my translation).

56. Gunthert, 'Les icônes du photojournalisme', pp. 19, 25. Gunthert explains that 'reflexive narratives about iconography' remained rare at the time when Capa's photographs of the Normandy landings, that would later become iconic, were first published (p. 25).

57. Zelizer, Barbie, *About to Die: How News Images Move the Public* (New York, NY: Oxford University Press, 2010), pp. 178–9.

58. Zelizer, *About to Die*, p. 179.

59. Raymond Demoulin, cited in Zelizer, *About to Die*, p. 179.

60. Capa, Robert, *Images of War* (London: Paul Hamlyn, 1964), pp. 20, 22–3.

61. Dubois, Philippe, '*La Jetée* ou le cinématogramme de la conscience', in Dubois (ed.), *Recherches sur Chris Marker, Théorème 6* (Paris: Presses Sorbonne Nouvelle: 2002), pp. 8–45 (p. 30).

62. Ibid., p. 30.

63. Audrey Leblanc and Dominique Versavel, 'Histoire visuelle de Mai 68: une construction médiatique et culturelle', in Leblanc and Versavel (eds), *Les Icônes de mai 68*, pp. 11–18 (p. 12).

64. Wollen, Peter, 'Fire and Ice' [1984], in Campany (ed.), *The Cinematic*, pp. 108–13 (p. 112).

65. Wollen, *Signs and Meaning in the Cinema*, pp. 116–54.

66. See, for example, Eco, 'Critique of the Image'; Webster, *The New Photography*; and Maynard, 'The Secular Icon'. While Wollen responds to *Camera Lucida*, other contemporary writings on photography that deal explicitly with the icon, such as Webster's book, return instead to Barthes's earlier political Saussurean works.

67. Barthes, Roland, *Camera Lucida*, trans. Richard Howard (London: Vintage [1980] 2000), pp. 76–7, 78.

68. Wollen, 'Fire and Ice', pp. 108, 113.

69. Barthes, *Camera Lucida*, p. 78.

70. Wollen, 'Fire and Ice', p. 110.

71. Ibid., p. 112.

72. Ibid.

73. Ibid., p. 113.

74. Ibid., pp. 113, 110.

75. Bellour, *Between-the-Images*, pp. 16.

76. Ibid., p. 153. The essay in which Bellour links *La Jetée* to the 'Falling Soldier', entitled 'L'Interruption, l'instant' (translated as 'The Film Stilled'), was originally published in 1987.

77. Bellour, *Between-the-Images*, pp. 152–3.

78. Ibid., p. 152. Bellour returns to the link between Capa's and Marker's falling soldiers in 'Concerning "the Photographic"', trans. Chris Darke, in Beckman, Karen and Jean Ma (eds), *Still Moving: Between Cinema and Photography* (Durham, NC: Duke University Press, 2008), pp. 253–76 (p. 258).

79. ffrench, Patrick, 'The Memory of the Image in Chris Marker's *La Jetée*', *French Studies*, 59: 1 (2005), 31–7 (36).

80. 'A Great War Reporter and His Last Battle', *Life*, 36: 23 (7 June 1954), 27–33 (29).

81. ffrench, 'The Memory of the Image', p. 36.

82. Ibid., p. 36.

83. For discussion of photographs of 'this first substantial expression of modern air war', see Sliwinski, Sharon, 'Air War and Dream: Photographing the London Blitz', *American Imago*, 68: 3 (Fall 2011), 489–516 (496–8).

84. ffrench, 'The Memory of the Image', p. 35.

85. Ibid., pp. 34, 37.

86. Ibid., p. 35.
87. Cooper, Sarah, *Chris Marker* (Manchester: Manchester University Press, 2008), p. 48.
88. ffrench, 'The Memory of the Image', p. 36.
89. For comment on perceptions of the militiaman as 'Christ-like', see Zelizer, *About to Die*, p. 178.
90. For brief discussion of eurocentric aspects of photojournalistic practice, see an introduction by exhibition curator Mark Sealy, 'Human Rights, Human Wrongs', http://www.thephotographersgallery.org.uk/images/Mark_Sealy_HRHW_essay_54d4be1c76ea8.pdf (last accessed 4 July 2016).
91. Carter, J. Kameron, *Race: A Theological Account* (Oxford: Oxford University Press, 2008), p. 13.
92. Ahmed, Sara, *Queer Phenomenology: Orientations, Objects, Others* (Durham, NC: Duke University Press, 2006), p. 5. Compare the Spanish militiaman, who, in the words of one veteran of the civil war, 'loses his life but retains his dignity', with Nguyen Văn Lém, another soldier, this time Vietnamese, whose dying moment became iconic not because of his expansive movement (his hands are restrained behind his back) but because of his expression of agony (Eddie Adams, 1968) (veteran interviewed in the documentary *Robert Capa: In Love and War* (Anne Makepeace, 2003)). For a penetrating analysis of the claim made by these two photographs to portray a moment that is both 'singular' and, like the instants that succeed each other in a narrative film, 'absolutely consequential', see Mieszkowski, Jan, *Watching War* (Stanford, CA: Stanford University Press, 2012), pp. 117–22 (p. 18).
93. Gunthert, 'Les icônes du photojournalisme', p. 19.
94. Stuart Cooper in 'Capa influences Cooper' (2007), photo essay on the Criterion DVD of *Overlord*.
95. Sobchack, Vivian, 'The Violent Dance: A Personal Memoir of Death in the Movies', *Journal of Popular Film*, 3: 1 (Winter 1974), 2–14 (8).
96. Similarly drawn out and eventually cruciform are the death throes of Sergeant Elias (Willem Dafoe) fleeing a patrol of Vietnamese soldiers in *Platoon* (Oliver Stone, 1986) (as satirised by the prolonged collapse of Tugg Speedman (Ben Stiller) in the controversial *Tropic Thunder* (Ben Stiller, 2008)). Elias's anguished reaching skywards with both arms and the place where he falls recall Greenspon's photo (mentioned earlier in this chapter) more than Capa's. According to Marita Sturken, *Platoon* also evokes the iconic photos of Brigadier General Nguyen Ngoc Loan's shooting of Văn Lém and of the mass killing of Vietnamese civilians by US military at My Lai (Ron Haeberle, 16 March 1968), and Guy Westwell has shown how the film 'rescripts' their initial connotation for Americans of defeat to redeem the invading nation's trauma (Sturken, *Tangled Memories: The Vietnam War, the AIDS Epidemic and the Politics of Remembering* (Berkeley, London: University of California Press, 1997), p. 100; Westwell, *War Cinema: Hollywood on the Front Line* (London: Wallflower, 2006), pp. 78–9). The overt Christian symbolism of Elias's end,

which unfolds in a series of frontal slow-motion tableaus, continues this work of redemption and pits agentic American death against the portrayal of the Vietnamese as victims that Sturken observes is 'not incidentally' a repeated feature of the war's photo-icons (*Tangled Memories*, p. 93).

97. See Debray's essay on Capa's photo, 'La belle mort'.

98. Roger Smithers in 'Mining the Archive', on the Criterion DVD of *Overlord*.

99. Debray, 'La belle mort', p. 147.

100. Capa, Robert, *Slightly Out of Focus* (New York: Henry Holt & Co., 1947), pp. 142–51.

101. Cooper in 'Capa influences Cooper'.

102. Sobchack, 'The Violent Dance', p. 8.

103. Boyd, William, *Sweet Caress* (London, New York: Bloomsbury, 2015), p. 275.

104. Ibid.

105. Zelizer, *About to Die*, p. 179.

106. Jones, Kent, 'Man Versus Machine', in booklet accompanying Criterion DVD of *Overlord*, pp. 5–9 (p. 7).

107. For an account of the production and broadcast of this footage, see Bailey, George A. and Lawrence W. Lichty, 'Rough Justice on a Saigon Street: A Gatekeeper Study of NBC's Tet Execution Film', *Journalism Quarterly*, 49: 2 (1972), 221–9, 238.

108. Denby, David, 'Boys at War', *New York* (31 August 1981), p. 52. Campany also sees 'traces' of the iconic photo in *Gallipoli*'s freeze-frame (cited in Campbell, Neil and Alfredo Cramerotti (eds), *Photocinema: The Creative Edges of Photography and Film* (Bristol: Intellect, 2013), p. 15).

109. Campany, *Photography and Cinema*, pp. 55–6.

110. See Zelizer, *About to Die*, p. 179.

111. Bellour, 'Concerning "the Photographic"', p. 258. For brief comments on differences between freeze-framed violence in European art cinema and American commercial cinema in the late 1960s and early 1970s, see Rust, 'Hitting the "Vérité Jackpot"', 51.

112. Campany, *Photography and Cinema*, p. 56.

113. Bellour, *Between-the-Images*, p. 15.

114. Zelizer, *About to Die*, pp. 173–217.

115. Daney, Serge, 'La dernière image', in Raymond Bellour, Catherine David and Christine Van Assche (eds), *Passages de l'image* (Paris: Éditions du Centre Pompidou, 1990), pp. 57–60 (p. 58) (translations from this text are mine).

116. Ibid., p. 58.

117. For a discussion of the freeze-frame's disruption of sound, see Campany, *Photography and Cinema*, pp. 56–7.

118. Campany, *Photography and Cinema*, p. 55; Daney, 'La dernière image', p. 57.

119. Campany cited in Campbell and Cramerotti (eds), *Photocinema*, p. 15.

120. Bergala, Alain and Jean-Jacques Henry, introduction to dossier, 'Photographies', *Cahiers du cinéma*, 268–9 (1976), 39 (translation mine).

121. De Baecque, Antoine, *Les Cahiers du cinéma: histoire d'une revue, Volume II, Cinéma, tours détours 1959–1981* (Paris: Cahiers du cinéma, 1991), p. 301.
122. Bergala, 'Le pendule (la photo historique stéréotypée)', 41.
123. Ibid., 41.
124. Ibid., 41.
125. See Chapter 4 for further discussion of the relationship between the individual, the crowd and the icon.
126. Bergala, 'Le pendule (la photo historique stéréotypée)', 46, 44.
127. Ibid., 44.
128. Ibid., 44.
129. Ibid., 44.
130. Alain Bergala in 'Cinema Through the Eye of Magnum' (BBC, 17 September 2017). This documentary sets out a relevant context for understanding the 'Falling Soldier' and other iconic images by addressing the ties between the photography agency that Capa co-founded, Hollywood and other cinemas.
131. Bergala, 'Le pendule', 42.
132. Ibid., 42.
133. Ibid., 46.
134. For analysis of the icon's potential to catalyse collective action and social change, see Ghosh, *Global Icons*.
135. Westwell, 'One Image Begets Another', 326.
136. Translations from the film are mine. A version of Freund's comment is also cited in Bellour, 'Concerning "the Photographic"', p. 270.
137. Wall, Jeff, 'Photography and Liquid Intelligence' [1989], in *Jeff Wall: Selected Essays and Interviews* (New York: Museum of Modern Art, 2007), pp. 109–10 (p. 109).
138. Ibid., p. 110.
139. Silverman, *The Miracle of Analogy*, p. 69.
140. Ibid., p. 70.

CHAPTER TWO

The Double Life of the Gestapo Informer

One of the women looks ready to explode with rage. She has flung her arm out and is baring her teeth ferociously. In contrast to her puffed-up stance, the woman at whom she is glaring has hunched over slightly, lowered her gaze and clenched her fist. The two women differ not only in posture but also in dress: the angry one draws herself up in a smart, well-fitting outfit buttoned all the way to the collar, which enhances her air of authority, while the other one slouches in a dusty, crumpled uniform as strands of hair escape from her chignon. In the foreground, a man sitting at a table takes notes. In the background, a crowd looks grimly on, seemingly sharing the gesticulating woman's contempt. This is the first of several crowds that play a prominent role in this book, either because they feature in iconic images, or because they are carrying reproductions of them. What has provoked the fury of the crowd surrounding the two women? There are a handful of clues, such as the insignia on identity papers on the table and the striped uniform of one of the bystanders, but not enough to obviate the need for an explanation. 'No caption needed' proclaims the title of Hariman and Lucaites's study of iconic photographs and yet this intense but ambiguous image would not have endured without the verbal descriptions that have accompanied its publication and exhibition.[1] These commentaries have revealed that the photograph was taken in Dessau-Kochstedt in one of the centres for reclassifying and repatriating displaced people set up by the Allied armies at the end of the Second World War, and shows a liberated deportee unmasking the person who denounced her to the Gestapo. The image has recurred in magazines, exhibitions, catalogues, books and online digital archives of different kinds and most recently a graphic novel. According to the art theorist Rosalind Krauss, 'it has joined a kind of communal memory bank along with the burning Vietnamese girl running down the road and the little boy from the Warsaw Ghetto'.[2] The filmmaker and writer Thomas Tode, who has dated the picture to June 1945, concurs that it achieved the status of 'a photographic icon of the twentieth century'.[3] Like the 'Falling Soldier', this second gestural rendering of an explosive wartime moment, widely known as the 'Gestapo Informer', has fuelled discussion of the distinctive properties of photography, including its capacity to sum up seismic historical events.

To write about this iconic image only as a photograph, however, would be to overlook defining aspects of its form and history. Next to the photographer taking pictures of the informer's interrogation stood a film camera operator. The showdown between the deportee and her betrayer plays out across two series of images: still ones by Henri Cartier-Bresson and a moving sequence shot by an (unidentified) member of the American army crew with whom he was collaborating on a film about the liberation and journey home of prisoners and forced labourers after the defeat of Germany.[4] The film reveals that the deportee is in the process of slapping the informer. A photographer and a movie cameraperson working side by side, a scenario that recurs in each of the following chapters, provide an emblem of this book's project of writing cinema back into photojournalistic icon histories. The public lives of Cartier-Bresson's photograph and the documentary he was in Dessau to direct, the 33-minute *Le Retour* (*The Return*), intertwined for several years at least. The future photo-icon first appeared on 20 October 1945 in a magazine article about the film, which would premiere in the Champs-Elysées cinema in Paris the following January.[5] The snapshot's cinematic connections continued to inform commentary on the New York Museum of Modern Art's exhibition of Cartier-Bresson's stills in 1947, even as its exceptional qualities were increasingly attracting attention.

This chapter builds on recent research into the interdependence of photography and film in Cartier-Bresson's work by reappraising the 'Gestapo Informer' from the perspective of iconic image studies. The first section rethinks the photo's iconicity in terms of gesture and pathos, and stillness and movement. I draw here on a recent book by the art historian and philosopher Georges Didi-Huberman which revolves around another iconic photograph of women with agitated arms and contorted faces.[6] Didi-Huberman compares these gestures with formulas for expressing grief that link ancient and modern art and Christian and Muslim images. He borrows his method from the art historian Aby Warburg, whose fascination with Renaissance portrayals of 'life in motion' and especially the figure of the moving woman also informs my discussion of the iconic force of gestures of violent retribution.[7] While this part of the chapter adds a dynamic dimension to the debate over (usually Western) painting and sculpture as a source of templates for photojournalistic icons, the next section returns to the relationship between photography and film. Whereas Didi-Huberman explores Warburg's art historical concept of *Nachleben*, 'this word that signifies "afterlife" or "living afterwards"', the 'Gestapo Informer' and *Le Retour* thematise survival in the more straightforward sense of not dying in the National Socialist camps and sites of forced labour.[8] *Le Retour*'s treatment of former prisoners and enslaved workers exemplifies cinema's distinctive capacity to enrich our appreciation of the qualities that elevate certain photographs into icons, which I discuss throughout this book. The documentary's reluctance to distinguish between the different kinds of survivor who make up its migrating masses helps us understand the deportee's iconic gestures in the context of efforts to reunify post-Liberation France and gendered imagery of collaborators. The third section reconsiders the iconic photo in the light of Cartier-Bresson's cinephilia and compares reproductions of it in this post-war era of renascent French humanism to film stills. The chapter as a whole develops two linked claims: that the pathos of gestures that survive from art historical images links photo-icons to cinema's bodies in motion; and that the iconicity of the 'Gestapo Informer' has as much to do with the moving crowds in *Le Retour* as with a frozen rictus of rage.

Gesture and Pathos

The book that Didi-Huberman published in 2019 about an iconic photograph announces itself as an 'essai sur la mémoire d'un geste' (essay on the memory of a gesture). Like the partly visible hand of the accusing woman in Cartier-Bresson's image, the hands of the woman at the centre of the 'Wake in Kosovo' are in motion. The manual and facial expressions of grief that Georges Mérillon pictured on 29 January 1990 in the village of Nagafc after the murder of a young Kosovan separatist by Serbian police reminded Western commentators of a *mater dolorosa* or *pietà*. Didi-Huberman, however, situates the World Press Prize-winning photo in a larger 'atlas of lamentations'.[9] His study of this picture of pain extends his engagement with Warburg's attempts to trace through montage the recurrence of particular kinds of movement in still images from different ages. Nearly two decades earlier, Didi-Huberman's *L'Image survivante* (*The Surviving Image*, 2002) introduced *Nachleben* as an alternative to Johann Joachim Winckelmann's understanding of Renaissance art as determined by the imitation of ancient Greece's ideal models. Didi-Huberman asks:

> Might there not be a *time for phantoms*, a return of the images, a 'survival' (*Nachleben*) that is not subject to the model of transmission presupposed by the 'imitation' (*Nachahmung*) of ancient works by more recent works? [. . .] Might there not be a type of resemblance that is not the one imposed by the 'imitation of the ideal', with its rejection, in Winckelmann's formulation, of *pathos*?[10]

The two approaches to art history between which this passage distinguishes – one that emphasises ideal origins and one that unearths 'survivals' and 'metamorphoses' – involve different attitudes to pathos.[11] Winckelmann repudiates pathos, Didi-Huberman explains, because it 'deforms bodies and thus ruins the *ideal*'.[12] Pathos 'changes the features of the face, and the posture', and so disturbs the tranquil forms idealised by Winckelmann, who describes stillness as 'the state most appropriate to beauty'.[13] By contrast, Warburg devotes sustained attention to the *Pathosformeln* (pathos formulas) of the Renaissance, which Didi-Huberman defines as 'those gestures that are intensified in representation through the artists' recourse to the visual formulas of Classical antiquity'.[14]

A concern with pathos recurs in Hariman and Lucaites's influential study of photographs that have become icons in the United States. These images 'are described', they report, 'as being especially emotional'.[15] One of the defining features they ascribe to this class of photograph is the display of expressive bodies which 'provide dramatic enactment of specific positionings, postures and gestures that communicate emotional reactions instantly'.[16] For example, the stances of the children flanking Dorothea Lange's 'Migrant Mother' (1936) 'with eyes averted, give the scene its deep Christian pathos'.[17] Iconic pathos helps to account for the frequent comparisons these exceptional images provoke, as noted in my discussion of the 'Falling Soldier', with artistic renderings of emotion through posture and gesture in the Western tradition of still images. Hariman and Lucaites are struck, for instance, by the resemblance between Lange's photo and William Adolphe Bougeureau's painting 'Charity' (1865). Both follow 'the template of the Madonna and child that has been reproduced thousands of times in Western painting' and excite pity by depicting Mary as a poor woman draped with barefoot offspring.[18] It is not only icons originating in Spain and the US that have reminded viewers of Christian iconography. Another scene of Marian pathos supplied the design, according to European newspapers, for a photograph of Oum Saâd, an Algerian woman transfigured by shock and anguish at a massacre of civilians in Bentalha in the night of 22 to 23 September 1997. Seven years after Mérillon, Hocine Zaourar also won the World Press Photo prize for an image of Muslim grief that controversially acquired a Christian moniker: in this case the 'Madonna of Bentalha'. In a book devoted to this image, Juliette Hanrot discusses how its best-known, tightly cropped version 'strikingly concords' with paintings and sculptures of the Virgin grieving her dead son 'from the fifteenth to the seventeenth century, a period during which artistic translation of Marian piety reached peak expressivity'.[19] Oum Saâd's body slumped against a wall, the sideways tilt of her head and her distorted face express her agony. The woman next to her helps to 'concentrate and direct emotions', to quote from Hariman and Lucaites's description of photo-icons, by resting her hand on Oum Saâd's chest.[20] Hanrot relates this gesture of support and sympathy at the centre of the photo to the emphasis on Mary's breasts and by implication her role as a mother in paintings such as Sandro Botticelli's 'Lamentation Over the Dead Christ' (1490–2). Renaissance and baroque images of Jesus's corpse surrounded by distraught family and friends also play an important role in Didi-Huberman's discussion of movement in the contentiously nicknamed 'Pietà of Kosovo'.[21]

The risk of 'colonising' a Muslim tragedy by situating its iconic image in an exclusively Christian artistic tradition provides the point of departure for Didi-Huberman's discussion of Mérillon's photograph.[22] The name *pietà* implies a moral appeal to a Western audience. It also has the potential, Didi-Huberman argues, to accentuate the affect of the picture to which it quickly stuck while distracting from its politics. To tackle these problems, he suggests in an essay that returns to Warburg's concept of *Nachleben*, we need to recognise that '*images imply a duration* that goes well beyond the time that they represent or document'.[23] Placing an image in its historical context only gets us so far; we must attend to the 'formal relations' and 'long term temporal circulations' that become visible when we put it next to other images.[24] Like Hanrot considering the 'Madonna of Bentalha', Didi-Huberman discusses correspondences between an iconic photo – in this case the 'Wake in Kosovo' – and Renaissance paintings, drawings and sculptures of mourners surrounding the body of Christ, including a bronze relief by Donatello showing him lying beneath the cross (around 1460). Rather than limiting his comparisons to Christian images, however, Didi-Huberman draws attention to their '*classical* sources', by which he means 'tragic' and pervaded by 'corporeal and psychic *intensity*'.[25] It was this survival of antique 'pathos formulas' in Renaissance art that Warburg studied using montage in the *Bilderatlas Mnemosyne* (*Mnemosyne Atlas*) (1927–9). Didi-Huberman highlights the particular relevance of panels 41, 41a and 42 to Mérillon's still image of lamenting gestures and 'corporeal energy': 'from pagan Bacchae to Christian mourners, passing via the Jewish *kinah* or the Muslim ululation, it is the – essentially tragic – motif of a *Ninfa dolorosa* that Warburg sketches in the panels of his atlas'.[26] In contrast to the *mater dolorosa*, the figure of the *ninfa* (nymph) mixes the sacred 'sometimes scandalously' with the profane.[27]

How the bodily effects of despair and disaster, as displayed by the movements of the *ninfa dolorosa*, mutate in the modern period matters particularly to this chapter's study of photographic and cinematic images of 'corporeal and psychic intensity', which builds on my analysis of the 'Falling Soldier', whose gestures express the pathos of the moment between life and death. It is to nineteenth-century history painting that Gunthert compares iconic photography's 'incarnation' of a significant event or moment.[28] This artistic genre evolved when Goya replaced its traditional panoramas with more intimate perspectives on gestural extremes in his 'Disasters of War' series of prints (first published in 1863). Didi-Huberman draws a parallel between Goya's *'gesture of approach'* and Capa's conviction that getting closer makes for better photos, as put into practice with his iconic image of the militiaman, which I compared to the Spanish artist's 'Third of May, 1808'.[29] The 'Falling Soldier' and the photograph and film of the deportee striking the informer show close-up gestures illustrating or responding to the horrors of war. *Le Retour* belongs to an epoch ushered in by Goya's 'Disasters'. The heroes on which history painting had traditionally concentrated made way in Goya's images for what Didi-Huberman describes as 'human beings disfigured and destroyed by their fellows'.[30] Didi-Huberman makes a link between these pictures of affliction and the *'photographic figures of the human disfiguration* practised in the Nazi camps' that Władysław Strzemiński incorporated into the series of collages he made soon after the war ended, 'To My Friends the Jews'.[31] Human beings (nearly) destroyed by concentration camps, footage of which Cartier-Bresson sourced from archives, amass in the first quarter of his compilation film from the same era. They are still fresh in the mind of the viewer as she watches the documentary's several scenes showing confrontations with Nazi collaborators. It is to avoid pictures of the skeletal survivors 'engulfing our representation of the world' and to 'neutralise' their 'trauma' that *Le Retour* juxtaposes them, argues Tode, with '"counter-images", which are their exact opposite'.[32] Following Tode, we can think of the blow that the deportee lands on the informer in the DP camp as 'countering' the brutality that has been inflicted on the survivors in Wöbbelin and Dachau, to whom moving causes pain.[33]

This section of the chapter has concentrated so far on manifestations of extreme pain in order to sketch out a framework in which to explore gestures that link icons to both still and moving images. I want to suggest that the figure of the nymph is also relevant to bodily and emotional agitation in Cartier-Bresson's photograph and film. The protagonist who epitomises the *ninfa dolorosa* in Renaissance images of mourners collected around the dead or dying Christ, such as Bertoldo di Giovanni's bronze relief of the 'Crucifixion' (around 1485), a reproduction of which hangs on panel 42 of Warburg's atlas, is Mary Magdalene. It is due to the 'spectacularly excessive pathos' of her grief, as Didi-Huberman points out, that other art historians have described her as a 'maenad under the cross'.[34] Worshippers of Dionysus also known as Bacchae, maenads also congregate on the previous panel of *Mnemosyne*.

One of the themes of panel 41, according to Warburg, is 'Nympha als Hexe' (the nymph as witch). As Didi-Huberman explains, it presents 'a set of images where the motif of femininity dangerously approaches violent and murderous negativity'.[35] It is particularly through pictures of women that this and the previous panel, in the words of Christopher D. Johnson, 'stress how classical images of violence and woe recursively trouble the Renaissance imagination'.[36] Unlike the so-called 'maenad under the cross', who rips out her hair in sorrow, the two in a copper engraving by an unknown artist from Ferrara (from around 1465) that appears on panel 41 raise their arms in rage. The essay in which Warburg first proposed the concept of *Pathosformeln* (originally a lecture given in 1905) singles out the portrayal of Orpheus in this and analogous Renaissance reworkings of 'antique superlatives of gesture' as he tries to protect himself from the women who will tear him apart.[37] The 'gestural rendering of emotion' by the maenads, whose motives for punishing Orpheus vary between different versions of the story, escaped commentary in Warburg's lecture but has caught the attention of other art historians.[38] Isabella Woldt describes the 'pregnant' moment shown in the drawing Albrecht Dürer based on the Italian engraving in 1494: 'both maenads have already lifted their sticks and are about to perform their deadly attacks'.[39] Classicists have also underlined the significance of the maenads' expression of intense emotion in written versions of the myth. Genevieve Liveley, for example, argues that Virgil's retelling of the story accords 'remarkable authority [. . .] to angry women seeking retribution and settled scores'.[40] She points out that 'fierce feminist responses' to the narrative, such as H. D.'s poem 'Eurydice' (1917), reinforce the importance of female anger by 'glanc[ing] back [. . .] to the first fierce audience of women to respond to (or, rather, to resist) Orpheus: the bacchants'.[41]

What survives of the gestures of the 'witchy nymphs' of which Warburg collected images in Cartier-Bresson's iconic photograph of Dessau? Like the maenads, the woman in the makeshift law court convulses with anger and pursues retribution. As Tode argues of the film version, the blow she gives the informer provides a 'counter-image' to or amounts to 'a reversal of the violence that the deportees have suffered for such long years'.[42] A man in the striped uniform of a concentration camp prisoner in the front row of the crowd in the photograph is holding what looks like a baton. Like Orpheus, the woman accused feared that an angry mob would kill her, as we can surmise from Cartier-Bresson's note, on the back of a photographic print of a later moment in the trial, that she pleaded for her life.[43] Tode observes that male collaborators who Cartier-Bresson photographed and filmed as they were tried by the same court seem to have met this fate.[44] Other photos in the sequence and the matching film footage reveal that the deportee who lashes out at her betrayer, like her predecessors in art, is armed with a whip. And like the Bacchae, she appears in the middle of dealing a blow, as we can infer from her outstretched arm, braced stance and contorted face.

As evocative of her paroxysm of anger as her arm gesture is the movement of her mouth. Women and girls most often open this part of their body in photo-icons to give muted voice to physical or psychological pain. Think, for example, of the wails of the student beside the anti-war protestor shot dead at Kent State University by soldiers of the Ohio National Guard (photographed by John Filo on 4 May 1970), the screams of Kim Phúc covered in burning napalm, the lamentations of relatives and friends at the 'Wake in Kosovo' or the 'howl, groan or sigh' of Oum Saâd in response to the killings in Bentalha.[45] Oum Saâd's mouth amplifies the art historical echoes of Zaourar's news photograph. It reminds Hanrot particularly of the woman in 'Guernica' (Pablo Picasso, 1937) throwing back her head to wail in despair at the death of her baby.[46] The recurrence in iconic photographs of female cries of distress reinforces the pernicious gendering of pain that Jane Blocker has noticed in philosophical writing on still images of the mouth. Lessing's comments on the sculpted scream of Laocoön seem to imply, she suggests, that 'to exist in a state of pain is to exist helplessly in the body itself with no means to transcend it, as though one were a child or a woman'.[47]

The expressive mouth of Oum Saâd, however, has a different connotation for the artist Pascal Convert, who has turned Zaourar's photograph into a wax sculpture ('Pietà du Kosovo', 1999–2000). According to Convert, this detail in the picture 'transports us from Christian iconography and its imagery of pain to Greek tragedy and its rhetoric of vengeance. The *Mater dolorosa* becomes Medea.'[48] Along with the maenads, Medea is one of the 'nymphs as witches' featured on panel 41 of the *Bilderatlas Mnemosyne*. The desire for revenge takes the shape, in Cartier-Bresson's photo as in Convert's characterisation of Zaourar's, of a mouth. The deportee hitting the informer bares her teeth in a wrathful grimace. Anger manifests itself in her oral and dental – as much as manual – movements. The photograph illustrates the writer Georges Bataille's claim that 'on important occasions human life is still bestially concentrated in the mouth', whose meaning is 'violent'. Just as 'terror and atrocious suffering turn the mouth into the organ of rending screams', so too 'rage makes men grind their teeth'.[49]

The published English translation of Bataille's comments on the moving mouth reinforces the age-old cultural association between masculinity and violence. By contrast, an enduring tradition of image-making idealises women, in Marta Zarzycka's terms, as 'carriers of peace and reconciliation'.[50] Zarzycka has discussed, for example, how a photograph of mainly female protestors voicing their fury at President Hosni Mubarak in Tahrir Square in 2011 exploits these gendered codes. Against the prevalent tendency to denigrate anger – especially that of women – as 'unreasonable and destructive', this image mobilises the stereotype of femininity as pacific 'to suggest a national uprising where anger is contained and constructive rather than violent and excessive'.[51] The open mouths of these demonstrators, writes Zarzycka, 'connect anger to a speech act'.[52] While *Le Retour* shows the deportee testifying against the informer, the photograph of them that has become iconic isolates the moment when speech cedes to a snarl of hatred. The image breaks with the tradition that aligns femininity with non-violence by depicting a woman exacting revenge, not seeking reconciliation, and by rendering anger as violent gesture.

Didi-Huberman's 'essay on the memory of a gesture' helps us understand the pathos of iconic photographs in the context of the history, not only of still images, but also of moving ones. For Warburg, writes Didi-Huberman, 'an image, every image, is the result of movements that are provisionally sedimented or crystallized in it. These movements traverse it through and through, each one having its own trajectory [. . .] starting from a distance and continuing beyond it. They oblige us to think of the image as an energy-bearing or dynamic *moment* [. . .].'[53] This is the way in which Woldt approaches Dürer's picture of the angry maenads: 'the gestures of the raised arms as well as the billowing vestments – called [in Warburg's writing on other images] "moving accessories" (*bewegtes Beiwerk*) – whose flowing lines flatter the body and are blown away by the wind, contribute to emphasize the energy in the bodily movement'.[54] The gestures of these women, accentuated by the fluttering of their long, full, beribboned dresses, exemplify the rapid motion that animated the still image of Warburg's crucial motif of the nymph.[55] The question of the nymph's 'pictorial reproduction in early Humanism', Barbara Baert explains, 'opens a discourse on movement and wind in the visual medium'.[56] But this figure had particular resonance in the historical epoch when Warburg was studying her passage through Renaissance art. According to Philippe-Alain Michaud, Warburg's approach to still images was 'entirely based on an aesthetic of movement that was expressed at the end of the nineteenth century by the nascent cinema'.[57] Kathleen M. Gough has argued that not only photography and early film, but also 'the fin de siècle New Woman asserting her right to "unrestricted movement"', especially by wearing looser clothes, helped inspire the art historical preoccupation with the 'unmanly' nymphic image.[58] As I return at this juncture in the chapter to the relationship between photography and cinema, I seek to keep the moving woman, not only as an artistic motif, but also as a historical figure, in the foreground.

The women's gestures that link Mérillon's photograph to a vast panoply of still images recur in film and video. Didi-Huberman's account of the *ninfa dolorosa* mentions, for example, the transformation of mourning into protest, and of 'despondency into uprising', in films including *La Rabbia* (*Anger*; Pier Paolo Pasolini, 1963).[59] He also alludes to Jean-Luc Godard's use of moving bodies befallen in Goya's images by disaster as a 'leitmotif' in the video essay *Histoire(s) du cinéma* (1988–98).[60] The grieving women of Nagafc themselves appear in video recorded by a French television crew directed by Véronique

Taveau. Didi-Huberman stresses the connection between the video and photographs, the two media supposedly 'bearing witness to the *same scene*, that's to say, the same bodies, the same space and the same duration'.[61] Even so, film and video play a marginal role in Didi-Huberman's essay, as I have suggested they also do in theorisations of iconic camera images. The rest of this chapter aims to show why cinema needs to occupy a central position in an account of the iconicity of another photograph of a scene simultaneously recorded in movement, though on film rather than video.

STILL AND MOVING CROWDS

What unique resources does *Le Retour* bring to our understanding of the iconic power acquired by Cartier-Bresson's photograph of a gesture of retribution? This section of the chapter develops my discussion of the 'Gestapo Informer' by comparing it with the equivalent scene and other prominent images of still and moving bodies in Cartier-Bresson's film. In so doing, I seek to complicate an assumption about the relationship between photography and cinema that recurs in scholarly and journalistic writing on iconicity. As I have noted, Susan Sontag and Gisèle Freund observed in the decade or so after the Vietnam War, with reference to emblematic pictures of this conflict, that a photograph is more likely than moving images to stick in our memories, in spite of television's ever-swelling flood of pictures. As Sontag subsequently put it, 'memory freeze-frames'.[62] This is partly because photographs are better, suggested the narrator of Teri Wehn-Damisch's film about Freund, at summing up and throwing light on bewildering and complex events. The question of why a clutch of photographs of protestors against political violence in Vietnam and soldiers and civilians caught up in it have become more famous than any moving footage of the war arose again at the end of the century in Marita Sturken's study of camera images and memory. One of Sturken's reasons echoes Wehn-Damisch's commentary in attributing to the photograph of Kim Phúc a greater capacity than the equivalent piece of film to elucidate a confusing episode, especially by delineating facial expressions.[63] Like Hariman and Lucaites, whose insights into iconic pathos I discussed earlier in this chapter, then, but by implication, Sturken associates iconicity with ways of evoking emotion that are particularly photographic. In her account, photography clarifies film, whose role, in Patrick Hagopian's discussion of another icon of the war in Vietnam, the so-called 'burning monk', is merely to 'enhanc[e] the significance of the photos'.[64] By contrast, this section of the chapter suggests that Cartier-Bresson's film clarifies the iconic appeal of his photograph, while the final section examines how the photograph enhanced the significance of the film.

About a third of the way through *Le Retour*, during a sequence about what the narrator calls 'provisional centres of reclassification and repatriation' created by the Allies, such as those in Dessau-Kochstedt, the supposed informer walks into the frame. The still camera, the lack of synchronous sound and the improvised feel of the proceedings may give a viewer today the sense of watching the subjects of the famous photograph taking their places for it. A guard leads the woman under arrest to a table at which sits the camp's commander, Wilhelm van der Velden. Behind them stand a large crowd of liberated prisoners, into which her accuser for the moment blends. The film cuts to a high angle, tighter shot of the three main protagonists. The woman who has recognised her betrayer has stepped forward and is speaking. Her whip hangs threateningly from her folded arms.[65] The camera moves nearer still to capture the blow. The plaintiff strikes so hard with her weapon that she knocks the other woman, reeling, momentarily out of the frame. While the assault continues in Cartier-Bresson's photographs, the film moves quickly on to the interrogation of two other suspected collaborators, who are men. The giving of evidence against the woman takes less than half a minute.

Krauss remarks on this condensation when comparing the film to the photo-icon: 'the scene in the movie is over before we can even figure out what it's about. The slap has no resonance. Something's off about the drama.'[66] Why does the film sequence lack the photo's 'violence' and 'memorableness', wonders Krauss, given that they frame the testimony and the blow in roughly the same way? Tellingly, she prefaces her discussion with Freund's observation that 'it's always the still image and not the one in motion that stays etched in our minds, becoming ever after part of our collective memory'.[67] Like the television images from Vietnam considered by Sturken in her book of 1997, the footage from Dessau, according to Krauss's article of the same year, lacks the equivalent photograph's iconic force. The main difference between the two versions of the scene, she concludes, is that the stasis of the photo lets us pore over details in it. Whereas the two women monopolise our attention in the film, the photo 'gives us the time to notice the motley crowd of onlookers'.[68] Krauss spots, for example, that one of these spectators is looking 'not at the drama itself but at the camera capturing it'.[69] The 'tangle of metallic zipper appearing and disappearing along the side of the denunciating woman's dress' also catches her attention.[70] Krauss's careful description of this fastening not only shares the concern with material detail that leads Gough to read Warburg through the lens of the loosening of women's attire at the *fin de siècle*. Both these accounts of art or art history pay attention to the clothes of historical women (though from different periods). It also anticipates Claire Gorrara's analysis of Lee Miller's images of the liberation of France as offering 'a reflection on the intersection of fashion, war photography and the female body' that 'encouraged a largely female civilian readership to recognise the gendering of war experience'.[71]

It is in features such as the metal strip that outlines the deportee's waist, Krauss reminds us, that Roland Barthes finds an 'obtuse' or 'third meaning', different from the 'obvious' (first and second) informational and symbolic levels of an image.[72] Barthes comes up with this notion, however, in an article originally published (only a few years before Sontag's discussion of photographic and television coverage of the Vietnam War) by *Cahiers du cinéma* that excavates the supplementary meanings not of photographs, but of film frames or photogrammes.[73] The 'third meaning', then, has to do with the relationship between still and moving images. In other words, the very element of the photo that makes it more 'memorable', in Krauss's reading – its revelation of detail – leads, via its 'obtuse' meanings, back to film.

The details that fascinate Krauss are indifferent, she points out, to the 'decisive moment' that Cartier-Bresson has been famous for capturing since the publication of the English language version of his first book of photos, even if some suppose Capa to have invented the concept.[74] In *Images à la sauvette* or *The Decisive Moment*, the 'Gestapo Informer' is one of around twenty pictures that spread across two whole pages. The book selects it as an important image, anticipating its future status as an emblem, like the 'Falling Soldier' before it, of a special property of photography. What the caption describes as 'the strong, sharp light of rage' that 'illuminates' the accusing woman's face recalls Cartier-Bresson's reference in the foreword to photography's distinctive capacity to fix 'things which are continually vanishing': 'what is there more fugitive and transitory than the expression on a human face? [. . .] The decisive moment and psychology, no less than camera position, are the principle factors in the making of a good portrait.'[75] Most of Cartier-Bresson's 'decisive moments', as David Campany points out, render 'eventful' the everyday.[76] 'While news-photographers specialize in catastrophe, the photo-finish of some aspect of shock', wrote Lincoln Kirstein in 1947 in what was to my knowledge the first book that reproduced the 'Gestapo Informer', 'Cartier-Bresson's pictures are seized in the middle norm of a run of action [. . .].'[77] Exceptionally, however, his iconic image of fury and revenge fixes a 'decisive moment' in history; as Campany observes, it is 'a momentary depiction of something momentous'.[78]

The popular and enduring idea that photography ought to arrest the moment when 'the elements in motion are in balance', as Cartier-Bresson puts it, was inspired by its encounter with cinema.[79] It is this idea – the 'decisive moment' – that leads Campany, writing about a decade after Krauss, briefly to compare the 'Gestapo Informer' with *Le Retour*. What 'compels' Campany about the photo are not the obtuse meanings that intrigue Krauss but its 'fragmentary incompleteness'.[80] 'The film', he suggests, offers 'a more comprehensive account of the scene [. . .]. While its individual frames show less than the photograph, the unfolding film can explain more of what is going on.'[81] Whereas, for Krauss, the photo helps us make sense of the film, for Campany, the film helps us make sense of the photo. More than this, *Le Retour* also throws light, I will argue, on the features that made the photograph iconic.

Le Retour helps us appreciate how what has become a universal icon resonated with the concerns of a particular nation. Whereas Didi-Huberman places the 'Wake in Kosovo' in its historical context before relating it to images from other times, this chapter inverts his method. Having begun by linking the 'Gestapo Informer' to art history, I turn now to the circumstances of its creation, which were inextricable from the film. The sleeping partner on *Le Retour*, as Tode has revealed, was the Mouvement National des Prisonniers de Guerre et Déportés (National Movement of Prisoners of War and Deportees), a resistance group closely tied to the Ministère des Prisonniers, Déportés et Réfugiés (Ministry for Prisoners, Deportees and Refugees) of the provisional government established in France after its liberation from Germany.[82] Sylvie Lindeperg has argued that *Le Retour* takes up 'the unitary and unifying discourse of [this] ministry according to which all those who had been away belonged to the same category and should be neither separated nor divided'.[83] It was rifts not only between resisters and collaborators but also between different groups who had fought the Germans and between distinct classes of former prisoners that the humanism renascent in this country in the aftermath of the war sought to bridge. Nina Lager Vestberg describes this contentious ideology as 'the small plot of common ground where the political tensions of post-Liberation France could be resolved momentarily'.[84] Lists of pioneers of the photographic form of this humanism, which Vestberg links to freelancers' financial need to take pictures that would sell to both the Catholic and the Communist press, usually include Cartier-Bresson. Like Capa's 'Falling Soldier' and Vestberg's case study, Robert Doisneau's 'The Kiss at the Hôtel de Ville' (1950), the 'Gestapo Informer' exemplifies the interest in ordinary people that became a hallmark of humanist photography in both its French and American strains.[85]

Le Retour uniquely contributes to our understanding of this photograph, I suggest, by placing the iconic gesture of retribution in the context of visual and verbal depictions of mass movement that elide differences. While the previous section of this chapter focused on the figure of the moving woman, the main motif of *Le Retour*, through which it plays down divisions, is a moving (and mainly male) crowd. A minute or so into the film, the commentary by Claude Roy, a survivor, like Cartier-Bresson, of a stalag or German prisoner of war camp, lists several of the categories of people who have been absent from wartime France: POWs, forced labourers and 'opponents of Hitlerian fascism, deported, condemned to a slow death in the camps or a tragic death by torture, in a gas chamber or at a stake'.[86] There is no mention of the Jewish genocide, or of the distinction between *Konzentrationslager* (concentration camps) and *Vernichtungslager* (camps of destruction or extermination), which is not unusual in documentaries and newsreels produced in the immediate aftermath of the war that refer to those enslaved and murdered by the National Socialists.[87] As Lindeperg notes, the film de-emphasises the distinctions between these categories of prisoner and deportee, whether or not it names them.[88] We recognise survivors of the concentration camps, whose images accumulate in the first part of the film, as I suggested earlier, by their minimal, painful movements. After these images of near stillness come shots of multiple bodies in motion. Described by the male narrator simply as 'liberated captives', some of the men trudging along country roads in a montage of footage lasting several minutes wear uniforms that suggest they were POWs. But it is hard to be sure from what kind of camp or labour site many of the exhausted, hungry and ragged marchers who appear throughout the film are returning.

The narrator in fact draws attention to the propensity of these moving masses to obscure the difference between victims and perpetrators. He tells us that the female informer under arrest in Dessau was 'trying to disappear into the flood of deportees'. This crowd, he later observes, mixes 'traitors' with 'innocents', 'torturers' with 'victims' and 'denouncers' with 'the denounced'. Only 'a small handful' of such 'wretches', however, in his account, have sought refuge in these migrating masses, and several scenes depict their exposure and punishment.

How do the images of mass movement, especially home to France, that accumulate in Cartier-Bresson's film elucidate the iconic power of his photograph? Like these scenes of travel, those of denunciation and retribution reinforce what Lindeperg calls *Le Retour*'s 'hymn to a united France'.[89] Although, as Krauss points out, the photograph gives us more chance to scrutinise the crowd of displaced people than the counterpart images in the film, the sequence twice cuts away from collaborators on trial to sections of the crowd of onlookers. These shots exemplify what Campany describes as Cartier-Bresson's habit of picturing history's 'decisive moments' indirectly by 'shooting bystanders rather than the main attraction'.[90] But they also turn 'bystanders' into 'the main attraction'. For Tode, the scene of the female informer's interrogation depicts the DPs as 'a questioning and judging mass' organising themselves into a '"primitive democratic" assembly actively participating in the pursuit of Nazi criminals and the new French Republican postwar order which is ideologically underpinned by an identification with the Resistance'.[91] The power of the photograph derives from its depiction not only of an individual gesture of violence but also of disparate inhabitants of a transit camp united in the prosecution of their former persecutors. An early account in the *New York Times* of one of Cartier-Bresson's photos of the crowd of DPs watching the informer's trial underlines this unity by describing them as French.[92]

In reading this photo-icon, through the lens of the film, as showing a unified crowd, I am not suggesting that the punishment of collaborators helped to heal divisions in post-Liberation France. The 'Gestapo Informer' recalls another iconic photograph of a vengeful mob surrounding a woman who has suffered violence for alleged collaboration with the Germans. Capa took this analogous picture in Chartres less than a year earlier on 18 August 1944, the day of the city's liberation. A shaven-headed woman clutching a baby is paraded along a street decorated with a *tricolore* flag by a crowd of townspeople who encircle and mock her. In an essay on the photographic 'iconography of the ends of wars' (which does not mention the 'Gestapo Informer'), Ulrich Hägele suggests that Capa's image 'could be read as a form of symbolic catharsis, allowing viewers to liberate themselves simultaneously from the National Socialist occupier and de facto compromises of principle under the Vichy regime'.[93] As Gorrara has explained, however, the first historical accounts of the head shavings as cathartic and guilt-assuaging for the nation were complicated by later interpretations of this ritual as 'scapegoating women and thereby avoiding confrontation with individual and collective crimes of collaboration'.[94] While Cartier-Bresson's photograph of a female collaborator also became iconic, five of the six 'wretches' singled out in *Le Retour* and his other stills of Dessau as perpetrators are male. These two image repertoires fixate, however, on individual collaborators, while depicting resistance as collective.

THE 'GESTAPO INFORMER' AS FILM STILL

Having discussed, in the previous section, what distinguishes these still and moving images of individual perpetrators and justice-seeking crowds and how *Le Retour* sheds light on the 'Gestapo Informer', I turn now to the cinematic qualities of this photograph. In Chapter 1 I noted that the dynamism that makes the 'Falling Soldier' so memorable unsettles the boundary between the photograph and the film frame. The Leica, which pioneered the use of film stock for stills and helped deepen the dialogue between photography and cinema in the late 1920s and 1930s particularly, enabled Capa to capture an image of the militiaman's sudden and dramatic collapse. Cartier-Bresson used the same camera in what Tode describes as his lifelong exploration of the 'open space' between these two media.[95] The intermedial terrain in which he prospected has attracted increasing attention in the new millennium. An important reappraisal of his stills through a cinematic lens, by the photography historian and theorist Michel Frizot, only fleetingly touches on his images of the end of the Second World War.[96] Drawing on Frizot's essay, this section discusses how one of the photographs that became icons of this historical moment resembles and circulated in the guise of an image from a film.

The still and moving images of the collaborator trials at Dessau epitomise what Frizot characterises as Cartier-Bresson's 'permanent hesitation' between the professions of photographer and filmmaker.[97] Frizot traces this vacillation back to the late 1920s and early 1930s, when Cartier-Bresson was starting his career and cinema supplied the 'the great model hanging over photography'.[98] Not only did Cartier-Bresson begin to make films in 1936; cinephilia also shaped his photographic practice. In order to explain how, Frizot turns to the film magazines that sprang up in France at the end of the 1920s. The pages of these antecedents of the 'paper cinema' that first animated the 'Falling Soldier' are filled with film stills, that is, photographs taken during filming (not to be confused with film frames). Frizot ponders the specific properties of this 'cinematographic photography': 'you know you're seeing cinema-images, on account of the fact that they are in a specialist publication. But, sooner or later, you see photography first, you grasp it as equivalent to other photographs, and perhaps you forget the film that is its source.'[99] Unlike other kinds of photograph, however, these ones involve staging and choreography, as revealed by their protagonists' looks and gestures.[100] Frizot suggests that film stills that circulated in the new kinds of lavishly illustrated magazines anticipate Cartier-Bresson's later photographs, which he took as if he were making cinema, 'like an unconscious of the gaze to come'.[101]

To what extent do the 'photographs of cinema' that began to proliferate in interwar magazines foreshadow Cartier-Bresson's post-war icon?[102] The film still conventionally presents a scene that is unfolding on a film set. Obviously, Cartier-Bresson could not avail himself in the DP camp at Dessau of the lighting, props, costumes and make-up that benefited the so-called 'stillmen' who Steven Jacobs construes as 'a typical product of the industrial organisation of the film studios during the classical era (ca. 1912–1960)'.[103] Nevertheless, there are significant similarities between the specialised labour of film still production and the practices that produced the 'Gestapo Informer' and certain later icons of photojournalism, including several discussed in this book. Like a film still, the iconic photo from 1945 portrays an instant from a motion picture from a similar perspective to that adopted by the film camera.[104] The positions of Cartier-Bresson's Leica and, even closer to the main protagonists and slightly higher, the film apparatus operated by his colleague, which afford an advantaged view, arouse the suspicion that someone has planned the scene, like those in on-set photographs, with the cameras in mind. As Jacobs explains, the lenses with smaller maximum apertures and the inferior stock used by film photographers in comparison to cinematographers meant that for much of the classical period 'the suspension of the action and posing for stills guaranteed more satisfying results' than pictures hazarded during takes.[105] Cartier-Bresson's dynamic photograph instead foreshadows the appropriation by Hollywood still photographers in the 1950s and 1960s when their profession was in decline of what Jacobs terms 'the snapshot aesthetics of photojournalism', so that 'stills turned into so-called *action stills*'.[106]

The 'Gestapo Informer' not only shares some key features with film stills but also began its public life in a similar way to this type of photograph. The primary purpose of these production stills, whether destined for newspapers, film magazines such as *Pour vous* and *La Revue du cinéma*, richly illustrated weeklies with wider remits such as *Vu* or lobby cards, was to promote films.[107] Like the 'Falling Soldier', which introduced frames from *The Spanish Earth* in *Life* and mutated into a poster for *Gallipoli*, as described in the previous chapter, the 'Gestapo Informer' participated in film publicity. What according to Tode was the first publication to carry Cartier-Bresson's future icon, *France Illustration*, extended the interwar tradition of paper cinema in a regular film column arranged around abundant large pictures that raised awareness of new releases. In the 20 October 1945 issue, for example, not insignificantly only the third since *L'Illustration* had morphed after the liberation, under the direction of Resistance member Georges Oudard, into the new title, a richly illustrated two-page article announces the forthcoming *Le Retour*. Seven snapshots of liberated prisoners and refugees passing through Leipzig, Halle and Dessau, which Cartier-Bresson took while gathering footage for the documentary, occupy more space than François de Roux's text, which overlaps with Roy's voice-over commentary. The piece neither mentions photography nor credits the pictures to Cartier-Bresson; it describes them instead as 'the most significant images' of the film, as if they were frames from it.[108] A caption underlines the 'drama' of the Gestapo informer's public unmasking, foreshadowing the special status that one of the two images of this scene that appear at the top of the piece would acquire.[109] Whereas iconic image studies has tended to view films as amplifying the importance of photographs, however, the magazine harnesses the power of the future photo-icon to highlight the significance of *Le Retour's* portrayal of liberated prisoners of all kinds working together to expose Nazi collaborators.

Less than a year and a half after this issue of *France Illustration* went on sale, an exhibition at MoMA would present several of the same photographs as worth attention in their own right, rather than merely as foretastes of a film. In a book appended to this display of over 150 of Cartier-Bresson's images, Kirstein insists on the specificity of their medium: 'Cartier-Bresson's best shots could not have been drawn or painted, but only photographed.'[110]

That the 'Gestapo Informer' is the sole picture of the exposure of so-called 'stool-pigeons' in Dessau reproduced in the catalogue hints that it was already recognised as one of these superior images, though it had not yet assumed the proportions it would in *Images à la sauvette*.[111] At the same time, writing about the show reinforces the connection between the photographs of the DP camp and the medium of cinema. It was not just that these stills overlap with *Le Retour*, which was screened at MoMA on the opening night of the exhibition, 4 February, and again later in the year by the museum's Film Library.[112] Their cinematic dimensions also caught Kirstein's attention over half a century before Frizot's discussion of the film still as the unconscious of Cartier-Bresson's photography. Contrary to de Roux's article in *France Illustration*, Kirstein stresses in a *New York Times* piece on the exhibition that Cartier-Bresson's 'still-photographs are by no means fragments cut out of a film'. 'Yet', he continues, 'they have their cinematic drama, a sharpness and – particularly in the scenes of denunciation of informers at Dessau – an almost classic ferocity.' While the photos of Dessau remind him of cinema, *Le Retour* leads him back to these same stills: 'much of the anguish in this film's almost insupportable emotion is clear in his still photographs of the denunciation of traitors and informers by the released French prisoners'.[113] Like the 'Falling Soldier', then, the 'Gestapo Informer' exemplifies the under-explored propensity of iconic images to provoke reflection on overlaps between photographic and filmic renderings of intense emotion through gesture.

CONCLUSION: COMPOSITE ICON

This chapter has tried to show how attention to gesturing bodies, moving images and film stills enriches our appreciation of a defining photograph of the end of the Second World War. A staple of collections of iconic camera images, this picture has circulated for over seventy years as a privileged example of photography's special propensity to crystallise what matters about a historical event in a single instant. Yet this approach to the photograph neglects the double life the 'Gestapo Informer' has led in and around the cinema, not only as part of the cast of *Le Retour* but also in images promoting the film. As is conventional in iconic image studies, I began by seeking precedents for the photograph in art history. Like Renaissance images of maenads about to rip Orpheus to pieces, in which antique gestural formulas survive, Cartier-Bresson's picture foregrounds female anger and retribution. The explosive emotions that made this image iconic are expressed through bodily movement: the deportee's arm preparing to deliver a blow, her grimacing mouth and her gnashing teeth. *Le Retour*'s suppression of divisions among crowds of liberated prisoners on the move elucidates the iconic resonance of their united resistance to collaborators. The circulation of the 'Gestapo Informer' in the 1940s as an image from *Le Retour* further bolsters this book's central claim that iconicity troubles the boundary between photography and film.

The still and moving images of the prosecution of suspected collaborators at Dessau soon parted ways. The photograph continued to turn up, especially in books and exhibitions, but lost its connection to *Le Retour*, which its captions stopped mentioning. Previously appended to the film, it became 'emblematic' of Cartier-Bresson's photographic style, 'a skilfully thought out image that was composed in an instant, never cropped'.[114] The documentary, meanwhile, faded into obscurity. By 1996, when Krauss saw it in Paris in a double bill with Cartier-Bresson's *Victoire de la vie* (*Return to Life*, 1938), it had turned into a 'rare' film.[115] One of the reasons why the debate about the 'Gestapo Informer' has revived in the past decade is the widespread public and scholarly interest in iconic photographs. Yet contemporary publications are also rediscovering the photo-icon's attachment to cinema. For example, Tode's essay from 2014 reunites the 'Gestapo Informer' with *Le Retour* by reproducing the photograph and three analogous film frames next to each other for the reader to compare.[116] Jean-David Morvan, Séverine Tréfouël and Sylvain Savoia recreate the same moment in their graphic novel, *Cartier-Bresson, Allemagne 1945* (2016), whose cover features the original snapshot.[117] Their drawing faithfully copies every detail in the photograph but widens the frame to incorporate the figures of Cartier-Bresson pointing his Leica and an American soldier filming. This fascinating amalgam of still and moving pictures supports Hariman and Lucaites's account of icons as composite images while highlighting the particular significance of photographic and cinematic components.

Notes

1. Hariman and Lucaites, *No Caption Needed*.
2. Krauss, '". . . And Then Turn Away?"', p. 163.
3. Tode, Thomas, 'Henri Cartier-Bresson: la liberté, le mouvement et l'instant', trans. Clara Bloch, in Morvan, Tréfouël and Savoia, *Cartier-Bresson, Allemagne 1945*, pp. 119–41 (p. 136). On the photo's date, see Tode, Thomas, 'Une larme sur la joue du temps: *Le Retour* d'Henri Cartier-Bresson', trans. Clara Bloch, *1895*, 74 (2014), 12–37 (21). (Translations from both these texts are mine.)
4. Cartier-Bresson was working with two camera operators supervised by Lieutenant Johnson. Contributions to the film by Johnson, Lieutenant Richard Banks and Captain Jerold Krimsky are detailed in Tode, 'Une larme sur la joue du temps'.
5. See Tode, 'Une larme sur la joue du temps', 18, 29.
6. Didi-Huberman, *Ninfa dolorosa* (translations from this text are mine).
7. Warburg, Aby, 'Dürer and Italian Antiquity', in *The Renewal of Pagan Antiquity: Contributions to the Cultural History of the European Renaissance*, trans. David

Britt (Los Angeles, CA: Getty Research Institute for the History of Art and the Humanities, [1932] 1999), pp. 553–8 (p. 555).

8. Didi-Huberman, Georges, *The Surviving Image. Phantoms of Time and Time of Phantoms: Aby Warburg's History of Art*, trans. Harvey Mendelsohn (University Park, PA: Penn State University Press, [2002] 2016), p.16.

9. Didi-Huberman, *Ninfa dolorosa*, p. 21.

10. Didi-Huberman, *The Surviving Image*, p. 11.

11. Ibid., p. 45.

12. Ibid., p. 9.

13. Winckelmann, cited in Didi-Huberman, *The Surviving Image*, p. 9.

14. Didi-Huberman, *The Surviving Image*, p. 25.

15. Hariman and Lucaites, *No Caption Needed*, p. 36.

16. Ibid., p. 36.

17. Ibid., p. 57.

18. Ibid., p. 56.

19. Hanrot, *La Madone de Bentalha*, p. 83 (translations from this text are mine).

20. Hariman and Lucaites, *No Caption Needed*, p. 36.

21. Didi-Huberman, *Ninfa dolorosa*, for example pp. 134–45. For further discussion of Western paintings of the dead Christ, which also crop up regularly in writing on Alborta's iconic photograph of Che Guevara's corpse, see Chapter 4.

22. Didi-Huberman, *Ninfa dolorosa*, pp. 18–19. Didi-Huberman only refers to Mérillon's and Zaourar's photographs as 'icons' in passing when discussing their acquisition of Christian titles (p. 19). He describes Joe Rosenthal's photograph of 'Flag-raising at Iwo Jima' (23 February 1945) as an 'image phare' (beacon image) (p. 35).

23. Didi-Huberman, *Ninfa dolorosa*, p. 19.

24. Ibid., p. 21.

25. Ibid., p. 136.

26. Ibid., pp. 21, 42.

27. Ibid., p. 150.

28. Gunthert, 'Les icônes du photojournalisme', p. 23.

29. Didi-Huberman, *Ninfa dolorosa*, p. 29.

30. Ibid., p. 29.

31. Ibid., p. 33.

32. Tode, 'Une larme sur la joue du temps', p. 15.

33. For an important discussion of the interplay between stillness and movement in another film that reappropriates archival images of concentration camps, *Nuit et brouillard* (*Night and Fog*; Alain Resnais, 1956), see Wilson, 'Material Remains'.

34. Didi-Huberman, *Ninfa dolorosa*, p. 150.

35. Ibid., p. 21.

36. Johnson, Christopher, *Metaphor, Memory and Aby Warburg's Atlas of Images* (Ithaca, NY: Cornell University Press, 2012), p. 90.

37. Warburg, 'Dürer and Italian Antiquity', p. 558.

38. Ibid., p. 556.

39. Woldt, Isabella, 'Ur-Words of the Affective Language of Gestures: The Hermeneutics of Body Movement in Aby Warburg', *Interfaces: Image, Texte, Language*, 40 (2018), https://preo.u-bourgogne.fr/interfaces/index.php?id=605 (last accessed 5 August 2019).

40. Liveley, Genevieve, 'Orpheus and Eurydice', in Vanda Zajko and Helena Hoyle (eds), *A Handbook to the Reception of Classical Mythology* (Malden, MA: Wiley Blackwell, 2017), pp. 287–98 (p. 293).

41. Liveley, 'Orpheus and Eurydice', p. 297.

42. Tode, 'Une larme sur la joue du temps', p. 20.

43. The handwritten note is reproduced in *Henri Cartier-Bresson: Scrapbook. Photographies 1932–1946* (Steidl: Göttingen, 2006), p. 229.

44. Tode, 'Une larme sur la joue du temps', p. 20.

45. Hanrot, *La Madone de Bentalha*, p. 94.

46. Ibid., p. 95.

47. Blocker, Jane, *What the Body Cost: Desire, History, and Performance* (Minneapolis, MN; London: University of Minnesota Press, 2004), p. 30. See especially her chapter on 'Mouths', pp. 19–52.

48. Convert, Pascal, 'Médée l'algérienne', *Art Press*, 286 (January 2003), 19–22 (20) (my translation).

49. Bataille, Georges, 'Mouth' [1930], in *Visions of Excess: Selected Writings, 1927–1939*, trans. Allan Stoekl (Minneapolis: University of Minnesota Press, 1985), pp. 59–60 (p. 59).

50. Zarzycka, Marta, *Gendered Tropes in War Photography: Mothers, Mourners, Soldiers* (London: Routledge, 2016), p. 25.

51. Ibid., pp. 23, 25.

52. Ibid., p. 23.

53. Didi-Huberman, *The Surviving Image*, p. 19.

54. Woldt, 'Ur-Words'.

55. Warburg, 'Dürer and Italian Antiquity', p. 555.

56. Baert, Barbara, 'Nymph: The Reproduction of a Phantom. A Contribution to the Study of Aby Warburg (1866–1929)', in Shigetoshi Osano and Milosz Wozny (eds), *Between East and West: Reproductions in Art. Proceedings of the 2013 CIHA Colloquium in Naruto, Japan, January 15–18, 2013* (Cracow: Irsa, 2015), pp. 167–90 (p. 167).

57. Michaud, Philippe-Alain, *Aby Warburg and the Image in Motion*, trans. Sophie Hawkes (New York: Zone Books, 2007), p. 39.

58. Gough, Kathleen M., 'Between the Image and Anthropology: Theatrical Lessons from Aby Warburg's "Nympha"', *The Drama Review*, 56: 3 (2012), 114–30 (120, 124).

59. Didi-Huberman, *Ninfa dolorosa*, p. 233. He also gives examples from *Battleship Potemkin* (Sergei Eisenstein, 1925) and *Entranced Earth* (Glauber Rocha, 1967).

60. Ibid., pp. 32–3.

61. Ibid., p. 16.

62. Sontag, *Regarding the Pain of Others*, p. 19.

63. Sturken, *Tangled Memories*, p. 90. I discuss Sturken's comparison of two iconic photographs from Vietnam with moving footage of the same violent incidents in more detail in the next chapter.

64. Hagopian, Patrick, 'Vietnam War Photography as a Locus of Memory', in Annette Kuhn and Kirsten Emiko McAllister (eds), *Locating Memory: Photographic Acts* (New York, Oxford: Berghahn, 2006), pp. 201–22 (p. 214).

65. Tode explains that the woman's weapon identifies her as 'a sort of investigator or public prosecutor representing the deportees' ('Une larme sur la joue du temps', p. 19).

66. Krauss, '". . . And Then Turn Away?"', p. 11.

67. Ibid., p. 10. Freund's remark is also cited in the introduction to this book.

68. Ibid., p. 11.

69. Ibid., p. 12.

70. Ibid., p. 12.

71. Gorrara, Claire, 'Fashion and the *Femmes Tondues*: Lee Miller, *Vogue* and Representing Liberation France', *French Cultural Studies*, 29: 4 (2018), 330–44 (331).

72. Krauss, '". . . And Then Turn Away?"', p. 12.

73. Barthes, Roland, 'The Third Meaning' [1970], in *Image Music Text*, pp. 52–68.

74. See Chapter 1 for a discussion of the 'Falling Soldier' as a 'decisive moment'.

75. Cartier-Bresson, *The Decisive Moment*, no page numbers.

76. Campany, *Photography and Cinema*, pp. 27–8.

77. Kirstein, Lincoln, 'Henri Cartier-Bresson: Documentary Humanist', in *The Photographs of Henri Cartier-Bresson* (New York: The Museum of Modern Art, 1947), pp. 7–11 (p. 8).

78. Campany, *Photography and Cinema*, p. 27.

79. Cartier-Bresson, *The Decisive Moment*, no page numbers.

80. Campany, *Photography and Cinema*, p. 28.

81. Ibid., pp. 28–9.

82. Tode, 'Une larme sur la joue du temps', p. 27.

83. Lindeperg, Sylvie, *Les Écrans de l'ombre: la seconde guerre mondiale dans le cinéma français* (Paris: CNRS, 1997), p. 223 (translations from this text are mine).

84. Vestberg, Nina Lager, 'Robert Doisneau and the Making of a Universal Cliché', *History of Photography*, 35: 2 (2011), 157–65 (59).

85. Vestberg, 'Robert Doisneau', 159, 161.

86. Translations from the commentary of *Le Retour* are mine.

87. For a detailed discussion of the critical difference between these kinds of camps, see Pollock, Griselda and Max Silverman, 'Introduction', in Pollock and Silverman (eds), *Concentrationary Cinema: Aesthetics as Political Resistance in Alain Resnais's 'Night and Fog'* (New York, Oxford: Berghahn, 2011), pp. 8–13.

88. Lindeperg, *Les Écrans de l'ombre*, p. 223.

89. Ibid., p. 223.

90. Campany, *Photography and Cinema*, p. 27.

91. Tode, 'Une larme sur la joue du temps', p. 21. Tode reads the film as inserting images of concentration and DP camps into the larger context of the post-war democratic order.

92. Kirstein, Lincoln, 'Artist With a Camera', *New York Times*, 2 February 1947, 12. Morvan, Tréfouël and Savoia's graphic novel casts the alleged informer as Belgian and her denouncer as French (*Cartier-Bresson, Allemagne 1945*, p. 88). *Le Retour* shows a sign on the gate of the camp in Dessau identifying those waiting there to be repatriated as DPs from the Soviet Union, France, Belgium, Poland and the Netherlands.

93. Hägele, Ulrich, 'War is Over! Pour une iconographie des fins de guerres', *Revue des Sciences Sociales*, 'Nouvelles figures de la guerre', 35 (2006), 62–75 (65) (translations from this article are mine).

94. Gorrara, 'Fashion and the *Femmes Tondues*', p. 332. See also Alison M. Moore's discussion of the 'post-war mythologisation of collaboration as specifically feminine' in 'History, Memory and Trauma in Photography of the *Tondues*: Visuality of the Vichy Past Through the Silent Image of Women', *Gender and History*, 17: 3 (2005), 657–81 (658).

95. Tode, 'Henri Cartier-Bresson', p. 124 (translations from this text are mine).

96. Frizot, Michel, 'D'imprévisibles regards: les géométries subjectives d'Henri Cartier-Bresson', *L'Homme photographique* (Paris: Hazan, 2018), pp. 393–423 (pp. 404–13) (translations from this text are mine).

97. Ibid., p. 411.

98. Ibid., p. 405.

99. Ibid., p. 407.

100. Ibid., p. 408.

101. Ibid., p. 409.

102. Ibid., p. 408.

103. See Jacobs, Steven, 'The History and Aesthetics of the Classical Film Still', *History of Photography*, 34: 4 (2010), 373–86 (374).

104. On point of view in classical film stills, see Jacobs, 'The History and Aesthetics of the Classical Film Still', p. 374.

105. Ibid., p. 376.

106. Ibid., p. 378.

107. See ibid., p. 374.

108. de Roux, François, 'Le Retour', *France Illustration*, 3 (20 October 1945), 69–70 (69).

109. de Roux, 'Le Retour', 69.

110. Kirstein, 'Henri Cartier-Bresson', p. 11.

111. *The Photographs of Henri Cartier-Bresson*, p. 40.

112. *Henri Cartier-Bresson: Scrapbook*, p. 220; Kirstein, 'Henri Cartier-Bresson', p. 11.

113. Kirstein, 'Henri Cartier-Bresson', p. 11.

114. Morvan, Tréfouël and Savoia, *Cartier-Bresson, Allemagne 1945*, p. 3 (my translation).

115. Krauss, '"... And Then Turn Away?"', p. 10.

116. Tode, 'Une larme sur la joue du temps', p. 19.

117. Morvan, Tréfouël and Savoia, *Cartier-Bresson, Allemagne 1945*, p. 88.

CHAPTER THREE

Apocalyptic Stillness: The Self-Immolators

He sits still, in spite of the pain. He keeps his back straight and his head up, and he rests his hands in his lap. He hasn't made a speech; nor is he audibly praying. Other monks and nuns are moaning with grief. They are still forming a circle around him, protecting him from the police, keeping their distance out of respect and because of the heat. It is all happening so fast. Already, flames snake across the petrol on the ground and his robe and stream from his head like a golden mane. The journalist raises his camera. For a moment, the wind bends the fire away from the man, revealing his unharmed face. By the time the second picture is taken, the crowd has stopped moving and some people are on their knees. It is still going on. They smell and taste him burning. The flames wrap round him more tightly and the remains of his cloak and skin have turned black. Although the fire has destroyed his body, he looks more human now, less otherworldly. He is like them after all. But he hasn't changed position. They wonder if he is still alive.[1]

The series to which this pair of photographs belongs, taken by the American Malcolm Browne, fills in more of the story. On 11 June 1963, a demonstration by members of South Vietnam's majority Buddhist faith against their persecution by the government of the Catholic Ngo Dinh Diem culminated in Thich Quang Duc's self-immolation. Copies of the two pictures I have just evoked quickly proliferated around the world. While scholars of photography and visual rhetoric have researched the lives of these photos in detail, film footage of Buddhists who followed Quang Duc's example has remained in the margins of critical writing on history and images. Most references to these films merely contrast their alleged obscurity with the photographs' fame. The flame-wreathed Quang Duc has appeared in these frozen forms in newspapers, magazines, books and photography exhibitions, on posters, a rock album cover, in a digital photomontage and even in a recent sculptural relief. But moving images of Vietnamese monks and nuns who emulated him also reached mass viewers, through newsreels shown in cinemas and especially through television, whose unprecedented 'inundation' of the public with images of the war Sara Blaylock calls a 'global phenomenon'.[2] As Gunthert confirms, 'the publication of future [photographic] icons of Vietnam was preceded by the broadcast of filmed sequences on public television channels, whose audience was much larger'.[3] Breaking with the consensus, discussed in Chapters 1 and 2, that we forget filmic moments more easily than photographic ones because they are exchangeable rather than exceptional, Stanley Cavell in 1982 described footage of a Vietnamese priest burning himself as 'one of the most haunting images I know from television'.[4] During the 1960s, when the availability of television archives was fuelling cinematic experimentation, the recurrence of footage of these self-burnings in other films also helped secure their place in memory and elevate them above merely documentary status.

This chapter explores what cinema reveals about the iconicity of Buddhists who self-immolated in wartime Vietnam. It questions the conventional opposition of the iconic still to the forgotten moving image by pursuing pictures of these protests through the first generation of European and North American films – encompassing newsreels, documentaries, art and experimental cinema – that used them as emblems of violence on the other side of the world. One of Browne's pictures of Quang Duc reappeared in *Life* on 26 December 1969, which Gunthert judges the first issue to pair 'the classical function of representing the event' with 'the project of incarnating history through photography'.[5] I suggest that filmmakers were already turning the Vietnamese self-immolators into emblems or symbols several years earlier and that the iconisation of Quang Duc was part of the same process. I discuss how films juxtapose this footage with photos, reinforcing this book's argument that to understand the iconic image we need to heed interactions between the two media, rather than isolating a single fixed image as is traditional in work in this field. One way in which intrusions of photography into cinema, particularly American films of the late 1960s, have been interpreted is as harbingers of the apocalypse. The intense violence and massive destruction with which the 'Falling Soldier' became associated in *La Jetée*, *Overlord* and *Gallipoli* reinforce this connection. It was not still images of the self-immolators but their still figures, I argue, that fuelled Western cinematic fantasies of catastrophe, which elided the protestors' politics and agency by using them to symbolise the end of history.

Exemplary Postures

Accounts of Buddhists protesting by immolation during the war in Vietnam always remark how still they stayed. According to Browne, Quang Duc 'remained upright, his hands folded in his lap, for nearly ten minutes' as he burned.[6] Michael Biggs adds that Quang Duc and other middle-aged, experienced monks 'demonstrated almost superhuman self-control by sitting motionless while burning to death'.[7] Of course, none of Browne's photographs shows this immobility. To see this display of courage, strength and dignity, we must turn to moving images, like the narrator of Philip Roth's novel *American Pastoral* (1997), who is haunted by television pictures of a self-immolator who 'did not so much as move a muscle'; there was 'no screaming, no writhing', instead 'his posture remained exemplary, [. . .] meditative, serene'.[8] Roth's evocation of these mesmerising – and apparently moving – pictures hints at film's important and distinct role in the West in elevating burning Vietnamese protestors into icons who exceed the bounds of fixed images.

The received view, by contrast, that we more easily recall stills recurs in an endnote to one of Bellour's essays on stasis in cinema. For Bellour, the affinity between the fixed picture and memory is illustrated by 'the [. . .] image, in both film and photography, of the self-immolating Buddhist monk on a Saigon street'.[9] However, Bellour's writings on interactions between the two media support my proposal that moments in film can haunt us like photographs and turn into icons. Building on Deleuze's argument that cinema's procession of snapshots 'reproduces movement as a function of any-instant-whatever', Bellour suggests that the forms of paralysis, such as photographs and freeze-frames, that proliferated in films in the early 1960s accentuate 'exceptional or fundamental' moments instead, as exemplified by *La Jetée*'s apparent allusion to the 'Falling Soldier'.[10] Around the same time that cinema was multiplying immobile images in this way, it began to offer glimpses of the unforgettably still self-immolators.

The fundamental moments that halt film's movement include, according to Garrett Stewart, that of the apocalypse.[11] In its 'lowercase' form of 'ultimate scourge', the apocalyptic, he explains, has a privileged relation to photography. The 'unique purchase on disaster' that he ascribes to this medium might seem to bolster the prevalent idea that, since the 'Falling Soldier' at least, it has had an exclusive claim on historical iconicity. However, it is cinema, in Stewart's account, that conjures the 'longer tradition' of the apocalypse centring on 'terminus and telos, death but also judgement' by revealing the still frames of which film is composed. In this sense, he argues, 'the constituent photogram stands to the film track as cinema's ruin and its truth at once' and sometimes aptly exposes itself when apocalyptic violence engulfs the narrative.[12] Stewart's first example is the freeze-frames that identify members of a lynch mob when film is used as courtroom evidence in *Fury* (Fritz Lang, 1936). This stop action footage and especially victim Joe Wilson's (Spencer Tracey) description of the attack as like 'watching a newsreel of myself getting burned to death' eerily foreshadow the still and moving pictures of flame-engulfed Buddhists that would become news three decades later. There are of course significant differences between the two sets of images: Lang's armed, hate-filled crowd is replaced, in the photos and films from Vietnam, by protests conceived, we shall see, as non-violent. And whereas *Fury*'s mass frenzy evokes what Stewart calls a 'fiery day of judgement', as implied, for example, by a crowd member's recital of the Lord's prayer, the self-immolators didn't bear witness to an end time but demanded an end to oppression.[13]

By the time images of the Buddhist protests had gained currency, the apocalyptic interpretation of photogrammes was compounded in the US by a particular constellation of fears. Amy Rust has examined how incursions of stasis into commercial American cinema in the late 1960s and early 1970s figure 'the era's apocalyptic fantasies of violence'.[14] Rust's discussion provides another important framework for exploring the relationship between photography, cinema and incipient iconicity at this historical moment that is this chapter's concern. One of the signs of this apocalypticism that she identifies is the allusion by full-frame stills in a film such as *Night of the Living Dead* (George A. Romero, 1968) to photographs of real barbarism, including the lynching of African Americans.[15] The murderous racism whose spectre *Fury*'s freeze-framed attack on a white man summons without confronting is evoked more directly by the stills at the end of *Night*. Fantasies about violence and race interact as the historical images to which Romero alludes 'revive lost instants to stand, like zombies, as apocalyptic icons'.[16] This reading of the film 'through the spectre of photography', to borrow a phrase from Bellour, leads Rust to reflect on other 'privileged icons of the era's apocalyptic self-conception', including the recursive photojournalistic moments of brutality by or against Nguyen Ngoc Loan, Nguyen Văn Lém and Phan Thi Kim Phúc.[17] This chapter suggests that European and North American films from the second half of the 1960s view footage of the Vietnamese self-immolations through the same lens; that is, they help to turn the Buddhists' non-violent attempts to secure a better future for their compatriots into symbols of the world's end. I suggest that this modification of the meaning of these protests distracts from the self-immolators' agency and shores up the imperial power structures they condemned. If for Rust, apocalyptic and racialised violence throws light on stalled movement in cinema, it remains photographs that serve as icons. In what follows I explore instead how films of immobile protestors gained iconic resonance and how their association with 'terminus and telos, death but also judgement' (in Stewart's words) obscured the self-immolators' political aims.

'WE, TOO, PROTEST'

The story of pictures of the self-immolators initially reinforces the traditional view that photography alone is capable of producing images of iconic power. In the summer of 1963, the motionless silhouette of Quang Duc, charred but still seated, spread across newspapers, banners and flyers. As Michelle Murray Yang has traced, Browne's picture took on different symbolic meanings when mobilised in North Vietnam and China and by groups in the US protesting against their country's involvement.[18] Lisa Skow and George Dionisopoulos stress the 'aesthetic power' of what appeared to Americans as Browne's 'riveting but surreal images from a mysterious place'.[19] Attempts to explain what makes them so arresting have drawn, as accounts of photo-icons frequently do, on the notion of the pregnant moment (discussed in Chapter 1). Barbie Zelizer, for example, categorises the last photo of Quang Duc before he collapsed (the second described above), alongside Capa's falling soldier, as an 'about to die' image.[20] One permutation of the broader trope in news photography of 'impending action', characterised by the potential for change, the 'about to die' picture, Zelizer notes, often turns a moment of 'intense human anguish' into the iconic image of an event.[21] Alternatively, rather than the final seconds of Quang Duc's life, the photograph, as Yang suggests, may show him immediately after death.[22] In her account, it is not the present moment that is unforgettable but 'what has been', whose image has the power to 'promote agency and civic engagement'.[23]

Painstaking reconstruction of the history of Browne's photos, especially their first few months in circulation, has isolated them from the medium of film. Yet in the US and Europe stills of Quang Duc soon mixed with moving images. Not only did they appear on television; it is likely that within a month or two at least one of them also entered cinemas. A shot-by-shot description of a newsreel compiled in August 1963 by the French company Pathé, for example, places a photo of an (unnamed) Buddhist self-immolating next to footage of other scenes related to protests by his religious community in Saigon.[24] Whether or not the creators of this film had access to moving images of a self-burning, their insertion of a still whose subject was already familiar to viewers around the world reaffirms the idea that photography has a special power to sum up an event. At the same time, the film adjusts the photo's meaning, divesting the pictured moment of pregnancy. The self-immolator is no longer, in Zelizer's phrase, 'about to die', yet just conceivably saved. Rather, shots of an (again unnamed) monk's funeral preface his appearance, emphasising that his life has ended. Whereas Yang stresses the 'transformative potential' of photographs of the dead, which can 'provoke questions concerning future action', the frozen picture of burning concludes the newsreel, connoting both pastness and finality.[25]

Cinema not only raised the profile and altered the significance of photos of Quang Duc ablaze but also generated its own versions. From 6 November 1963 (less than a week after Diem was overthrown and assassinated in a coup d'état), another Pathé newsreel confronted audiences with a Vietnamese self-immolator in 36 seconds of footage sourced from the international film agency Visnews.[26] How do these six shots compare with Browne's iconic stills? According to Marita Sturken, one reason why 'photographic images in general have a greater capacity than moving images to achieve iconic status' is that the former kind can be clearer.[27] As examples, she sets side by side the fixed and filmic versions of two other scenes from the Vietnam War, where Loan shoots Văn Lém at point-blank range and the scalded Kim Phúc runs from chemical-laden bombs. The stills have become icons, Sturken suggests, in part because they show more distinct facial expressions and the film of the children is more confusing than the corresponding photograph.[28] This observation echoes Vicki Goldberg's claim, supported by her study of the also iconic images of Lee Harvey Oswald's assassination, that photos enriched television news 'overviews' in the early 1960s by 'fill[ing] in the details'.[29] Following the same pattern, even though Quang Duc is some distance away, we can discern one of his closed eyes and his frown in the earliest of Browne's two best-known photographs, whereas the Visnews film registers the face of a burning monk only as a dark blur. Perhaps Quang Duc's facial display of determination and courage in one of the photos contributed to its eventual displacement of the other, where flames have all but devoured his features, as the exemplary image of the Buddhist resistance movement and, in Patrick Hagopian's phrase, one of the 'emblems of the war's wrongness'.[30] Both stills have more potential to clarify faces than the moving images because they are in sharper focus. The film shots are also harder to understand insofar as they are unsteady, shift between several points of view and capture rapid motion: passers-by hurry towards the protestor and a policeman darts around him. Compounding this, the film itself rushes by, unless of course the viewer manipulates its speed. As Hagopian comments of films of an immolation and Văn Lém's execution, 'compared with the time we can spend studying a photo, the existence of a moving image is a fleeting thing'.[31]

Sturken's further observation that the film of Văn Lém's execution is more gruesome and therefore less appropriated or remembered than the equivalent still does not, however, straightforwardly extend to images of the self-immolators.[32] One iconic photograph of Quang Duc visualises his injuries more graphically than the Visnews footage, which exhibits more unbearably the prolonged nature of its flame-enveloped subject's suffering. If the stills are richer in spatial detail, including the contours of faces, bodies and wounds, the moving images are richer in temporal detail about the evolving event. Moreover, Pathé's editing of these brief, silent shots accentuates the 'about to die' – or, more accurately, 'about to collapse' – moment. Although, at first glance, the newsreel appears to unfold chronologically, elements of the second shot – photographers crouching in the background and the protestor, who has maintained the lotus posture, eventually falling over – recur in the sixth, revealing that they show the same seconds from different perspectives. At least two cine-camera operators, one of whom is visible at the edge of the second shot, circled around the self-immolator. Like the lingering iconic close-up of Settela Steinbach, which Sylvie Lindeperg calls a 'cine-photograph', the repetition and resulting extension of his last moment seated heightens the sense of what Lessing, writing on painting, calls pregnancy, in this case a quality of the still body, not the still image.[33] The policeman's apparent intent to intervene keeps open the possibility, as does the 'about to die' photo, that the imaged subject might be saved.

'Each time we see the footage, we may remember the photograph': Hagopian's remark about moving versions of the iconic snapshots of Quang Duc and Văn Lém recalls Bellour's idea of a cinema haunted by still images.[34] While the Visnews footage may bring Quang Duc's self-sacrifice to mind, I will argue that film played more than what Hagopian calls (as also cited in the previous chapter) 'a supporting role, enhancing the significance of the photos', in the transformation of the self-immolators into icons.[35] Capturing the work of photographers and a cine-camera operator incidentally and marginally, these film shots not only attest to the close proximity in which the two kinds of picture-making increasingly took place and which compels my project of writing cinema back into iconic image history. They also encapsulate film's autonomous import by using it as a frame, rather than mere support, for photography, and by being quoted more widely than stills of the scene. As later sections of the chapter will demonstrate, whether or not this footage reinforced the power of Browne's celebrated snapshots, it soon began to take on characteristics of an icon itself. In effect, the repetition – or rewinding and replaying – of the 'about to die' moment in the Pathé montage initiated an iterative process which would valorise the film as more than a straightforward document.

In spite of frequent reuse of the footage, key facts about it have been forgotten. While iconic images often temporarily separate from their referents, today we know exactly who, where and when most photo-icons show (the 'Falling Soldier' and the 'Gestapo Informer', whose names are unknown, are exceptions).[36] The Gaumont Pathé Archive records that the Visnews sequence originated in Saigon in October 1963.[37] However, no source I have found provides a more precise location or date for the footage or names the burning man (except those that misidentify him as Quang Duc).[38] Similarities between these moving images and a photograph in the Getty Archive reveal that he is Ho Dinh Van, a 42-year-old monk who set himself on fire on a broad, tree-lined pavement facing the city's Catholic cathedral on 27 October.[39] Dinh Van and the other Vietnamese self-immolators who appear in film from this era remind us that Quang Duc's self-sacrifice was just the first to galvanise a political movement. The nearly exclusive scholarly focus to date on the older monk as photo-icon risks obscuring the at least one hundred other protests by immolation that engulfed the country in several waves between 1963 and 1975 as well as the participation of nuns and laypeople, and the smaller number of self-burnings by anti-war activists of several faiths in other countries.[40] The circulation of footage of the Vietnamese demonstrations helps to redress iconic photography's preference for showing individual victims rather than mass agency (a tendency criticised by Bergala). At the same time, the loss of and difficulty of recovering the identities of these self-immolators, at least one of whom discussed in this chapter I haven't managed to name, heighten the danger of objectifying them. Whereas Browne's photos helped to elevate Quang Duc into what Ghosh calls a 'bio-icon' whose life story and words have circulated widely, Dinh Van and the other people in the footage have become detached from biographies.[41] Like the Wolof woman in a chronophotographic film from 1895 directed by the French physician Félix-Louis Regnault, these Vietnamese men and women have been, in Fatimah Tobing Rony's words, 'rendered nameless and faceless' and so their body may be 'deemed the most significant datum'.[42] The ethical problem of their forgotten names and inaccessible subjectivities is compounded in Western appropriations which all too often 'reify' non-Western indigenous people 'as specimens, metonyms for an entire culture [. . .]'.[43] The individuality of the filmed self-immolators is further obscured when commentators confuse them with Quang Duc or mistake dramatic reconstructions for documentary records. As we shall see, the histories of these iconic and anonymous imaged subjects intertwine.

SENSATIONAL IMAGES: *IN HOMAGE TO NICÉPHORE NIÉPCE*

Why does film of two of these self-immolators appear in a 9-minute documentary made for Pathé's 'Magazine' series to mark the 200th anniversary of the birth of photography's inventor? And what light does this contextualisation throw on encounters between still and moving images? *En homage à Nicéphore Niépce* (*In Homage to Nicéphore Niépce*, 1966) opens by honouring the experiments that led to what has recently been dubbed an 'icon of our time'.[44] Pre-empting this status, the film presents 'View from the Window at Le Gras' (c. 1826), often considered the first photograph, as both inaugurating and symbolising what the voice-over calls 'the civilisation of the image'.[45] By extension, this screen memorial also casts Niépce as an icon, a term sometimes applied, as Audrey Leblanc and Dominique Versavel observe, to photographers.[46] Not only photography, however, the film suggests, but also cinema has the capacity to define an era. Rather than playing a subordinate role to stills, the work of Louis Lumière, proposes the commentary, marks the beginning of the age of 'reportages d'actualité' (filmed news reports or newsreels). According to the voice-over, he devises this genre with his images of a photographers' congress in Lyon in 1895, which reminds us that one of the first films encapsulates the two media's interrelatedness. Later, we glimpse photographers in another piece of footage belonging to the same tradition of cinematic *actualités*. However, the documentary turns these images of Dinh Van from journalism into examples of film's capacity to capture exceptional moments that lodge in our memories.

Whereas Freund would maintain fifteen years later that the more we watch moving pictures, the more we remember stills, *En homage à Nicéphore Niépce* suggests, by contrast, that in an image-saturated world we are more likely to retain 'sensational' filmic scenes. The first example of what the voice-over also calls 'shock' imagery, given halfway through the film, is footage of car crashes. Shots of accidents at race tracks in France and the US, where vehicles smash into each other or crowds at high speed, and deliberate collisions by stunt-man Gil Delamare pile up on the screen. What is arresting about these images is the spectacle of movement and its violent cessation. The next sequence moves to Vietnam and is unforgettable instead for its portrayal of stillness, that of two Buddhists sitting and lying on the ground as they are consumed, like the wrecked cars, by flames. The shots of both burning vehicles and people also seem to assert the importance of moments by prolonging them: just as slow motion reveals details of bending and shattering metal, so too what we imagine the protestors to be suffering makes glimpses of them feel interminable. In other words, these 'sensational' images are memorable for capturing movement, stillness and time in ways that photographs cannot.

According to Ludovic Cortade, the 'spectacularisation of motion' in American cinema of the 1950s registered an apocalyptic cultural preoccupation with time accelerating.[47] It is conversely the arrest of time in the freeze-frame or photopan across films from other decades or countries that Rust and Stewart, as explained above, read as apocalyptic. In *En homage à Nicéphore Niépce*, a sense of disaster links the shocks of movement and immobility. The sequences about accidents and immolations both accumulate death and destruction. For example, we see footage of a tragedy at Le Mans in 1955 in which over eighty people perished. That Delamare lost his life during a stunt just before the film's release, as the voice-over informs us, turns the scenes of his work into a form of 'about to die' image, a category into which the pictures of the Buddhists' fatal protests also fall (as Zelizer and Yang discuss with reference to photos of Quang Duc). The sight of lethal technology and fiery ends and the sound of screeching and screams inspire horror and give this part of the documentary a catastrophic feel. Simultaneous commentary about the *cinéaste's* search for provocative images illustrates Stewart's apocalyptic conception of filmic self-revelation by reflecting on the medium. The car crashes also exemplify the eruptions of violence that – for both Stewart and Rust – characterise apocalyptic cinema. But the Buddhists' acts do not. As Karin Fierke explains, Mahāyāna Buddhism, the main form of the religion practised in Vietnam, prohibits violence and conceives self-immolation instead as a 'representation of violence committed by an "other"'.[48] As testimonies to suffering inflicted on the Vietnamese by the government in the South and its allies abroad, these protests concern history, conceived in accordance with the Buddhist view of existence as cyclical, rather than apocalyptically signalling its end.

Not only does the film ignore the politics of a movement it reduces to *images choc*; it also seems to mix up different self-immolators. 'We remember the trance-revelation of the first suicide of a Vietnamese bonze, in the era of Diem', says the narrator as Dinh Van, not Quang Duc, burns before us. This discrepancy between words and image strengthens my claim that photos and films of these waves of self-burning can't be properly understood in isolation from each other. The commentary doesn't name either of the Buddhists who we see in flames. Based on the evidence I have found – the voice-over's reference to 'female suicides' and details in film footage, photos and written records – the second self-immolator is likely to be Ho Thi Thieu and a subsequent image probably shows mourners watching the self-sacrifice of Thich Nu Thanh Quang, two nuns who set themselves on fire on 28 May 1966 in Saigon and Hue respectively. Nor does the documentary explain why they did this. Bearing out Fierke's understanding of self-immolation as presenting an image of, rather than perpetrating, violence, Nu Thanh Quang's letters explain that she will protest against the spilling of 'the blood of [her] compatriots' during two decades of 'war without reason', and in the 'massacre of bonzes' by forces working for Prime Minister Nguyen Cao Ky, which, she claims, the US government implicitly endorsed.[49] Contrastingly, *En homage à Nicéphore Niépce* pays no attention to what links (in the narrator's words) the 'build-up of the dreadful [. . .] around the pagodas' to French colonialism and American imperialism, even though these violent projects were inextricable from what the film's subtitle calls the 'era of the image' because they were buttressed by the camera. There are similarities between the shots of the self-immolator Thi Thieu and another set of images that relate to France's colonial history but appear in the film as examples of the work for which Marc Garanger won the Niépce prize. Like the Vietnamese nun, the Algerian women forcibly pictured by this French army photographer in 'grouping villages' or camps (*villages de regroupement*) in 1960 for identity cards have been divested of names and biographies in the course of the dissemination of their images. Moreover, all these female subjects bear witness to colonial or imperial violence and racism: just as Thi Thieu's smouldering body denounces (in her words) 'the inhuman actions of Generals Thieu and Ky, henchmen of the Americans', so too the Maghrebi women express what Garanger describes (in the absence of records of their words) as 'mute, violent protest' against the French.[50] Like the rooftop at Le Gras, Garanger's immobile portraits have become icons, inspiring artistic remakes. In helping to elevate moving images of self-immolators to this status, Pathé's short film turns out to pay homage as much to Lumière as Niépce.

FIRE AND ICE: *PERSONA*

Having turned from a news item into an inerasable image in the Niépce tribute, Dinh Van's self-sacrifice recurs in both these guises in a feature film released several months later. In Spring 1966, a second wave of Vietnamese Buddhists set themselves on fire in protest against Ky's government and its American collaborators, making self-immolation topical again and generating new pictures, some of which made their way into Pathé's documentary. Nevertheless, as this compilation film does too, *Persona* (Ingmar Bergman, 1966) returns to images of the self-burning three autumns earlier and in so doing contributes to making them iconic. Moreover, like *En homage à Nicéphore Niépce* again, Bergman's film juxtaposes these moving pictures with fixed ones. For Bellour, *Persona* is a landmark film because it exemplifies how photography 'invaded' cinema in the 1960s.[51] One reason why is that its protagonist Elisabet Vogler (Liv Ullmann) takes and studies photographs. Bellour compares the print that she contemplates for longest, whose origin in the Holocaust was already well known by 1966, to the footage of the self-immolating Buddhist: 'between these two pictures cinema burns and is reborn [. . .]; it becomes postwar cinema, where movement is not guaranteed any more than is speech, subject to a paralysis that can at any moment condemn them to come to a standstill.'[52] (As we will see, iconic images play a role in the film's exploration of speechlessness.) The ghosts of war also threaten to halt cinematic motion in Stewart's commentary on *Persona*, his second example, after *Fury*, of a film that 'aligns lowercase apocalypse with the self-revelation of its own medium of record and (psychic) projection'.[53] What Stewart describes as the film's 'reassemblage' of the genocide photo into 'a protocinematic montage' of interacting stills reminds viewers of the material basis of the medium.[54] Focused on photographs and photogrammes, Bellour and Stewart say little and nothing respectively about Bergman's treatment of the barely moving Dinh Van. *Persona's* coupling of the Nazis' crimes against humanity with Vietnamese resistance to religious discrimination and American imperialism warrants further exploration from the perspective of iconic image studies.

Elisabet's encounter with the picture of Jewish civilians and German soldiers reinforces the traditional link between photography and icons. On its first publication in a report for senior SS members, the image documented the emptying of the Warsaw Ghetto in 1943. *Persona* separates it from the collection of photos to which it originally belonged and mobilises its symbolic potential. According to Frédéric Rousseau, not until three years after the release of Bergman's film, when the still recurred on the front cover of the British edition of Gerhard Schoenberner's *Der gelbe Stern* (*The Yellow Star*), did it encapsulate the whole genocide.[55] However, as Richard Raskin has demonstrated, a cluster of publications and an exhibition were already raising its international profile in 1960.[56] Sontag's interpretation in an essay written in 1967 of *Persona's* incorporation of the 'famous photograph' as a reference to 'the Six Million' confirms that by then it connoted a wider event.[57] The film does not simply repeat the image but suggests that it has a special power. Someone valued it enough to keep the copy that Elisabet discovers tucked into a book. We don't know how the print got there, but we know how the image did. Elisabet's lingering gaze at the photo dramatises and participates in its iconisation. To borrow from Hariman and Lucaites's definition of photojournalistic icons, her absorption suggests that it 'activate[s] strong emotional identification [and] response'.[58] As well as connoting the Holocaust, in line with Gunthert's claim that photo-icons evolve from documents into allegories, it also symbolises the fraught affective bonds between women and children in Bergman's story.[59] As other critics have noticed, the frightened boy in the foreground recalls Elisabet's son, whose photograph she earlier, in a chilling gesture accented by the music, tore into pieces, and, more obliquely, an abortion by the other heroine, Alma (Bibi Andersson). A boy also strokes blown-up images of women's faces in a much-cited preface accompanied by an ominous, alarm-like crescendoing semitone trill that recurs as Elisabet contemplates the historical still. Stewart's construal of the Holocaust picture as a 'tempting emblem' of the female protagonists' 'common denial of a child' illustrates how the rhetoric of photo-icons tends to reinforce normative expectations about gender, such as the conflation of women and mothers.[60]

Like the Nazi genocide, the Vietnamese self-immolations produced widely recognised photographs, including the one by Browne of Quang Duc that was awarded the 1963 World Press Photo of the Year; but *Persona* alludes to the Buddhist resistance in film footage instead. In contrast to the standard view of iconic images, Bergman's film suggests that moving pictures can sometimes be as haunting and rich in symbolism as still ones. Similarly, while making *Persona*, Bergman drew no distinction between photography and cinema in a written note about the pictures from Warsaw and Saigon: 'I am unable to grasp the large catastrophes. They leave my heart untouched. [. . .] But I shall never rid myself of those images.'[61] Nor will Elisabet, judging by the way they transfix her. The footage of the monk startles her as she watches television.

Insofar as it is contained within a news broadcast, it has documentary status. The televisual frame and motion pictures present the self-burning as a recent event, just as Pathé did a week or so after it occurred, distinguishing it from the wartime photo that Elisabet comes across later. What was significant about TV for Bergman at this time was its 'immediate closeness to what is going on all over the world', as a result of which the news was taking over art's traditional role as incitement to political action.[62] The interviewer to whom he said this agreed, recalling Jack Ruby's shooting of Harvey Oswald, 'which we actually saw happen' in another piece of footage that joined with photographs to form a composite icon.[63] As Bergman admitted, however, his films don't 'often [. . .] depict current events'; or as Sontag put it, he was 'not a topical or historically oriented filmmaker'.[64] Although the commentary accompanying the report from Vietnam refers to American military action there roughly contemporary to the film and although the surge of self-burnings by Buddhists in May–June 1966 was a fairly fresh memory for the audience at *Persona*'s Stockholm premiere in October, the footage of the fiery protest turns out to be several years old: an anachronism, a found image like the Holocaust photograph. *Persona*, I suggest, is less interested in documentary actuality than in indelible imagery, whether still or moving.

Unlike *En homage à Nicéphore Niépce*, *Persona* avoids explicit commentary on the meaning of the immolation footage and its relationship to other images in the film. As Seung-hoon Jeong observes, 'we can only grope for the dark link between this real political trauma and the heroines' pathological trauma [. . .]'.[65] Cavell reads Dinh Van's act as figuring Elisabet's suffering and sense of culpability: she stares at him 'both as if she has been given an image of her pain, even a kind of explanation of it, and as if she is the cause of such pain in the world, as of its infection by her'.[66] The monk also provides an emblem of Elisabet's protest. Her fascination with him lends weight to the idea that her sudden, unexplained refusal to speak and reluctance to move express dissent. Bergman too discerns in her muteness 'a strong person's form of protest', although silence is also selectively imposed by colonial and patriarchal power structures that *Persona* doesn't explicitly address.[67] Her doctor's remark that she has chosen speechlessness and stillness over the uglier alternative of killing herself perhaps strengthens Elisabet's link to Dinh Van by indirectly echoing the inaccurate designation by contemporary Western journalists of self-immolations as 'suicides'. While writing on stasis often explores the trope of death, Dinh Van's upright posture evokes instead what Fierke, referring to Vietnamese Buddhists who immolated themselves in the attempt to stop violence and killing, calls 'a gesture for life'.[68] His stance would have found sympathy in Sweden, *Persona*'s country of origin, where the political establishment and grassroots groups opposed the Vietnam War.[69] As much as the paralysis of speech and motion that connects the footage of Dinh Van to the Holocaust photo in Bellour's account, it is protest – religious, political and existential – that threatens to bring *Persona* to a standstill.[70] The analogy between Dinh Van's and Elisabet's experiences has conspicuous limits, however. In stark contrast to the monk, who sacrificed himself in an extreme political action, the affluent, privileged, famous actress withdraws from public life, seeks bespoke medical treatment and succumbs to inaction.

The film also renews the apocalyptic connotation with which Pathé invested Dinh Van's image, diverting attention from his intent and agency. *Persona* evokes catastrophe not only by referring to Nazi atrocities but also by borrowing the iconography of horror. The famous opening montage announces the film's connection to this genre. A skeleton in a scary old film, a hairy spider, intestines ripped from a living sheep and a nail hammered into a hand steadily build up a sense of menace that will colour our perception of the self-immolation. These alarming visions give way to disconcerting shots of grey bodies in a morgue, intact but not quite dead. Disorientatingly framed upside down, a woman opens her eyes and looks straight at us, making us jump. Her zombie-like existence between life and death (a motif of apocalyptic horror) resonates with the earlier 'about to die' pictures of the lamb and Christ and anticipates the footage of Dinh Van's last moments as well as the photo of Jewish people held at gunpoint. As Bellour puts it, in this pre-credit sequence, 'neither life nor death is sure, no more so than the immobile (or immobilised) picture and the moving picture are sure'.[71] The boundaries between the living and the dead and between stillness and motion remain creepily unsettled as Dinh Van and Elisabet perform their different protests; later on, she will lie so quietly and motionless in her hospital bed that we might mistake her for a corpse, or long close-ups of her face for fixed images. These uncertainties established in the prologue persist during the credits, where we first glimpse the Buddhist monk in a subliminal image of the kind popularised by horror films (classic examples include sinister pictures that flash up for a few frames during *The Exorcist* (William Friedkin, 1973)). Bergman pre-empts this technique by inserting between credits shots so fleeting that they lean towards photographs. One of these isolates the moment when Dinh Van, filmed from behind, collapses, perhaps the most horrible in the footage, accented by drums and xylophones playing Lars Johan Werle's modernist score. This image startles and disturbs particularly because it has no evident relation to earlier ones. The sacrificial flames burst suddenly into the bleak, ice- and snow-bound world that accommodates the morgue. For Wollen, the difference between these elements resembles that between film and photography: 'film is like fire, photography is like ice. Film is all light and shadow, incessant motion, transience, flicker [. . .]'.[72] Instead of a 'frozen tongue of fire', the image that Wollen uses to explain the paradoxical look of Capa's iconic photo of the *event* of

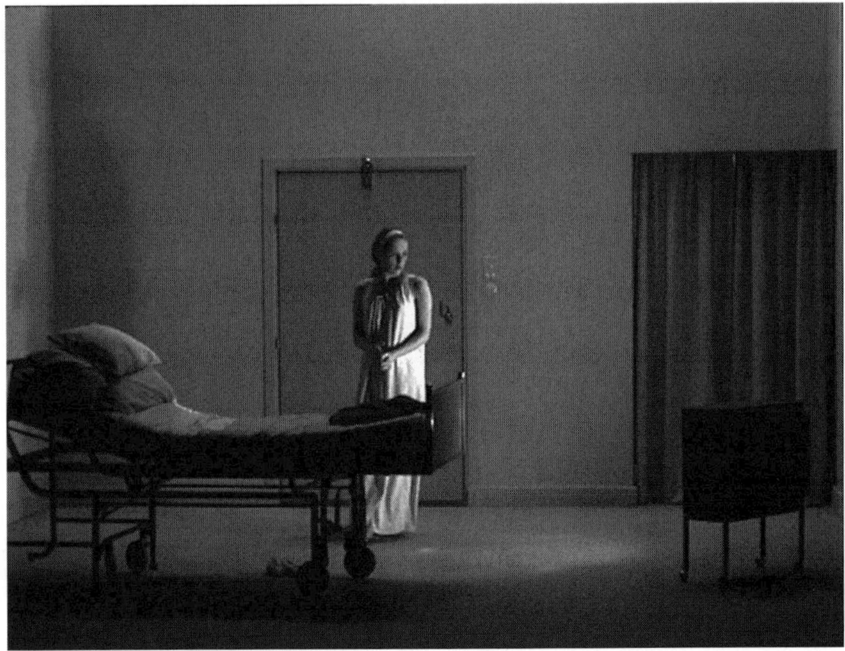

Figure 3.1 *Persona* (dir. Ingmar Bergman, Sweden, 1966).

the soldier's fall and one that Browne realises literally in picturing Quang Duc, Bergman films an enduring *state* – that of death, icily gripping humans and nature – and juxtaposes it with ephemeral flames.[73] Dinh Van's protest may also awaken memories of women being burned alive as witches in *The Seventh Seal* (Bergman, 1957), which alludes to the Christian apocalypse, and *Day of Wrath* (Carl Theodor Dreyer, 1943).

Persona interrupts this gendered pattern by casting a woman as witness to, rather than offering rendered through, an immolation by fire, while repeating classic cinema's habitual attempt, in Kaja Silverman's words, 'to extract a cry from the female voice'.[74] The curtains of Elisabet's hospital room are drawn against the night and she paces anxiously in the half darkness. Unable to open the door, she is imprisoned with pictures from another, unfamiliar world, whose chaos penetrates her ordered surroundings. In the 1963 Pathé newsreel, shots from different angles prolong Dinh Van's suffering, which Bergman extends further by inserting cutaways to Elisabet's reaction and repeating twice more the footage of the monk falling or fainting. Whereas 'about to die' photos appear to pause pain by stopping time, which, as Zelizer has shown, is conducive to their iconisation, Bergman's expansion of this moment and addition of the roar of flames make it more unbearable and heighten suspense – will

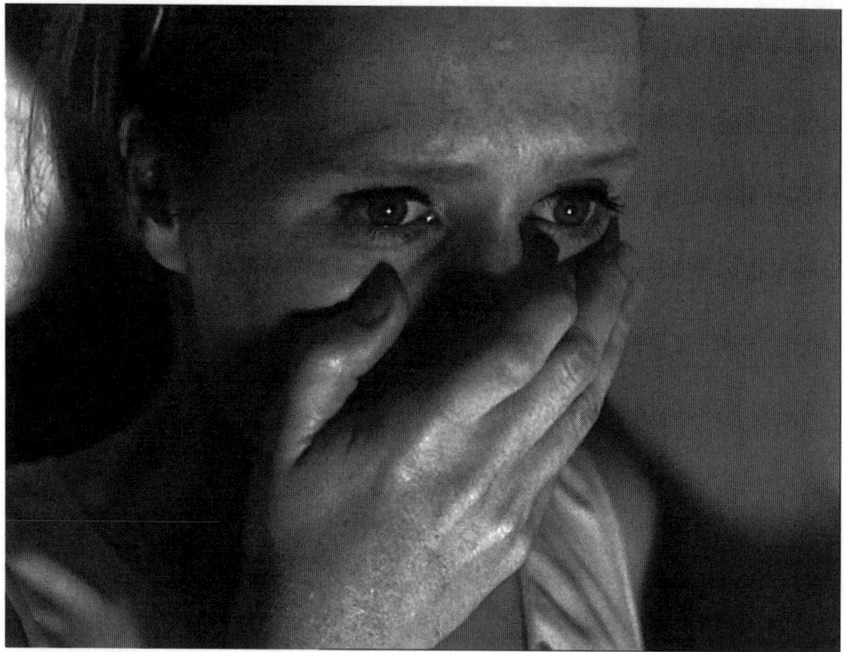

Figure 3.2 *Persona.*

the monk be saved? As Elisabet backs away from the television and covers her mouth with a hand as if to stifle a scream, the camera closes in, trapping her. Her long white nightdress and gestures of dread recall those of Eleanor Lance (Julie Harris) similarly cornered in a ghost-infested mansion in *The Haunting* (Robert Wise, 1963). Elisabet's expression also prefigures the 'mute fear' that is all Deleuze reads on the composite visage into which her and Alma's faces later merge.[75]

Deleuze calls 'the set [. . .] of the affect and the face', 'icon'.[76] This definition looks back not only to the history of Christian art but also, like other theorists of photography and the image more generally writing in the 1970s and 1980s, to the approach to signs developed by Peirce in the late nineteenth century.[77] It also foreshadows Ghosh's discussion of the icon's intense affective charge.[78] *Cinéma 1: L'Image-mouvement* explains why the concept of the icon is useful for thinking about film. Elisabet's face oscillates between the two poles of Deleuze's icon: the immobile 'reflective unity' that turns the aforementioned close-ups of her resting into photos; and the 'intensive series' animated, at the sight of the burning Buddhist, by expressive micro-movements.[79] By contrast, Dinh Van earns no venerating close-up – or, to use Deleuze's synonym for this kind of shot, 'affection-image'.[80] These images of Elisabet and Dinh Van chill-ingly converge halfway through the film in a photogramme with a hole scorched where Alma's face should be; as Deleuze puts it, Bergman 'burns the icon'.[81] The symbolic violence to Alma coincides with exposure of the combustible material from which the film is made, exemplifying Stewart's 'apocalyptic model of filmic self-disclosure'.[82] The melting celluloid that destroys Alma's countenance also threatens to finish the film – or return us to its beginning, which depicts a projector's arc lamp, a film strip and a room full of corpses suggesting a disaster has already taken place. If Western icon culture, as Deleuze discusses, has a privileged relationship to the face, Bergman's horror scenes remind us that this face is usually white and European (as do his close-ups of figures in the photo from Warsaw), while other subjects are reduced to bodies. The physically dam-aged, suffering Dinh Van also perpetuates a pattern that iconic images derive from photojournalism, as Mark Sealy explains: 'the black figure, the non-European subject, is often photographed in the most broken of conditions [. . .] whereas there is an absence of images that show us the European subject on the edge of life in the same way'.[83] By idealising the white European face, Bergman's portrayal of Vietnamese experience fuels Mondzain's critique of the iconic image (discussed in this book's Introduc-tion) as an instrument of (Christian) imperial power.[84]

ICONOCLASM: *THE EIGHTH DAY*

En homage à Nicéphore Niépce and *Persona* aren't the only films of their era to associate burning Vietnamese Buddhists with apocalyptic destruction. The year after their release, a 14-minute collage of archival imagery of war and vio-lence featured shots of another self-immolation. Like *Persona*, *Le Huitième Jour* (*The Eighth Day*, 1967) conjures a sense that the world is ending by mixing still and moving images. Photographs not only dominate passages of the film but also filled parts of the installation for which Québécois artist Charles Gagnon created it in collaboration with an ecumenical consortium of churches. In 1963 the Notre Dame Cathedral in Saigon provided a symbolic site for Dinh Van's protest against a Catholic regime; four years later the Christian Pavilion at Expo 67, Montréal's world's fair, incorporated another flame-shrouded Buddhist. With the exception of this figure, the installation avoided religious iconography, but *Le Huitième Jour* recycles several pieces of footage, including the immolation sequence, that were transforming from newsreel into sacred – and iconic – cul-tural artefacts.[85] In different ways from Pathé's 'magazine' and Bergman's feature, Gagnon's handling of these images troubles the standard opposition between photography's exceptional moments and cinema's exchangeable ones.

Instead of isolating the instant when a 'major event' assumes 'the ideal iconographic form', to borrow from Leblanc and Versavel's definition of the photo-icon, *Le Huitième Jour*, as well as the installation to which it originally belonged, amasses images.[86] On their way to the film theatre and on leaving it, visitors to the pavilion passed walls and a lattice of cubes displaying over three hundred enlarged photographs mainly supplied by the agencies Magnum and Black Star. Although these included pictures by Capa and other celebrated war photographers, most depicted what Gary Miedema characterises as 'ordinary people in everyday life', rarely a fertile source of photo-iconic moments.[87] The first few minutes of the film continue this focus on the quotidian but increasingly through violent scenarios (such as high-speed car crashes, echoing Pathé's account of the 'era of the image'), preparing the way for a barrage of pictures and often distorted non-synchronous music and noises that progressively renders mass human death unexceptional.

The carnage of twentieth-century war and genocide is chronicled in footage located for Gagnon by researcher Judith Trotsky and stills from the Photo Library of the Defense Department in Washington. His selection and editing of these images validates cinema as more than a mere support for photography: as a superior means for analysing human and mechanical gestures of killing. In Gagnon's words, his interest in war as 'an active thing, [. . .] where actual movement leads people to further violence' was more suited 'to film than photography or any other medium'.[88] *Le Huitième Jour* is all about motion within and between images. In the archives from the First World War, for example, explosions fling earth everywhere, soldiers run and fall and a ship flips over in relentless quick-fire succession. In this sense, Gagnon's experimental montage provides a foil to the freeze-framed violence that was accumulating, as Rust explains, in contemporary commercial American cinema. When the film turns to photographs, in the middle of a section on the Second World War, it loses no momentum; like stop motion animation, the rapid sequence of stills barely interrupts the chains of falling bombs. This 'cinematisation' (to reuse Cortade's term) of the fixed image replaces the 'decisive' instant with merely successive ones.[89]

Gagnon also replays iconic moments in movement. His film includes shots of Mussolini and Hitler gesticulating during speeches and of clouds swelling into mushrooms that exemplify what David D. Perlmutter defines as 'generic icons', whose elements recur 'from image to image, so that [. . .] the basic scene becomes [. . .] a visual cliché'.[90] We also see the 'discrete icon' (to borrow Perlmutter's alternative category) formed by the TV footage of Harvey Oswald's murder, whose chaotic but 'definite set of elements' is even more dynamic.[91] And we glimpse a smudged print of a frame of Abraham Zapruder's also 'discretely' iconic movie of John and Jackie Kennedy's fateful drive through Dallas.

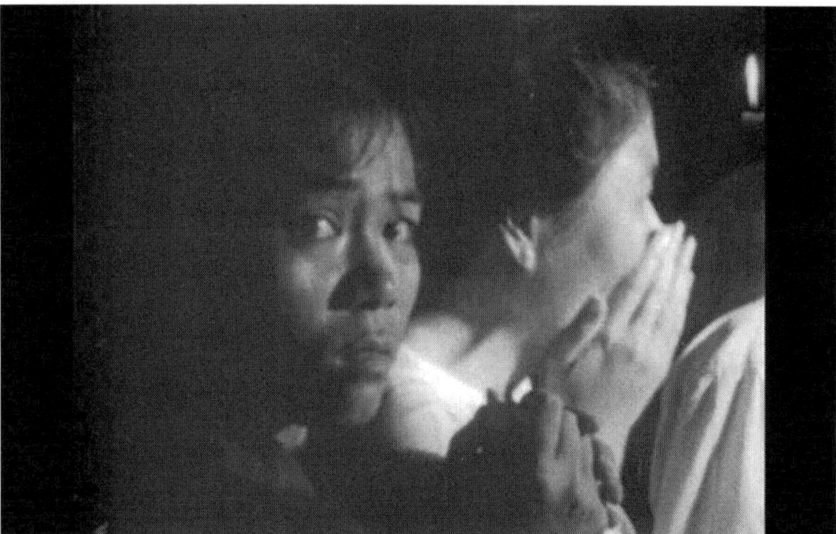

Figure 3.3 *Le Huitième Jour* (*The Eighth Day*; dir. Charles Gagnon, Canada, 1967).

The incorporation of these kinetic icons underscores the film's concern not only with different kinds of murder but also with their role in visual culture. Gagnon's reuse of filmic images of scenes that (with the exception of JFK's assassination) have circulated as well-known photos challenges the conventional view that the older medium provides the ideal and most meaningful versions.

The same is true of the moving images of the self-immolator, which appear a minute before the end of the film. Neither class of icons proposed by Perlmutter – generic or discrete – is adequate for describing this 11-second shot, prefaced by a 5-second shot of the distressed faces of onlookers (see Figure 3.3), which present both a singular and individual act, as Monika Kin Gagnon has pointed out, and part of a collective protest that has produced a collection of similar pictures.[92] Although the burning figure (whose gender we can't tell) rocks gently and, eventually, falls onto her back, this shot stands out as relatively still amid a frantic rostrum-animated rush of contemporary photos from the mass media or of mass-produced consumer objects. The sequence is accompanied by rhythmic rock guitar, which augments the critical distance between viewer and film, in contrast to the realist sound effects added to the footage of Dinh Van on fire in *Persona*. Visually and sonically, then, this section of Gagnon's film, which includes the aforementioned pictures of JFK, Harvey Oswald and the aftermath of an atomic explosion, buttresses Gunthert's claim that 1960s pop culture generates the iconic image, while suggesting that cine-icons were as important to this era as photo-icons.[93]

According to Kin Gagnon, the self-burning is an exceptional moment; while *Le Huitième Jour* belongs to a television-influenced tradition of found footage collage whose concern with disaster evokes what Catherine Russell labels an 'archival apocalypse', the immolation 'seems to open up the film suggestively to a less apocalyptic and more explicitly anti-war conclusion'.[94] The appearance of one of the Vietnamese people who burned themselves for peace bolsters Gagnon's trenchant critique of war. However, as I have argued in relation to other films in this chapter, placing images of self-immolation within an apocalyptic framework risks distracting the viewer from their politics. The apocalypticism of *Le Huitième Jour* owes little to the Christianity that the pavilion was supposed to promote. Rather, like Bergman, Gagnon adopts a humanist approach that differs from the photographic one encapsulated in the mantra of the 'decisive instant' (as discussed in Chapters 1 and 2) by showing how film too can capture moments that incarnate a phenomenon or era. In so doing, the cinematic humanism of *Le Huitième Jour* prioritises connections between different wars and instances of destruction over those between Buddhist activism, colonial Catholicism and imperialism.[95] The cycles of violence highlighted by the film largely exclude the brutal interventions of Europeans and North Americans in the global South. How the self-immolators were denouncing French and US actions in Vietnam receives closer attention in the final film considered in this chapter.

STATUES AND MANNEQUINS: *IN THE YEAR OF THE PIG*

The Buddhist monk or nun who flames devour at the end of *Le Huitième Jour* reappeared a year later, still burning, at the beginning of another film that makes pioneering use of news pictures. Like Gagnon, the American filmmaker Emile de Antonio surrounded this footage with topical photographs. *In the Year of the Pig* (1968) opens with a meditation on fighting for one's country that alternates, like *Persona*'s prologue, between stillness and motion. Both Bergman's fiction and de Antonio's documentary compilation also incorporate television, the medium through which film of the Buddhists' spectacular acts of resistance reached the widest audience. Whereas most of the 'found' footage in *Le Huitième Jour* predates the televisual, *In the Year of the Pig* draws extensively on the archives of the American Broadcasting Company. The film's implicit denunciation of mainstream media (which foreshadows Mondzain's concepts of an 'iconic empire' and an 'iconocracy') provides a critical frame for its presentation of the self-immolators.[96]

In the Year of the Pig's opening montage, like *Persona*'s, places a self-burning amid a procession of disparate images. Commentators have described the relationship between these pictures as 'dissonant and nonsynchronous' and the appearance of the person in flames as 'jarring'.[97] Half a decade after American and European newspapers 'struggled to contextualise' Browne's photos of Quang Duc, de Antonio's film, unlike the 'Pathé Magazine' newsreel discussed earlier but similar to *Persona* and *Le Huitième Jour*, avoids explicit comment on the meaning of immolation footage, which emerges instead through its juxtaposition with other images.[98] The sequence intersperses memorials to America's Civil War and an epitaph from its Revolutionary War with photos and film relating to the contemporary conflict in Vietnam. This implies a parallel between heroic American battles of the past and the Vietnamese struggle for independence. In other words, it is not only the statues of Union soldiers who appear here, in Sara Blaylock's apt phrase, as 'icons of patriotism', but also the self-immolator.[99]

The alternation between these sculptures, photographs and pieces of film mounts a critique of imperialism, which clearly distinguishes de Antonio's framing of Vietnamese self-immolators from their treatment by the other filmmakers discussed here. As Cortade explains, traditional (medieval) iconographies of power granted primacy to stillness as exemplified by the 'august pose' adopted by likenesses of the priest, monarch or emperor.[100] This correlation between power and immobility is reinforced by the film's initial images, not of sovereigns, but of soldiers, both heroic and brutal-looking. A carved Civil War sentinel leans nobly on his rifle; a GI crossing a rice paddy wears a helmet proclaiming 'make war not love', parodying a pacifist catchphrase, in a photograph that would itself inspire parody; an infantryman brandishing a bayonet leaps out of another monument to the nineteenth-century conflict; in another snapshot, a marine laden with belts of enormous bullets enters a helicopter; and a regiment of African American soldiers who fought for the Union marches across a bronze frieze, an allusion to a history of racism in which the film considers the violence in Vietnam another episode. As idealisations and allegories, the three memorials foreshadow photos not included in the film that – in spite of their debt to contingency – have also become patriotic icons, affirming nationalist perceptions of other sacred events (such as Joe Rosenthal's 'Flag-Raising on Iwo Jima', on which a memorial was modelled). By contrast, the warmongering poses and accessories of contemporary soldiers make manifest imperial brutality when conjoined here with still and moving images of Vietnamese witnesses. The lotus posture in which the flaming Buddhist sits with what Barbara Correll calls 'eerie dignity' until she runs out of strength represents not power but resistance to it.[101] Nor is her stillness monumental. For Correll, *In the Year of the Pig* exposes how traces of violence 'seep' from 'war's monumental discourse', attempting 'to make more visible [. . .] the bodies (in pain) that construct the war monument'.[102] The film of the Buddhist consumed by fire renders palpable the bodily suffering that the memorials elide.

This conflagration also stands in for the Vietnamese whose bodies were destroyed by American aggression, which is evoked not only photographically but also, throughout the prologue, by discordant revving and whirring remixed by composer Steve Addiss from films about combat helicopters.[103] Evoked, then, by both sound and image, the helicopter gunship became, as Guy Westwell notes in a discussion of American cinema, 'the singular icon of the Vietnam War'.[104] Its cacophonous music loosely links the self-immolator's image to the others in the sequence, while black leaders starkly separate them. These moments of darkness last at least as long as the intervals during which the screen is illuminated. The extended gaps between pictures draw attention to editing and exacerbate discontinuities between the images. They foreground the disparate nature of the 'found' materials that make up the film and prefigure its close without disturbing the stillness that prevails as it opens; in this way the black screens combine with the violence implied and represented by the images and sounds from Vietnam to conjure the idea of an apocalypse. *In the Year of the Pig* initially continues the pattern traced in this chapter of associating self-immolation by fire with a revelatory end.

Rust and Stewart describe as 'apocalyptic' the frozen gesture that interrupts filmic succession. An account of de Antonio's treatment of the Buddhist movement must similarly contend with the impact of still images, since commentators have regularly misidentified the burning figure at the start of the film as Quang Duc. His iconic status has made us more likely to overlook obvious differences between the photos that helped secure this and film of other self-immolators (for example, Quang Duc died in daylight, whereas the first self-immolation presented by *In the Year of the Pig* is taking place at night). Critics' habit of misrecognising Quang Duc in the footage repurposed by de Antonio further highlights the need to take account of film, as well as photography, to understand the construction of the icon of the so-called 'burning monk'.

This confusion about a scene in the prologue also foreshadows the gap between image and sound that persists when the film returns, halfway through, to the subject of the Buddhists' protests. *In the Year of the Pig* mediates self-immolation through white, Western gazes, like *Persona*, while relying, in contrast to Bergman's film, on almost exclusively male narration. As government official Roger Hilsman and journalist David Halberstam tell the story of Quang Duc's final hours, varied scenes unfold on the screen. The first shot of a monk sitting cross-legged on the ground, who is being doused with petrol, synchronises with the detail of Hilsman's narration. This is not because it is newsreel, for which it would be easy to mistake, but because it was extracted from a reconstruction of Browne's documentation of the event by Gualtiero Jacopetti and Francesco Prosperi for their Italian 'shockumentary' *Mondo Cane 2* (1963). Given that the real self-immolators are often admired as 'unflinching', an epithet repeated by Hilsman, it is ironic that the too-still mannequin set on fire in this re-creation confirms, for at least one critic, its fakery.[105] The fictional status of this footage is perhaps obliquely acknowledged a moment later, when Halberstam recalls Diem's false belief that Quang Duc's immolation was staged for American television. Then, when Hilsman mentions a 'suddenly [. . .] towering flame', the film cuts to a longer sequence from the footage of fire engulfing Dinh Van. Of discrepancy between sound and image in the cinema, de Antonio comments: 'there is an intensification, an intensity of hearing, when [. . .] the voice says one thing and the image another: it pulls you inside the film, it compels you to pay attention.'[106] Differences between the description of Quang Duc burning and the accompanying shots remind us that self-immolation was a collective phenomenon. A minute later, in an archival film frame stilled for our scrutiny, protesting monks carry a blown-up copy of one of Browne's famous stills of Quang Duc, which belatedly illustrates the earlier commentary. The sequence, then, refers to these iconic photographs in several ways: through verbal reconstructions of the event, a re-enactment based on Browne's pictures and, finally, film depicting the Buddhist community mobilising Quang Duc's image – or, in Ghosh's phrase, 'forg[ing] social bonds through the icon'.[107] This shot of a collective divests self-immolator images of the apocalyptic tenor – connoting the end of time – they acquired at the outset of the film and orients them instead towards the future. Browne's still is juxtaposed with moving images of similar but different scenes: a restaging of it and another self-burning (which also remind us of the figure on fire in the prologue). De Antonio's film thus complicates the traditional discourse around photo-iconicity by highlighting close ties between the stills of Quang Duc and moving images of other self-immolators which together form a composite icon. Although no moving images of his protest survive, this iconic monk and activist, *In the Year of the Pig* confirms, became part of cinema history.

Conclusion: Scandalous Peace

This chapter has tracked the incorporation of film of Dinh Van and still and moving images of other Buddhist activists into a French newsreel and cinemagazine, a Swedish fiction film, an American documentary and a Canadian installation between 1963 and 1968. It has sought to complement research on the itinerary of iconic photographs of Quang Duc by showing that film of other self-immolators recurred in European and North American cinema as emblems of the war in Vietnam or more generally of pain, shock or the power of images. Moving images attest that these protestors remained still, forming a distinctive part of the war's iconography. Yet the elevation of the burning figures in the films discussed here into apocalyptic icons risks diverting attention, I have suggested, from what sources including their published testimonies specify as their anti-imperial and pacifist politics.

The later of the two iconic stills of Quang Duc returned to French newsstands in the middle of the following decade on the cover of *Cahiers du cinéma*. The white flames engulfing him rise up towards the bright red masthead, whose final word stands out in large, bold capitals, renewing the association between the self-immolators and the moving image. The choice of this non-cinematic full-page cover picture (which announced the dossier containing Bergala's critique of 'stereotyped historical photos') and its juxtaposition with the ambiguous title 'spécial images de marque' ('special issue on mark-, sign- or brand images') disturbed the contributor Pascal Bonitzer, as he recounts in an essay in the following issue. Nevertheless, Bonitzer underlines the 'continuity [and] complicity between photography and cinema', whose 'central paradox' Mulvey would later describe as 'the co-presence of movement and stillness'.[108] Bonitzer is also riveted by stasis in the photograph: 'there is a *scandal* of this burning monk. [. . .] Scandal of this peace, of this immobility, of this inviolate attitude of prayer when the fire bares the whole tree of nerves, gnawing at and defoliating the tissues, intolerable contradiction which intolerably persists, o dreadful serenity!'[109] This scandalously peaceful figure bears witness not only against the past horrors of the American war, but also against the 'soft and cold war of information' relayed to us by television's 'interminable flux'.[110] Quang Duc's protest would continue to provoke reflection on the relation between still and moving images. For example, he resurfaces in Wehn-Damisch's documentary *Photographie et société: d'après Gisèle Freund* (1983) alongside an excerpt of the footage of Dinh Van for comparison. Moreover, his appearance in a digital photomontage on Chris Marker's CD-Rom *Immemory* (1997), in which the Hora of Spring from Sandro Botticelli's 'Birth of Venus' (c. 1485) tries to smother the flames, reminds the critic Vincent Jacques of 'Gustave'. This is the nickname film editors gave to an unidentified burning man in Second World War footage of Borneo, another 'symbol' or 'icon' who 'bears witness against war'.[111] Not only has cinema created iconic images of figures on fire; the history of the indelible pictures of Quang Duc's political self-sacrifice also illustrates how iconic photography intersects with a cinematic imaginary.

Notes

1. This description is based on two of Malcolm Browne's photographs of Thich Quang Duc's self-immolation and his written account of the event in *The New Face of War: A Report on a Communist Guerrilla Campaign* (London: Cassell, 1965), pp. 178–81.

2. Blaylock, Sara, 'Bringing the War Home to the United States and East Germany: *In the Year of the Pig* and *Pilots in Pajamas*', *Cinema Journal*, 56: 4 (Summer 2017), 26–50 (26). On television news coverage of Quang Duc's protest, see, for example, Moss, Georg Donelson, *Vietnam: An American Ordeal* (Englewood Cliffs, NJ: Prentice Hall, 1990), pp. 104–5. For confirmation that American television showed images of other Vietnamese Buddhist nuns and monks burning themselves, see, for instance, Franklin, *Vietnam and Other American Fantasies*, p. 54.

3. Gunthert, 'Les icônes du photojournalisme', p. 29. To support this claim, Gunthert cites Westwell, Guy, 'Accidental Napalm Attack and Hegemonic Visions of America's War in Vietnam', *Critical Studies in Media Communication*, xxviii: v (2011), 407–23.

4. Cavell, Stanley, 'The Fact of Television', in Rothman, William (ed.), *Cavell on Film* (New York: State University of New York Press, [1982] 2005), pp. 59–85 (p. 83).

5. Gunthert, 'Les icônes du photojournalisme', p. 23.

6. Browne, *The New Face of War*, p. 179.

7. Biggs, Michael, 'Self-Immolation in Context, 1963–2012', *Revue d'Études Tibétaines*, 25 (December 2012), 143–50 (146).

8. Roth, Philip, *American Pastoral* (London: Jonathan Cape, 1997), p. 153.

9. Bellour, 'Concerning "the Photographic"', p. 276.

10. Bellour, *Between-the-Images*, pp. 16, 153.

11. Stewart, *Between Film and Screen*, p. 19.

12. Ibid., p. 75.

13. Ibid., p. 75.

14. Rust, 'Hitting the "Vérité Jackpot"', 51.

15. Ibid., p. 66.

16. Ibid., p. 68.

17. Bellour, *Between-the-Images*, p. 135; Rust, 'Hitting the "Vérité Jackpot"', 70–1.

18. Yang, Michelle Murray, 'Still Burning: Self-Immolation as Photographic Protest', *Quarterly Journal of Speech*, 97: 1 (2011), 1–25 (15).

19. Skow, Lisa M. and George N. Dionisopoulos, 'A Struggle to Contextualize Photographic Images: American Print Media and the "Burning Monk"', *Communication Quarterly*, 45: 4 (1997), 393–409 (404–5).

20. Zelizer, *About to Die*, pp. 221–5.

21. Ibid., pp. 2, 24, 25.

22. Yang, 'Still Burning', pp. 15–16.

23. Ibid., pp. 1, 15.

24. 'Problèmes au Vietnam', Pathé Journal Actualité (1963), silent, black and white, Gaumont Pathé Archives.

25. Yang, 'Still Burning', pp. 15–16.

26. 'Suicide d'un bonze à Saigon', Pathé Journal Actualité (1963), sound film, black and white, 46 seconds, Gaumont Pathé Archives.

27. Sturken, *Tangled Memories*, p. 90.

28. Ibid., p. 90.
29. Goldberg, *The Power of Photography*, p. 225.
30. Hagopian, 'Vietnam War Photography', p. 219.
31. Ibid., p. 213.
32. Sturken, *Tangled Memories*, p. 90.
33. Lindeperg, *La Voie des images*, p. 187.
34. Hagopian, 'Vietnam War Photography', p. 214.
35. Ibid., p. 214.
36. For discussion of the detachment of the 'Marianne of '68' from the particular and unprecedented demonstration it documented, for example, see Leblanc and Versavel (eds), *Les Icônes de mai 68*, pp. 78–9.
37. See the newsreel's opening titles and the shot-by-shot description, Gaumont Pathé Archives.
38. To my knowledge, no moving film exists of Quang Duc's self-sacrifice.
39. See www.gettyimages.co.uk/detail/news-photo/flames-engulf-buddhist-priest-ho-dinh-van-in-front-of-the-news-photo/515512772 (last accessed 2 August 2018). British and American newspapers reported Dinh Van's self-immolation, and Browne later mentions it in passing (*The New Face of War*, pp. 180–1).
40. See Kin Gagnon, Monika, 'The Christian Pavilion at Expo 67: Notes from Charles Gagnon's Archive', in Richman Kenneally, Rhona and Johanne Sloan (eds), *Expo 67: Not Just a Souvenir* (Toronto: University of Toronto Press, 2010), pp. 143–60 (p. 157).
41. Ghosh, *Global Icons*.
42. Tobing Rony, Fatimah, *The Third Eye: Race, Cinema and the Ethnographic Spectacle* (Durham, NC, London: Duke University Press, 1996), p. 23. Tobing Rony notes the difficulty of recovering the subjectivity of people in ethnographic film without written records of their thoughts (p. 24). I quote later in this chapter from the only two testimonies by Vietnamese protestors who immolated themselves on film that I have been able to find.
43. Tobing Rony, *The Third Eye*, p. 24.
44. Joan Fontcuberta, 'Archive Noise', artist's statement, www.fontcuberta.com (last accessed 2 August 2018).
45. Translations from the film are mine. Like an icon, this photograph has periodically mutated, as detailed in Silverman's account of retouches to and remakes of it (*The Miracle of Analogy*, pp. 55–65).
46. Leblanc and Versavel, 'Histoire visuelle de Mai 68', p. 12.
47. Cortade, *Le Cinéma de l'immobilité*, p. 213.
48. Fierke, Karin M., *Political Self-Sacrifice: Agency, Body and Emotion in International Relations* (Cambridge, New York: Cambridge University Press, 2013), p. 184.
49. Nu Thanh Quang cited in Day Blakely Donaldson's book of self-immolators' biographies and testimonies, *The Self-Immolators* (2013), http://thespeaker.co/wp-content/uploads/2013/06/The-Self-Immolators.pdf (last accessed 10 July 2018), p. 42.

50. Thi Thieu cited in Donaldson, *The Self-Immolators*, p. 43; Garanger, Marc, *Femmes algériennes 1960* (Paris: Contrejour, 1982), p. 3 (my translation).
51. Bellour, *Between-the-Images*, p. 16.
52. Ibid., p. 145.
53. Stewart, *Between Film and Screen*, p. 76.
54. Ibid., p. 76. Rust too notes *Persona*'s association of violence with photogrammes ('Hitting the "Vérité Jackpot"', p. 51).
55. Rousseau, Frédéric, *L'Enfant juif de Varsovie: histoire d'une photographie* (Paris: Seuil, 2009), p. 157. Gunthert also cites Rousseau's claim in support of his history of the process of iconisation ('Les icônes du photojournalisme', p. 24). Schoenberner, Gerhard, *The Yellow Star*, trans. Susan Sweet (London: Corgi, 1969).
56. Raskin, *A Child at Gunpoint*, pp. 105–6.
57. Sontag, Susan, *Styles of Radical Will* (London: Secker & Warburg, 1969), p. 141.
58. Hariman and Lucaites, *No Caption Needed*, p. 27.
59. Gunthert, 'Les icônes du photojournalisme', p. 19.
60. Stewart, *Between Film and Screen*, p. 76. See also Ohlin, Peter, 'The Holocaust in Ingmar Bergman's *Persona*: The Instability of Imagery', *Scandinavian Studies*, 77: 2 (Summer 2005), 241–74.
61. Bergman, Ingmar, *Images: My Life in Film*, trans. Marianne Ruth (New York: Arcade Publishing, 1994), p. 59.
62. Bergman, Ingmar, *Bergman on Bergman*, trans. Paul Britten Austin (New York: Da Capo Press, 1993), p. 210.
63. Ibid., p. 210.
64. Ibid., p. 210; Sontag, *Styles of Radical Will*, p. 141.
65. Jeong, Seung-hoon, *Cinematic Interfaces: Film Theory after New Media* (New York: Routledge, 2013), p. 193.
66. Cavell, 'The Fact of Television', p. 83.
67. Bergman, *Bergman on Bergman*, p. 211.
68. Fierke, *Political Self-sacrifice*, p. 185.
69. See Salomon, Kim, 'The Anti-Vietnam War Movement in Sweden', in Christopher Goscha and Maurice Vaïsse (eds), *La Guerre du Vietnam et l'Europe, 1963–1973* (Brussels: Bruylant, 2003), pp. 327–38.
70. Bellour, *Between-the-Images*, p. 145. Connecting *Persona* to 'the tide of political conscience-raising' that swept through the 1960s, Lloyd Michaels reads the iconic images from Warsaw and Saigon as providing 'a resonance that transcends the idealist vision of [Bergman's] earlier historical melodramas and psychological case studies' ('Bergman and the Necessary Illusion: An Introduction to *Persona*', in Lloyd Michaels (ed.), *Ingmar Bergman's 'Persona'* (Cambridge: Cambridge University Press, 2000), pp. 1–23 (p. 17)).
71. Bellour, *Between-the-Images*, p. 144.
72. Wollen, 'Fire and Ice', p. 110.
73. Ibid., p. 110.
74. Silverman, Kaja, *The Acoustic Mirror: The Female Voice in Psychoanalysis and Cinema* (Bloomington: Indiana University Press, 1988), p. 93.

75. Deleuze, *The Movement-Image*, p. 111.

76. Ibid., p. 108.

77. For example, Eco also draws on Peirce's notion of the iconic sign in his 1970 essay 'Critique of the Image'.

78. Ghosh, *Global Icons*, for example pp. 184–5.

79. Deleuze, *The Movement-Image*, pp. 101, 108.

80. Ibid., p. 97.

81. Ibid., p. 111.

82. Stewart, *Between Film and Screen*, pp. 75, 79. See also Bingham, Adam, 'Apocalypse Now: Images of The End in the Cinema of Ingmar Bergman', in Virginie Selavy (ed.), *The End: An Electric Sheep Anthology* (London: Strange Attractor Press, 2011), pp. 236–50.

83. Sealy, 'Human Rights, Human Wrongs'.

84. Mondzain, *Image, Icon, Economy*.

85. Miedema, Gary, *For Canada's Sake: Public Religion, Centennial Celebrations, and the Re-making of Canada in the 1960s* (Montreal and Kingston: McGill-Queen University Press, 2006), pp. 163–4.

86. Leblanc and Versavel (eds), *Les Icônes de mai 68*, p. 12.

87. Miedema, *For Canada's Sake*, p. 163.

88. Gagnon, Charles, interview reproduced in booklet accompanying Spectral Media DVD, 'Charles Gagnon: 4 Films', pp. 33–5 (p. 33).

89. Cortade, *Le Cinéma de l'immobilité*, p. 220.

90. Perlmutter, *Photojournalism and Foreign Policy*, p. 11.

91. Ibid., p. 11.

92. As Kin Gagnon puts it, 'the effectiveness of such public acts of protest was the singularity and individuality of the act itself propelled for collective purpose' ('The Christian Pavilion at Expo 67', p. 157).

93. Gunthert, 'Les icônes du photojournalisme', pp. 26–8.

94. Russell, Catherine, 'Archival Apocalypse: Found Footage as Ethnography', in *Experimental Ethnography: The Work of Film in the Age of Video* (Durham, NC; London: Duke University Press, 1999), pp. 238–72 (p. 241); Kin Gagnon, 'The Christian Pavilion at Expo 67', p. 156.

95. For discussion of the humanist outlook of Gagnon's installation, see Miedema, *For Canada's Sake*, p. 173 and Kin Gagnon, 'The Christian Pavilion at Expo 67', p. 143. Kin Gagnon draws illuminating parallels between the pavilion and the 'Family of Man' photographic exhibition first mounted in 1955, drawing in particular on Janine Marchessault's reinterpretation of Edward Steichen's globe-trotting show 'not as a sentimental humanism that homogenized global difference into a harmonious unitary vision of humankind' but as a 'historical' and 'progressive' variant that alluded to racism (ibid., p. 153).

96. Mondzain, *Image, Icon, Economy*, pp. 151–2.

97. Correll, Barbara, 'Rem(a)inders of G(l)ory: Monuments and Bodies in "Glory" and "In the Year of the Pig"', *Cultural Critique*, 19 (Autumn 1991), 141–77 (156); Blaylock, 'Bringing the War Home', 34.

98. Skow and Dionisopoulos, 'A Struggle to Contextualize Photographic Images'.
99. Blaylock, 'Bringing the War Home', 34.
100. Cortade, *Le Cinéma de l'immobilité*, p. 240.
101. Correll, 'Rem(a)inders of G(l)ory', 156.
102. Ibid., 143.
103. See De Antonio, Emile, interview by Bernard Eisenschitz and Jean Narboni, *Cahiers du cinéma*, 214 (July/August 1969), 43–56 (51) (translations from this text are mine).
104. Westwell, *War Cinema*, p. 63.
105. Bentin, Doug, 'Mondo Barnum', in Gary D. Rhodes and John Parris Springer (eds), *Docufictions: Essays on the Intersection of Documentary and Fictional Filmmaking* (Jefferson, NC; London: McFarland & Co., 2006), pp. 144–53 (p. 149).
106. De Antonio, *Cahiers du cinéma* interview, 51.
107. Ghosh, *Global Icons*, p. 253.
108. Bonitzer, Pascal, 'La Surimage', *Cahiers du cinéma*, 270 (1976), 29–34 (29–30) (translations from this text are mine); Mulvey, *Death 24x a Second*, p. 12.
109. Bonitzer, 'La Surimage', p. 32.
110. Ibid.
111. Jacques, Vincent, 'Images floues, frontières troubles: la pratique photographique de Chris Marker', in Vincent Jacques (ed.), *Chris.Marker.Photographie* (Ivry-sur-Seine: Créaphis Éditions, 2018), pp. 85–105 (pp. 100–4) (translation my own). Jacques quotes references to the frequent reappropriation of the symbol of 'Gustave' in Alain Resnais's contribution to the anthology film *Loin de Vietnam* (*Far from Vietnam*; 1967), a segment scripted by Marker, and *Level Five* (Marker, 1995). Two decades after Quang Duc encountered a dynamic painted figure in *Immemory*, he turned back into the subject of a series of stills in the second episode of Ken Burns and Lynn Novick's *The Vietnam War* (2017). This documentary series frames the immolation and other war-time events as iconic images, explaining the process of their photojournalistic capture. The film's close-up exploration of the first of the most revered portraits of the monk recalls *Persona*'s detailing of the Holocaust icon, but adds movement by zooming out and panning across from flames to disclose the face and body from which they billow. Exemplified here, the animation effect with which Burns has become synonymous plays a key role in the following chapter's discussions of rostrum filmmaking. His and Novick's reframing of the photograph also anticipates moving images of Dinh Van on fire, which appear, in another visual echo of *Persona*, moments later.

CHAPTER FOUR

The Face of the Crowd: Che

The photograph singles out a face, strikingly framed by a beret, beard and curls. The most familiar, cropped version looks like a studio portrait; there's a stillness about him that resembles a pose. Yet the image derives from more contingent circumstances, as we know from the testimony of the photographer, Alberto (Díaz Gutiérrez) Korda, and his contact sheet. From the printed roll of film, we can infer that the picture's subject is on a podium packed with dignitaries, including Fidel Castro, Jean-Paul Sartre and Simone de Beauvoir. Korda remembers taking it on 5 January 1960 in Havana at a rally honouring the victims of an explosion ascribed to anti-revolutionary sabotage. Working for the newspaper *Revolución*, he scanned the raised platform through his viewfinder and at the moment when the mass of people parted to reveal Ernesto (Che) Guevara, he pressed the shutter.[1] The photograph, then, in Korda's account, owes its existence and form to the movement of a crowd.

Like iconic image studies more widely, scholarship on Guevara as icon has assigned a privileged role to photography because Korda's image, and to a lesser extent snapshots of the revolutionary's corpse, gained symbolism for groups around the world.[2] Writing on these and other iconic stills typically focuses on individual exemplarity. As discussed in Chapter 1, Bergala criticises the photographic 'stereotype' for promoting this by singling out an 'actor of History', 'most often a victim, preferably innocent', and, in so doing, repressing the historical agency of popular movements.[3] This chapter seeks to contribute to the conversation about iconicity, in which Guevara has played a defining role, by exploring emblematic images of this guerrilla fighter and revolutionary leader as composites of photography and cinema. If icons, in the traditional view, propose that individuals make history, my photo-cinematic approach throws light instead on the relationship between individuals and crowds. According to Jean-Hughes Berrou, photography imbues Guevara's face with the power to arrange these mass entities. In a snapshot from 1959 by Raúl Corrales, for example, suggests Berrou, this 'messianic' visage 'restores equilibrium' to a posse of commanders crammed precariously onto another podium in Havana's Plaza de la Revolución: 'perhaps it is just a question of *photogénie*. [. . .] Plunge Guevara into a crowd, and everything organises itself around his face.'[4] While the images on which Chapters 1 and 3 focused owe their power to full figures, whether moving or still, and corporeal gesture played a significant role in Chapter 2, popular and scholarly fascination has focused on Guevara's face (especially the one captured by Korda or outlines thereof), notwithstanding the iconicity of at least one photograph of the full length of his corpse. The theme of the face connects critical literature on Guevara's image to theological and philosophical writings on icons and representations of Christ.[5]

Yet *photogénie* refers, in French film theory of the early twentieth century, to a power specific to cinema, not photography, and is associated not only with faces, but also with crowds.[6] For the Hungarian Communist filmmaker and theorist Béla Balázs, writing in the 1920s, the crowd itself has a face, a metaphor that evokes the autonomous life and expressive gestures that cinematic portrayals of human 'masses' for the first time revealed. The notion of the mass face was also applied to photographs by a European interwar writer favoured at the opposite end of the political spectrum. Made between the late 1960s and the early 1980s in Cuba, Argentina and France, the newsreel, documentary and essay films discussed in this chapter revitalise this concept, I suggest, by staging encounters between mobile multitudes and still images. My aim is not to provide a comprehensive survey of the profusion of films that deal, in documentary or fictional mode, with Guevara as icon, but to reconsider a small selection of the most poetic and creative from the first decade and a half of his iconic afterlife. Along with Balázs's notion of crowd faciality, Christa Blümlinger's writing on the motif of the *défilé* (procession, march or parade) and Ghosh's reappraisal of the icon as a 'moving technology' orient and inspire my account of cinema's distinctive depictions of groups of people to which Guevara has given direction. Iconic images of Guevara have sometimes brought cinema to a halt, like those of the 'Falling Soldier' and the self-immolating Buddhists, but more often helped to build and sustain filmic momentum. While we traditionally think of cinema as setting still photographs in motion, it also offers unique insights, I argue, into the mobilisation of crowds by fixed images and, by extension, the appropriation of icons by social movements, which continues to matter today.

Filing Past

While the elevation of Korda's photograph into an icon, particularly in the aftermath of Guevara's assassination, has received detailed attention, how this process intersected with cinema remains little discussed.[7] A good place to start tracking the convergence of this still image with moving ones is the newsreel archive of the Instituto Cubano de Arte e Industria Cinematograficos

(Cuban Institute of Cinematographic Art and Industry, or ICAIC), which chronicles the photo's rise to prominence. For example, a cropped, painted and bannerised version dominates shots of a homage to Guevara, following his death on 9 October 1967, by President Osvaldo Dorticós that played in cinemas around the country in early November of that year.[8] Newsreels didn't merely document the spread and mutation of Korda's image, though. One of these films, ostensibly a report on the Cuban publication of Guevara's Bolivian diary, which further expanded the reach of the iconic image that recurred on its cover, also meditates on the relationship between cinema and photography.[9] The paramount role that an originally photojournalistic image plays in this 4-minute documentary recalls its director (and ICAIC newsreel production overseer) Santiago Álvarez's films *Now!* (1965) and *LBJ* (1968).[10] As Álvarez explained, '[I make] collages from American magazines because the Americans prevent us from getting live material.'[11] Like *Now!* and *LBJ*, which used a rostrum camera to animate press stills from sources such as *Life*, including iconic pictures (by Charles Moore and Zapruder respectively) of police dogs savaging African American civil rights activists in Birmingham, Alabama in spring 1963 and of JFK's shooting, the newsreel from 5 July 1968 turns Korda's still into a dynamic, moving image.[12]

The film's initial focus on the snapshot Korda dubbed the 'Heroic Guerrilla' fortifies the well-established links between photography, iconicity and the face. It opens with a newspaper clipping announcing the free distribution of Guevara's diary and illustrated by Korda's photo, which the camera moves to position in the centre of the frame. The ensuing sequence documents the reproduction of this notice on the front page of *Granma*, the official Cuban Communist Party paper formerly known as *Revolución* (which originally rejected Korda's picture). A cut to a close-up of a pile of Guevara's diaries being handed out prolongs the visual concentration on the photo's afterlife. As the camera pulls back to reveal a queue for the book that stretches out of sight and then begins to track it through the streets, the focus shifts from Guevara to thousands of people inspired by him. Not only in photos, then, as Berrou discusses, but also in films do crowds compose themselves around Guevara's face.

According to Balázs, writing in the 1920s, cinema alone among the arts 'showed us the true face of the masses'.[13] Not only can close-ups capture the play of expressions on a single countenance; the medium also makes crowds visible for the first time 'as living creatures with a shape and a physiognomy of their own'.[14] As Erica Carter explains, 'the mass [. . .] [has] a status, then, in Balázs's physiognomy that equals the significance of the human face'.[15] Essential to his notion of physiognomy is the capacity to show movement without arresting it that distinguishes cinema from photography. While photography, as Siegfried Kracauer would concur several decades later, 'was technically equipped to portray crowds as the accidental agglomerations they are', film alone, which

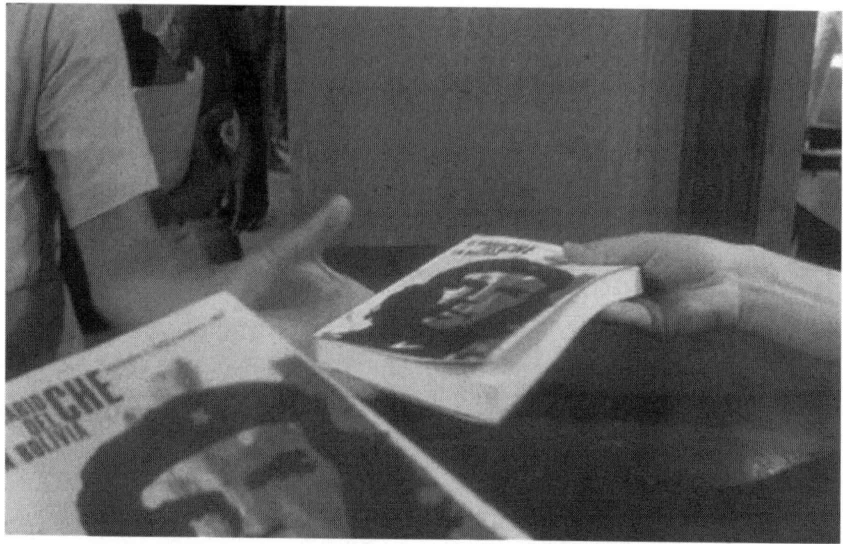

Figure 4.1 'Publication in Cuba of Che's Diary' (dir. Santiago Álvarez, 5 July 1968), *Noticieros: les actualités cubaines 1960–1970* (*Cuban Newsreels 1960–70*; Cuba, INA, 2017).

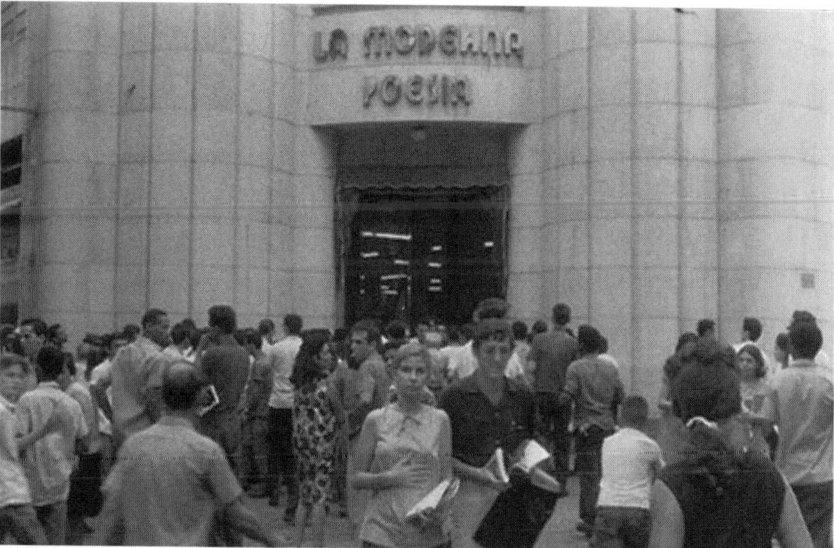

Figure 4.2 'Publication in Cuba of Che's Diary'.

embraced them as one of its main subjects, 'was equal to the task of capturing them in motion'.[16] And whereas theatre presents the mass facelessly, according to Balázs, as 'motion without form', cinema discloses the crowd's distinctive shape in close-ups that prevent it becoming 'inert or dead, like fallen rock [. . .]'

and 'ensure that the individual is not entirely forgotten or obliterated'.[17] Balázs singles out the portrayal of mass gestures and physiognomy in Soviet films such as Vsevolod Pudovkin's *Mother* (1926) as particularly revelatory.[18] The affinity between this national cinema in the late 1920s and Álvarez's documentaries in the 1960s derives not only from the significance both groups of films place on montage but also from the expressivity and autonomy they ascribe to crowds.[19] These characteristics manifest a revolutionary outlook that also inflects Balázs's approach to film after the First World War. In a series of long shots and close-ups in *Mother*, workers marching in protest against tsarist persecution break into what Balázs calls a 'mass smile'.[20] The queues for Guevara's diary in Álvarez's newsreel also appear from various angles and distances; sometimes the visage of a reader fleetingly fills the frame. But it is the face of the crowd, along with that of Guevara, that dominates the second part of the film.

The newsreel's accumulation of shots in which a series of people or images pass through the frame evokes a crowd-related motif that has oriented discussion of pre-digital photo-cinematic interaction. Since the late nineteenth century, films have used people filing through the visible field to symbolise the procession of photogrammes through a projector. As Christa Blümlinger explains, the French verb that describes this motif, *défiler*, 'not only means "to file" in the sense of to march past, but also, rather more generally and in a non-military sense, any moving past or passing by, including that of images'.[21] Álvarez's references to this aesthetic figure contribute to ICAIC's project of exposing the technical and formal workings of cinema for the purpose of making explicit how art encodes ideology.[22] The crowd in his film assumes the moving form of the *défilé* without arranging itself into a display of (military or state) power. Like Soviet films in Balázs's account, the Cuban newsreel shows 'not the *organised* mass visible in every disciplined regiment of soldiers, but the mass that has become an organism, a collective being, with a mind and heart of its own'.[23] This creaturely crowd and the diaries that have brought it together pass in close-up through four static shots that form a pattern.

The figure of the *défilé*, as Blümlinger states, is 'always linked to that of arrest'.[24] Álvarez's *mise-en-scène* of the journey of Korda's photograph illustrates this connection. The diaries' passage across the field of view rhymes visually with earlier shots of the icon in making travelling in multiplicate along conveyor belts and around cylinders at *Granma*'s printing plant. In both cases, the transport of versions of Korda's image across the screen mimics the 'photopan', Stewart's term for the 'lateral movements of ongoing cinematic record that cling to, linger over, and then disengage from serial photographic images in cinema's own procedural difference from them'.[25] The film plays instead between the still camera and the moving photograph, inviting us to think about cinema's sequencing of single immobile images.

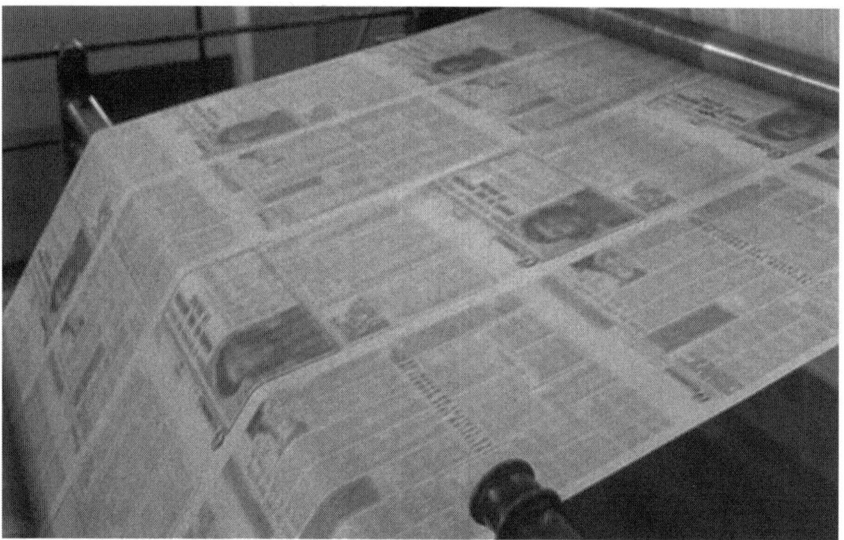

Figure 4.3 'Publication in Cuba of Che's Diary'.

The ribbon of uncut news pages is reminiscent of a filmstrip, and its accelerating passage through the machinery and past the camera evokes the movement of projected pictures.[26] The newsreel thus imaginatively prefigures the link between projection and procession that Blümlinger traces through films of the 1970s and 1980s by Jean-Luc Godard, whose examination with Anne-Marie Miéville of other versions of the same iconic image I will discuss later in this chapter. Álvarez's short draws an original analogy between the iteration of icons and the animation of stills. The immobile image shown at the start of the film turns into a mobile, travelling icon that in turn sets crowds in motion.

Posing and Passing Crowds

The mobilisation of Korda's picture in Cuban newsreels coincided with the repetition in other countries of more recent images of Guevara. Michael Chanan argues that this portrayal of the revolutionary as strong and dignified owed its power to another press still in which his executioners tried to depict him as weak and humiliated.[27] The image to which Chanan refers is the most acclaimed and widely reproduced of the at least fifty-six different photographs and film stills reproduced in Jean-Jacques Lefrère's photo-biography of Guevara that depict his corpse and those of two other executed guerrillas, Siméon Cuba (known as Willy) and Juan Pablo Chang (known as El Chino), which the Bolivian authorities displayed to international press on 9 and 10 October 1967 in the laundry of a Vallegrande hospital.[28] The best-known component of this most composite of icons is also among the most populous, accommodating two armed guards, two high-ranking military officers and four journalists.[29] Like Álvarez's close-ups of Havanans collecting their free Bolivian diaries, this iconic image supports Berrou's notion that photographed crowds arrange themselves around Guevara's face, which occupies the centre of the tableau, and suggests that this is more than a mere effect of composition. Like Korda's snapshot, this picture owes its shape to the gestures of a collective being. Its creator, Bolivian photojournalist Freddy Alborta, remembers his view being obstructed: 'I had the sense that I was missing lots of good shots thanks to these people who wanted at all costs to put the body on stage [*mettre le corps en scène*], as if it wasn't enough on its own'.[30] (The irony of their dominant positions in what would become his most famous photograph is not lost on him.) He recalls one of these would-be directors (who had nothing to do with Guevara's capture and killing), Bolivian Air Force General Oscar Adriazola, fingering a thoracic bullet hole: 'he was posing, quite simply'.[31]

Alborta's iconic photograph juxtaposes two different kinds of immobility: that of the dead body and that of the pose. John Berger discerns in this depiction of the revolutionary's corpse the same 'sense of global stillness' as in Rembrandt's portrayal of a partly dissected one in 'The Anatomy Lesson of Doctor Nicolas Tulp' (1632).[32] Rather than a painting, the photographed cadaver reminds Lefrère of a gisant, a sculpture recumbent on a tomb.[33] As well as remembering older artforms, Alborta's picture also anticipates the affinity between photography and death that particularly preoccupied French theorists in the 1980s. What 'pricks' Barthes in the photograph of Lewis Payne waiting to be hanged, for example, the *punctum* 'no longer of form but of intensity', is: '*he is going to die*'.[34] Just as Guevara's body was posed for the cameras, so too, in Alborta's photo and other images, do military and intelligence personnel pose around him. Invented in the nineteenth century and still popular today, the posed photograph has an intimate relationship, according to Sutton, with the end of life: 'however long the exposure of a photo-de-pose [. . .], the time within this image becomes that of *passing*: duration is depicted indexically and metaphorically enunciated by blurring eyelids, misdirected looks, blood-red retinas. We see the passage of the photons themselves in these photographs, and it is this passing of time and light, an evanescence from presence to absence, that renders the photograph steadily immobile with the silence of the funerary [. . .]'.[35] Like the corpse, the pose, photography's 'archetypal [. . .] temporality', reminds us of our transience, a word derived from the

Latin 'transire', whose meanings include 'pass' and 'pass through'.[36] This complicates Barthes's distinction between the phenomenology of the photograph, in which 'something *has posed* in front of the tiny hole' and of the cinema, in which 'something *has passed* in front of this same tiny hole: the pose is swept away and denied by the continuous series of images.'[37] Other images of the Guevara dead, as we will see, capture passing people.

At least three of Alborta's group portraits include a man filming with a Bolex H16 Reflex 16mm camera. Slung across his other shoulder is a synchronised tape recorder. Like the team that filmed Dinh Van's self-immolation, Alborta pictured photojournalists working alongside a filmmaker, underlining the heightened relevance of moving images to iconicity in a period when (as discussed in Chapter 3) photographs and television relied on each other for influence.[38] His best-known photograph coexists as a series of film shots of roughly the same crowd of soldiers – including Adriazola and the other (unidentified) military officer – and reporters poking and pawing the slain Guevara.[39] Although footage of the body's arrival in Vallegrande, its preparation and presentation has reached large audiences via television and cinema, and news agencies including the Associated Press continue to distribute it, far less has been written about these filmic images than photographs of the same scene. The previous chapter discussed Sturken's account of the obscurity of TV film of Văn Lém's execution and the burned Kim Phúc compared to the matching photo-icons, which came to prominence in the same broad era as the images on which this chapter focuses. I suggested in response that the capacity to represent duration directly enables film to produce icons of distinct power, rather than merely bolstering that of photographs, as illustrated by footage of extended protests by Dinh Van and other self-immolators. Not all of Sturken's distinctions between the two stills from Vietnam and their moving counterparts apply to the display of Guevara's body; the iconic photograph is no easier to look at than the film shot on the same day, nor does it further clarify facial expressions. But it exhibits the 'ability to connote completeness' that Sturken ascribes to still images, particularly when cropped, as is habitual, to remove the camera that intrudes at the edge on the right.[40] Just as this detail draws our attention outside the photograph's frame, so too the Bolex pans from Guevara's face to those leaning over him, and those below, dirty and destroyed, of El Chino and Willy, rendering off-screen space significant and the image lacunary. There are also shots of the scene that blur the boundary between film and photography.

Guevara appears in both media at a privileged moment in *La hora de los hornos* (*The Hour of the Furnaces*, 1968). The first part of Fernando Solanas and Octavio Getino's film concludes with pictures of his dead body. The stasis of this corpse in the half a minute of footage pre-empts that of his face in the filmed photo, the final image of Part One, which occupies the screen, accompanied on drums by the percussionist Domingo Cura, for 3 minutes.[41] Although Lefrère's photo-biography doesn't include this portrait, it contains other shots of varying tightness of Guevara's face after he had been killed, washed and coiffed, including one that shows soldiers comparing it with a magazine photograph taken while he was alive. The recurrence of facial close-ups among images from the laundry-cum-morgue not only reminds us of the authorities' concern to quell doubts about his identity, but also bolsters the idea that Guevara possesses the magical power that Berrou calls *photogénie*. The Argentinian film's reverent treatment of one such image foreshadows the comparisons of photographs and acheiropoietic icons by Maynard and Mondzain that I outlined in this book's Introduction. As Goldberg notes, Guevara's image reinvests the word 'icon' with religious connotations.[42]

The 'veronica' or true image and the photojournalistic icon that has more recently attracted critical attention have in common symbolic power that can be harnessed by ecclesiastical or secular authorities or social movements (sometimes they also share Christian iconography, as mentioned in Chapter 1). These two kinds of icon converge at the end of the first part of *The Hour of the Furnaces*. How do Solanas and Getino imbue a news photo with a religious connotation? As Mariano Mestman explains, the film interprets pictures of the dead Guevara in the light of 'an epochal discourse that brings guerrilla heroism and Christian martyrdom together'.[43] Like the 'Falling Soldier', whose repetition has perpetuated Christian theology's imperialist construction of whiteness as a privileged vantage point, Alborta's iconic snapshot has been compared to European paintings of martyrs.[44] For example, Berger draws attention to its resemblance to Andrea Mantegna's foreshortened portrayal of Christ's corpse (c. 1480–1500).[45] The photograph of Guevara's face over which Solanas and Getino's anti-imperialist film lingers is more reminiscent of images of the Shroud. Like the figure who appeared on the glass plates exposed in 1898 in Turin, captivating believers, the revolutionary has a beard and looks straight at us from a monochrome image. 'Photography', writes Barthes in a passage that intersects with Maynard's and Mondzain's reliquary discussions, 'has something to do with resurrection: might we not say of it what the Byzantines said of the image of Christ which impregnated St Veronica's napkin: that it was not made by the hand of man, *acheiropoietos*?'[46] Since the Shroud, for the iconophile, proves the resurrection, its cadaverous markings, argues Mondzain, become 'a sign of life' and photography, which reveals truth 'in the negative', participates 'in the work of animation, of reanimation', convincing us 'that this corpse is breathing, and that each image is fundamentally miraculous'.[47] In keeping with the narrator's claim, earlier in the sequence of *The Hour of the Furnaces*, that for revolutionaries 'death is no longer the end', the still image of Guevara that lingers on the screen, whose eyes, like those of Korda's 'Heroic Guerrilla', are open, performs this 'iconic magic'.[48] The scene in this sense contrasts with the apocalyptic photo-cinematic iconography generated by the deaths of the Spanish militiaman and the Vietnamese self-immolators.

Rather than attributing unique powers to photography, however, the sequence also incorporates four filmic close-ups of Guevara's face. The stasis of the Bolex and its subject during these moments unsettles the distinctions between film and photography and between the handheld shot and the icon made without human hands. The fourth close-up appears between long shots of inhabitants of Vallegrande filing past the body in a procession on 10 October that continued until nightfall. In a landmark essay published soon after they had finished the documentary, Solanas and Getino argue that the director should 'counter the film industry of a cinema of [. . .] individuals with that of masses [. . .]'.[49] In attempting this, they avoid the images of military officers leaning over Guevara's corpse, such as Alborta's celebrated picture, to which other Argentinian artists referred in roughly contemporary drawings and paintings.[50] In addition to these posed multifigure portraits, the cine-camera operator pictured by Alborta or perhaps one of the crews we glimpse in footage of journalists arriving at Vallegrande airport (not included in Solanas and Getino's film) captured more dynamic group formations. *The Hour of the Furnaces* cuts back and forth between Guevara's dead face and a crowd whose 'living creatureliness', to paraphrase Balázs, stands out by contrast, turning the setting of Alborta's fixed tableau into a passageway. The flow of people around a corpse displayed on a slab by the authorities connects two meanings of the English verb 'defile', to march in file (from the French 'défiler') and to desecrate or profane. This *défilé* foreshadows what I have argued is Álvarez's play with the motif half a year later in another filmic meditation on the revolutionary's capacity to draw crowds. Within roughly the same period, the parade around Guevara's body passed from television into cinema.

Solanas and Getino reconstruct the gesture of this crowd by splicing together four shots of local civilian men and women who function as onscreen surrogates for the film viewer. These images of visitors 'caught between simple curiosity and outright veneration' remind Mestman of Mantegna's painting, mentioned earlier, of the dead Christ 'similarly surrounded by peasants'.[51] But the distraught protagonists that Mantegna stations by Jesus are famous individuals (St John the Evangelist, the Virgin Mary and Mary Magdalene), whereas their unnamed counterparts who pass Guevara resemble a single collective organism. The previous sequence has followed another procession of mourners. It is as if this group stride out of Argentina's Juella-Jujuy Cemetery, where they are burying a loved one, straight into the hospital at Vallegrande to grieve – and learn from the example of – another of the epidemic of premature Latin American deaths that the commentary attributes to neo-colonial violence. These transitional moments in the film bring individual iconicity into view without losing sight of collective movement and agency, and in an attempt to inspire and mobilise the crowd of viewers.

ICONICITY AND ANONYMITY

Why did Godard, in the same year as the Argentinian directors, film a postmortem photograph of Guevara? The several snapshots of the political leader that appear in two 'film tracts' (May and June 1968) directed by Godard and in his feature *Le Gai Savoir* (*Joy of Learning*, 1969) participate in his analysis of contemporary news images. A second reason for appropriating these photographs was practical: although *Le Gai Savoir* underlines Godard's fierce interest in television, still pictures from newspapers and magazines were quicker to obtain and insert into films than moving footage. The tracts had to be assembled fast to spread awareness of the protests and inspire their continuation. In a guide for *ciné-tracteurs*, Chris Marker, who with Godard supervised the making of these silent black-and-white shorts, advocates the use of fixed images for a third purpose. It was easier to compose from stills than moving pictures since the films should not be edited after shooting.[52] But Godard's fourth and most pressing motive was to reflect and reinforce Guevara's exemplary – or what would later be called iconic – status for Parisian students and workers demanding social change. As Maria-Carolina Cambre notes, 'often the mobilisation of the iconic image of Che Guevara surges wherever and whenever people protest publicly'.[53] Although Godard's shorts of 1968 seek, like Solanas and Getino, to replace 'a cinema of [. . .] individuals with that of masses [. . .]', the French tracts and Argentinian film alike are concerned with the galvanisation of political movements by Guevara's words and images.

Film tract 12 comprises thirty-one shots of pages from magazines and cartoons, book covers and other images, including three photographs of Guevara, one of which shows him in iconic rigor mortis. No one has signed the photos or the 3-minute film that has incorporated them. The creators of the tracts rejected the bourgeois, romantic notion of the individual, named auteur, styling themselves instead as a collective of anonymous artists and activists creating artefacts that transmitted to the protestors the news the mainstream media omitted. To point out that the neat, curly handwriting in several of the tracts is unmistakably Godard's is therefore to read against their grain, but these traces of him help us understand how the films mediate between the individual and the crowd. Written on each image in tract 12 is a word, short phrase or assonant verbal cluster. These fragments of text build sentences as the images succeed each other. Like the film as a whole, this decomposed commentary lacks a signature but turns out to come from a letter by Guevara.

The main subject of this missive to the editor of a Uruguayan newspaper is the relationship between the individual and 'the mass', which Guevara describes as a 'multifaceted being', rather than merely 'the sum of elements of the same type', and which he repeatedly imagines in motion, for example in 'the image of the multitudes marching forward toward the future'.[54] This image recurs in the film tract, which begins and ends with photos of crowds at political rallies and during which other groups of demonstrators stride across the screen, descendants of the dynamic masses whose 'true face' was revealed, according to Balázs, by an earlier era of silent films. The combination of still pictures and moving protestors anticipates, in a different way from the other films I have discussed in this chapter, the motif of the *défilé* that Blümlinger tracks through the next two decades of Godard's work. Several of the other tracts go further and animate the battles between demonstrators and police in rapid sequences of photographs. Not only the mobilisation of the masses but also Guevara's description of it guide the selection and ordering of tract 12's images. Godard creatively pairs Guevara's words with pictures. For example, the proclamation 'we prepare [the youth] to take the banner from our hands' echoes across depictions of a group of soldiers in an unidentified African country ('nous'), the cover of the 5 June 1968 issue of the French militant journal *Action* ('la'), a magazine double spread of photos relating to the uprising in Paris ('prépare à prendre'), Guevara and Fidel Castro ('de nos mains'), a bandaged head ('le drapeau') and a young couple carrying flags.

The tract's final shot zooms out to reposition these student protestors in a rally shown in a second, larger photograph protruding from under the first. Sebastian Layerle identifies the outwards zoom as characteristic of 'the ciné-tract dynamic'; this perspectival widening 'conveys the profusion of movement in inscribing a face in the crowd of demonstrators'.[55] Tract 12 shows the crowd in both close-ups and long shots as a mobile organism that, in Balázs's words, which anticipate Guevara's, is 'more than the sum of the individuals who compose [it]'.[56] Just as pictures of crowds draw attention to what their members have in common, so too does the film give each image an equal status. The photographs of Guevara receive the same treatment as those of anonymous subjects, rather than participating in a star system. But by May 1968 the value of the portrait of him dead was already 'far more symbolic than referential', to borrow from Hariman and Lucaites's definition of iconic photographs, due to the repetition of news pictures of Guevara's corpse.[57]

Like the twelfth tract, the twenty-third cites Guevara's words from its very start while delaying his appearance. Copied out across an equally varied set of images are different extracts of the same letter. This borrowed text explains the importance of 'the masses' to the revolutionary vanguard: 'we know we draw all our strength from the mass of workers [. . .]'. Photographs packed with people attending huge rallies, protesting outside a Renault factory and raising French trade union confederation banners and fists reinforce this point by illustrating this source of power. But the sentence continues by indicating the dialectical relationship between these 'marching multitudes' and their leaders: '[this mass] can advance more rapidly if we inspire it with our example'. One of these exemplary individuals (and the author of the writing) comes into view at the beginning and end of this statement. He does so no longer in news photography, as in the earlier tract, but in posters. He appears in two designs that simplify and coarsen the detailed, grey-shaded features in Korda's snapshot. They transform Guevara from a documentary or referential image into a pure outline or symbol. Whereas tract 12 ends with an image of an anonymous crowd, number 23 concludes, like the first part of *The Hour of the Furnaces*, with a lingering shot of the iconic face, as reimagined in a photolithograph by Polish artist Roman Cieslewicz (1967–8), one of the earliest remakes of the 'Heroic Guerrilla', which appeared on the cover of the French magazine *Opus International* days before Guevara's killing.[58] Godard has written the final words of his citation, 'notre exemple' (our example), above the slogan 'Che si' (Che yes) with which Cieslewicz's collage replaced the eyes and nose. Guevara in this sense signs the anonymous tract.

The same iconic image returns in a different permutation in another visual essay about photography that Godard made with Miéville. In episode 3a of the television series *Six fois deux (Sur et sous la communication)* (*Six Times Two [On and Under Communication]*; 1976), *Photos et cie* (*Photos and Co.*), Guevara has separated from the facialised masses beside which the tracts placed him but remains a mass-mediated face. Rather than using film, like the *ciné-tracteurs*, to animate crowds, Godard and Miéville use video to analyse photos that, since they mostly come from the capitalist printed press, isolate individuals.[59] Whereas the multitudes in the tracts express demands for social transformation, mass communication, suggests *Photos et cie*, bolsters the status quo. As Michael Witt explains, Godard and Miéville's work in the 1970s registered dismay that 'industrialised countries had been colonised by the mass media, their citizens subjected to steady streams of conventional representations'.[60] They also considered the 'sheer quantity of images' or 'mass of reproductions' in circulation as impeding communication and understanding.[61] Korda's iconic photograph, the dissemination of which to crowds Álvarez's newsreel tracks, and which features in *Le Gai Savoir*'s critique of the media, also plays a central role in Godard and Miéville's provocative take on photojournalism.

Photos et cie condemns mass-distributed photographs and their creators for increasing the flow of capital rather than that of information, turning crowds, in effect, into consumers. While Miéville's criticism in voice-over of the 'profession reporter' refers obliquely to Locke's (Jack Nicholson) work for television in Michelangelo Antonioni's *The Passenger* (originally titled *Professione: reporter*, 1975), another European film from the same period that addresses the ethics of news pictures, the video singles out the commodification of still images for particular censure. It also takes aim at images of commodities, opening with a procession of camera adverts and closing with a scene in which adverts are ripped from a magazine. This framing of Guevara's iconic face reminds the viewer of the debt of political art to advertising, on whose visual 'grammars', as Prestholdt explains, the 'global left' began to draw in the early 1960s.[62] As we look through another pile of photos in the middle of the programme, a male voice laments that magazines around the world got rich from pictures of the war in Vietnam and wonders how much their subjects earned. The passage of images and the humans they depict through the frame offers yet another variation on the *défilé*, a motif that Blümlinger, as mentioned earlier, considers essential to the French director's work in this period. The film doesn't distinguish between the photograph of the naked, crying, running Vietnamese girl that had appeared in newspapers around the world and won the Pulitzer Prize and the pictures of anonymous subjects in the procession.

This image of Kim Phúc, though revealingly none of Guevara, also illustrates another critique of photographs for buttressing dominant ideology in *Cahiers du cinéma*'s issue of July–August 1976, exactly the period when *Six fois deux* was broadcast. (The journal would discuss Godard and Miéville's series in its November issue.[63]) Whereas Godard and Miéville flick through photos in loose mounds and magazines without discriminating between different kinds, Bergala separates out those that have appeared repeatedly and become 'emblematic of a historical event'.[64] The picture of Kim Phúc, reproduced twice more in miniature in the margins, exemplifies his argument, also discussed in Chapter 1, that these images single out an individual 'actor of History', 'most often a victim, preferably innocent'.[65] In so doing, they 'repress' the notion that 'the masses make History'.[66] The wide-angle lens through which they were often captured 'isolates the person', while 'the other actors in the event are driven into the background, insignificant and dissociated witnesses'.[67] This chapter explores, in a sense, how films turn this crowd of 'witnesses' back into historical 'actors' and return them to the foreground.

Godard and Miéville frame the 3-minute sequence in the middle of their programme that deals with Guevara as a flashback to 1968. But the crowds inspired by his example to march and fight in the *ciné-tracts* have dispersed.

The video oscillates between a black-and-white version of Korda's photograph in a book or journal and a cluster of two-tone prints of this image in different colours and sizes. Although less pointedly than Gerard Malanga's vibrant-hued serialisation of the 'Heroic Guerrilla' (1968), this artwork recalls Andy Warhol's silk screens of iconic photographs (such as the testimonies to police racism by Moore mentioned earlier in this chapter) and of photographs of icons (from Monroe to Mao).[68] As Thierry Gervais notes, Warhol repurposed 'images that were widely circulated by the mass media to simultaneously contest and celebrate 1960s consumer culture'.[69] Guevara turns from a news photograph in film tract 12 via the 'heroic guerrilla' in tract 23 into what Eduardo Grüner calls an 'icon – Warholian at best – [. . .] of consumer society' in *Photos et cie*.[70]

The programme also questions the capacity of the single image, much vaunted by scholarship on the photo-icon, to incarnate a historical experience. The information apparatus turns what Bergala provocatively dismisses as a 'miniscule and derisory sample of the real' into an emblem of 'the complex, multiple, disproportionate scene of a historical event like the war in Spain or Vietnam'.[71] Or in Goldberg's later formulation, cited in the Introduction, the 'secular icon' of photography 'stand[s] for an epoch'.[72] But *Photos et cie* casts doubt on the historical import of the individual picture by cutting and dissolving between iterations of Korda's icon and other images. Guevara's face is superimposed over war planes and another distraught Vietnamese girl (not Kim Phúc). Miéville's voice-over connects these apparently disparate pictures: 'he didn't see [. . .] that if you create one, two, three Vietnams, you also create one, two, three Americas'. Had Guevara listened to the child's cries, Miéville suggests, he might have realised that his call for other countries to follow the example of the North Vietnamese would mean more American bombers. In seeking to reveal what Guevara overlooked (in contrast to the more reverent film tracts), these photographs of instruments and a victim of war also cast doubt on the individual image's ability to elucidate history.

Didi-Huberman has also questioned the image's historical insight with reference to Godard. He argues that the photographs taken in Birkenau by *Sonderkommando* members provide knowledge and promote imagination only when made to 'resonate with [. . .] other sources, other images, and other testimonies'; 'the knowledge value could not be intrinsic to one image alone'.[73] This project of 'putting the multiple in motion, isolating nothing, showing the hiatuses and the analogies [. . .]' contrasts with accounts of camera icons, which conventionally set a handful of images apart from others.[74] The secluded picture also concerns photography studies; as Didi-Huberman points out, 'the phantasm of the *one image* is supported by a phantasm of the *absolute instant*: in the history of photography, which is true for the very notion of the snapshot.'[75] The concept of the privileged or exceptional moment has also preoccupied writing on iconicity, as discussed in the previous chapters. But Didi-Huberman pays as much attention to film as to photography. Godard's *Histoire(s) du cinéma* illustrates his claim that knowledge of a process or event emerges through montage by 'allow[ing] something to escape that is not *seen* in any one fragment of film but *appears*, differentially, with the force of a generalized haunting memory'.[76] *Photos et cie* anticipates this later video by prioritising the plural image – a serigraphic and videographic montage – over the singular icon. Since this montage speaks to Miéville about Guevara's death, what '*appears*, differentially' without being seen is the 'haunting memory' of the other iconic images that concern this chapter: those of his lifeless body.

CHE AS MOVING TECHNOLOGY

One response to the commodification of photography denounced by Godard, Miéville and Bergala arrived several years later in cinematic short form. Together with *Photos et cie* (1976), Bergala's essay from the same year and Wehn-Damisch's *Photographie et société: d'après Gisèle Freund* (1983), which I discussed in Chapter 1, *Una foto recorre el mundo* (*A Photo Travels Around the World*, 1981) helped to establish a canon of exceptional news photographs that had become symbols of abstruse phenomena, such as war, violence or revolution, for large groups of people. The circumstances in which a photograph was taken and how it spread, of which this film's director, Pedro Chaskel, pioneered the investigation, became a staple concern of iconic image studies from the 1990s. Working in exile from Chile at the ICAIC, Chaskel tracked down the creator of the globetrotting picture in question, Korda, and quizzed him about its capture.[77] Unlike Godard's and Miéville's TV programme, Chaskel's 13-minute documentary celebrates, rather than critiques, photojournalism not only for reporting on but also for participating in socioeconomic change. Both works use Korda's photo-icon to 'flash back' to the 1960s (though Godard and Miéville don't name the photographer). While a sense of disappointment at the failure of 1968 pervades the French programme's semiotic analysis of photographs, Chaskel's less theoretical film provides a rousing reminder of the ideals that turned the Cuban revolution into an inspiration for a generation of left-wing activists in Latin America and beyond. In contrast to Godard and Miéville's isolation of Guevara from depictions of social movements, Chaskel inserts him back into crowds, both literally, in depicting the sea of faces from which Korda's camera fatefully picked him out, and figuratively, in depicting multitudes brandishing his image.

     No Power Without an Image

Although the title announces Chaskel's intention to track the journey of the photograph, the film begins instead by following a crowd. A river of people with Castro and Guevara at the front pours through a street, introducing the theme of popular mobilisation. The crowd continues, in Balázs's apt phrase, to 'teem with life' when wrapped around the platform on which Korda photographed Guevara.[78] The moving footage then dissolves into a still shot of the massive gathering, which provides a transition into a sequence about the creation of the iconic image. In paying attention to the photo-icon's origin in this rally for victims of anti-revolutionary violence, by including pictures of the event and an interview about it with Korda, the film counteracts consumer capitalism's efforts to detach Guevara's image from collective action. The crowd imagery that comprises the main part of the documentary has the same effect, highlighting his status as an icon for the global left in the late 1960s and 1970s. The revolutionary reappears on banners and placards surrounded by crowds in the several years after his death. Chaskel amasses pictures of protestors all over the world gathered around images of Guevara's face.

As mentioned in the introduction to this chapter, critical debate about the revolutionary's iconicity has dwelt on his face. For example, Cambre asks whether Emmanuel Levinas's assertion that the face of the Other 'at each moment destroys and overflows the plastic image it leaves me' can help explain the 'ethical possibilities' of pictures of Guevara.[79] Another characteristic of Levinasian alterity – that no-one can stand in or substitute for the Other – is more relevant to my appraisal of Guevara's role in crowd imagery.[80] Levinas only once refers to a crowd in *Totalité et infini* (*Totality and Infinity*, 1961), disparaging its 'disordered din'.[81] However, Simon Critchley has discussed Levinas's ethics as a response to the Holocaust and other twentieth-century atrocities that, in dehumanising the Other, reduced her to a 'faceless face in the crowd'.[82] The Other whose 'calling into question of the same' Levinas names 'ethics' contrasts, in Critchley's account, with Martin Heidegger's approach to the other person as 'just one of the many: "the they", [. . .] the mass, the herd.'[83] How does *A Photo Travels Around the World* negotiate the risk of reducing its protagonists to such a status? Although the high-angle panning shots that emphasise the vastness of the rally of 5 January 1960 obscure its details, the depictions of crowds more often reveal internal difference than reduce individuals to a homogenous mass.

The first half of the film's middle section about protests achieves this through a succession of still images. Presumably Chaskel used the best pictures he could find of the iconic image's global journey, a large proportion of which were photographs. These stills look nothing like the frozen parades and

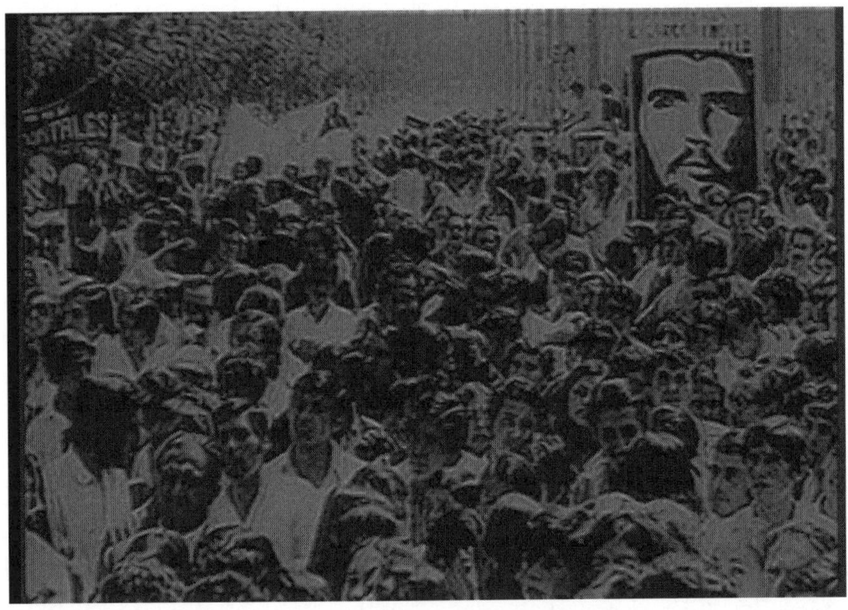

Figure 4.4 *Una foto recorre el mundo* (*A Photo Travels Around the World*; dir. Pedro Chaskel, Cuba, 1981).

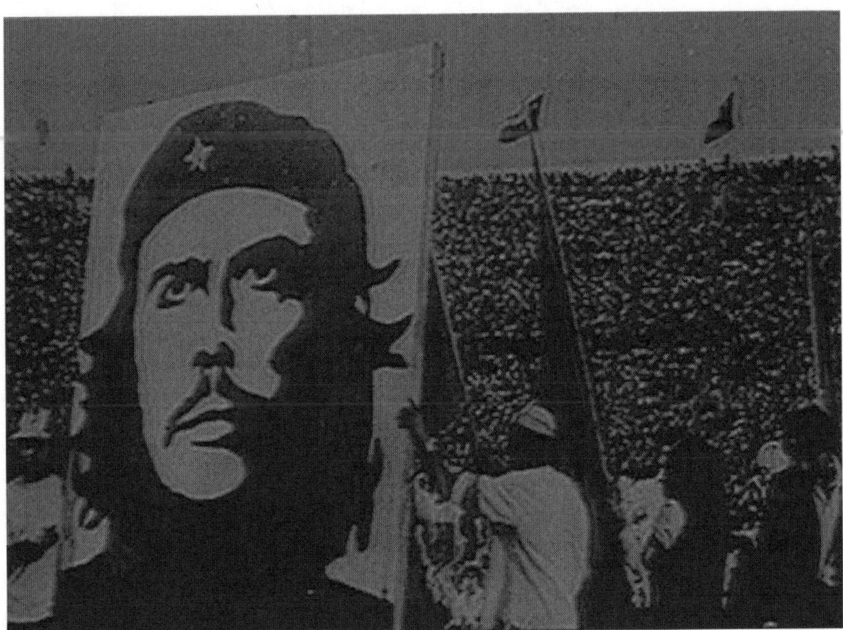

Figure 4.5 *Una foto recorre el mundo.*

rallies of the 'voluntarily uniformed' making unison gestures that illustrate one aspect of what future Third Reich soldier Ernst Jünger and his collaborator Edmund Schultz saw as the 'changed face of the mass' in Germany, the Soviet Union and the UK between the world wars.[84] In contrast to these rows of obedient types, the collective protagonists of Chaskel's film are disparate and autonomous, more like the other aspect of the 'mass face' exemplified in Schultz and Jünger's photo-book by unemployed British men and women being trampled by police horses and in the *ciné-tracts* by the rebels of May 1968.[85] The crowds in the Cuban short are 'organic', rather than 'organised' (in the senses with which Balázs invests these terms) and 'multifaceted' (to use Guevara's word), rather than uniform. We notice differences within and between crowds in the fixed images that we might miss in moving footage. We also see signs of protestors' creativity, such as small variations in Guevara's features; no two posters modelled on the iconic photograph are quite the same. The rostrum camera repeatedly enlivens the protests by zooming out from close-ups of these crowd-borne images, proximate views that Balázs suggests keep crowds alive, to frame whole gatherings, a movement that Layerle, as mentioned above, considers defining of the 'dynamic' of the *ciné-tracts* of over a decade earlier.[86] Chaskel too uses the outwards zoom to position a face amid a multitude and add motion to still photography. The rhythmic transitions between images heighten the momentum of the photographic montage. Sounds also help to bring the stills to life. Unlike the silent crowds in Jünger and Schultz's 'picture primer' and the stop-starting tracts from Paris, the demonstrators in the Cuban film chant and cheer.

The photographs give way, halfway through the film, to footage in which these vocal crowds bearing portraits of Guevara leap into motion. Of all the films discussed in this chapter, the archival footage in *A Photo Travels Around the World* provides the most dramatic and powerful portrayal of crowd motions – or what Balázs describes as 'mass gestures' – inspired by Guevara's example (as opposed to merely alluding to such movement in a sequence of photographs, like the French film tracts and sections of the Cuban documentary). Massive protests march or run through the frame in one shot after another. Chaskel mixes distant views of these supra-individual entities with shots recorded inside them that register single faces, accentuating what Balázs sees as the crowd's living material and further disturbing the opposition between the exemplary individual and the anonymous mass.[87] The figure of the *défilé* is useful for understanding this film because, like the others considered in this chapter, *A Photo Travels Around the World* plays on the relation between processions of people and of images. Focused, like Álvarez's newsreel, on an itinerant photograph, whose story it uses mainly found materials to tell, the short exemplifies the 'symptomatics of passage' that Blümlinger

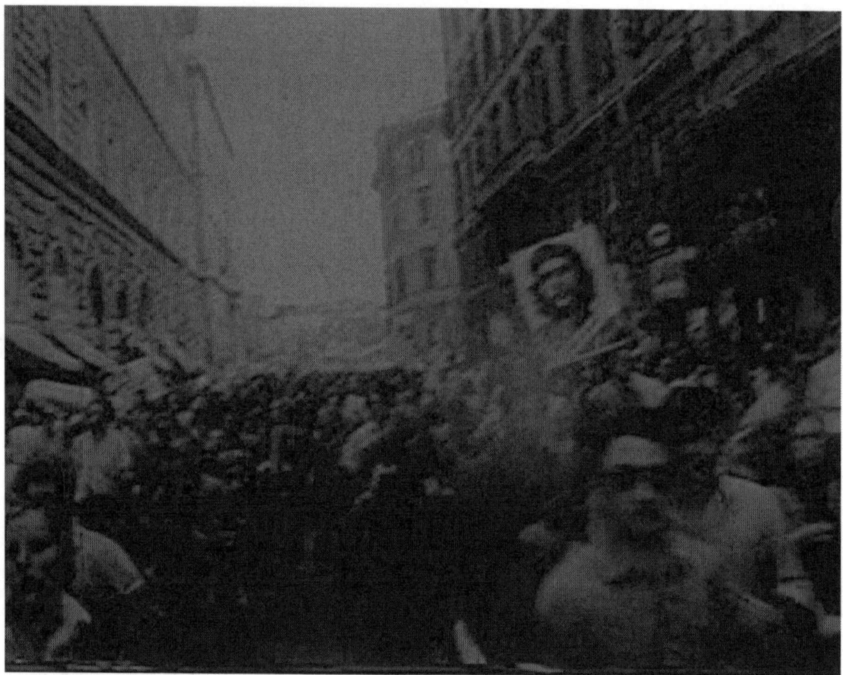

Figure 4.6 *Una foto recorre el mundo.*

discerns in 'second-hand cinema', which consists of images that have travelled through other sites of display.[88] The passing demonstrators also recall the parade of stills through the projector and cause Guevara's image to file past, sweeping it along with them. Just as the icon mobilises the crowds, so too the crowds mobilise the icon.

The dynamic interaction between images and those who venerate them that we see in Chaskel's film foreshadows Ghosh's redefinition of the icon as a 'moving technology'. Like the 'mass face' described by Balázs nearly a century earlier, Ghosh's account of icons seeks to elucidate the relationship between images and large groups of people. But while Balázs concentrates on the specific properties of cinema and dwells on 'physiognomy', Ghosh considers the particular qualities of iconic images and prioritises corporeality over faciality. Moving beyond semiotic approaches, she draws on feminist accounts of matter to emphasise the materiality of both the icon and its devotee. She views their encounter through the lens of theories of 'corporeal dynamism', of 'the body or the corpus (returning to matter as corpse) as abundant matter, a life force [. . .]'.[89] The manipulation of the corpse of Guevara (discussed earlier in this chapter) and other dead (bio-)icons exemplifies the transformation of their 'corporeal substance' into a 'treasured fetish'.[90] Ghosh is particularly interested in the occasions when these apparently magical artefacts can 'move subjects towards the social'.[91] 'Under historical conditions of possibility', she writes, 'the icon's potentialities are actualized to forge a popular mobilization against hegemonic institutions, and the moving technology opens into a social configuration [. . .]'.[92] What is mobilised can take the form of a crowd; all three of the bio-icons discussed in Ghosh's book – Phoolan Devi, Mother Teresa and Arundhati Roy – 'incorporat[e] the crowd into their image'.[93] For example, the 'febrile crowds' who turned out to mourn the death of Mother Teresa 'refused the elaborate choreography of the media spectacle'.[94] In Ghosh's conception, the crowd's corporeality becomes visible as it 'flows toward and into the icon'.[95]

Ghosh's discussion of star bodies like Guevara's exemplifies how film studies provides resources for thinking about icons. The films considered in this chapter suggest that cinema is particularly well equipped to explore the icon not only as a star image but also as a 'moving technology'. The mourners who surged towards Mother Teresa's body in Ghosh's account recall the lines of readers in Álvarez's newsreel, who snake towards free copies of Guevara's diary, covered with a version of Korda's image. While this film concentrates on the 'social configurations' into which the icon opens in Cuba, Chaskel's documentary, another of ICAIC's montages of still and moving images, tracks this 'popular mobilisation' across several continents.[96] Discussing the recurrent photographic framing of Roy, another 'global icon', within groups of activists who began to 'push', 'press' and 'obscure' her, Ghosh comments: 'the potentiality of the crowd staked its claim, even in a mass media obsessed with individuated celebrity'.[97] In Chaskel's film about Guevara too, where 'the singular iconic image [is] always harnessed to its social others', bodies push and press against the icon and carry it along, their energy conveyed most powerfully in the moving footage. Like Ghosh, *A Photo Travels Around the World* highlights the movement and dynamism that define our encounters with icons both as individuals and members of a crowd.

Conclusion

Chaskel devotes the last few minutes of his film to the kind of image around which discussion of Guevara's iconicity has typically revolved. The crowds of surging bodies retreat from view, leaving the whole space of the frame to art works based on the famous photograph of his still face. Although this sequence lacks the dialectical construction of Godard's and Miéville's appropriation of other versions of the picture in *Photos et cie*, the relationship between images remains significant. Chaskel's montage of posters and book covers joined by dissolves that make the face morph underlines the recursive and mutable nature of the iconic photograph that has formed the dominant concern of writing on Guevara's symbolic power. Such scholarship has dwelt on the affective appeal of this visage, which is intensified at the end of the film by the ennobling accompaniment of a song based by Gian Franco Pagliaro on Paul Éluard's poem 'Liberté' and performed by Nacha Guevara. No longer a (mere) face in the crowd, it becomes a 'holy face' (to borrow from Mondzain's account of acheiropoiesis), an image revered in stillness rather than brandished by marchers.

While Cambre focuses on Korda's photograph and its appropriations, her discussion of the affect expressed by the 'Heroic Guerrilla' hints at the relevance of cinema to iconic images that I underline throughout this book. To explain the viewer's relationship to this portrait, she borrows from Deleuze's account of the intensive and reflective poles of the face, which I have discussed in relation to his definition of the icon.[98] This passage of *Cinéma 1* draws inspiration from Balázs's writings on the close-up as expression. Deleuze cites Balázs: 'when a face that we have just seen in the middle of a crowd is detached from its surroundings, put into relief, it is as if we were suddenly face to face with it'.[99] Although Balázs's various comments on the relations between faces and crowds in cinema predate by several decades the incorporation of photo-icons into street protests and rallies that became habitual in the 1960s and persists today, he provides a useful framework, I have suggested, for analysing this development. Rather than the 'isolated face' that, according to Balázs, 'abolishe[s]' 'our sensation of space', this chapter has focused on faces around which crowds assemble and those that belong to these mass entities, that is, on iterative and collective visages.[100] To elucidate the way in which an icon mobilises and facialises crowds, I have argued, was a unique and vital contribution of cinema in the first era of Guevara's visual afterlife to our understanding of iconic images.

Several of the films and sequences on which I have based this claim refer to the conventional view of cinema as adding movement to photographs. To recap: Álvarez's news bulletin, for example, tracks the journey of a photograph through a printing press and into the hands of Havanans on a newspaper and book cover respectively, drawing an analogy between the passage, or *défilé*, of images and that of people across the field of view. Similarly, Godard and Chaskel zoomed out from photographs in order to convey the dynamism of demonstrating crowds. Like the newsreel about the publication of the diary, *A Photo Travels Around the World* also uses moving footage to reconstruct the icon's migration along streets and between continents. As this film exemplifies, cinematic montage is a particularly apt means to explore how the iconic image, in Cambre's words about the 'Heroic Guerrilla', 'link[s]' protests 'across time and space'.[101] Like the circulation of photos of Quang Duc burning in Vietnam and China that I mentioned in Chapter 3, the documentaries from Cuba and Argentina through which I have tracked Guevara's picture offer further confirmation that not only in Western democracies, such as France and the US, the countries on which Hariman's and Lucaites's and Gunthert's influential accounts of photo-icons concentrate, have exceptional news images acquired this status since the 1960s. Yet what is most interesting about the films considered in this chapter from the perspective of iconic image studies is their common attention to the relationship between fixed pictures and moving crowds or, in the case of Godard's and Miéville's television programme, mass mediation. Cinema's capacity (shared with video) to combine still and moving images has equipped it to open perspectives on the interaction of mass formations with their icons that complement exhibitions of and scholarship on iconic photography. The final chapter of the book continues to explore the trope of the crowd face, and the Epilogue suggests that it can help to illuminate images that have become icons of our contemporary era of protest.

Notes

1. Alberto Korda interviewed in *Una foto recorre el mundo* (*A Photo Circles the World*, Pedro Chaskel, 1981).
2. See, for example, Goldberg, *The Power of Photography*, pp. 156–9.
3. Bergala, 'Le Pendule', p. 41.
4. Berrou, Jean-Hughes and Jean-Jacques Lefrère, *Che: images* (Paris: Fayard, 2003), p. 340 (translations from this text are mine). The group photographed were waiting for Fidel Castro in Havana's Plaza de la Revolución in May 1959.
5. On the importance of the face in Judaic, Christian and Islamic thinking about the legitimacy of the visible, see, for example, Mondzain, Marie-José, *Homo spectator* (Paris: Bayard, 2007), pp. 50–1.
6. See, for example, Delluc's essay 'The Crowd' [1918], trans. Richard Abel in Abel (ed.), *French Film Theory and Criticism: A History/Anthology, 1907–1939*, vol. 1, 1907–1929 (Princeton, NJ: Princeton University Press, 1988), pp. 159–64, a longer version of which appeared in his book *Photogénie* (Paris: Brunoff, 1920).
7. See, for example, Kemp, Martin, 'Che', *Christ to Coke: How Image Becomes Icon* (Oxford, New York: Oxford University Press, 2012), pp. 167–96.
8. 'Homage to Che', 6 November 1967, *Noticieros: les actualités cubaines 1960–1970*, INA, 2017.
9. 'Publication in Cuba of Che's Diary', 5 July 1968, *Noticieros: les actualités cubaines 1960–1970*, INA, 2017.
10. See Chanan, Michael (ed.), *Santiago Álvarez*, BFI Dossier no. 2 (London: British Film Institute, 1980), p. 4.

11. Álvarez cited in Wilson, Kristi M., '*Ecce Homo Novus*: Snapshots, the "New Man" and Iconic Montage in the Work of Santiago Alvarez', in *Social Identities: Journal for the Study of Race, Nation and Culture*, 19: 3–4 (2013), 410–22 (418).

12. For discussion of Álvarez's innovative collages of iconic photographs, see Wilson, Kristi M., '*Ecce Homo Novus*: Snapshots, the "New Man" and Iconic Montage in the Work of Santiago Alvarez', *Social Identities: Journal for the Study of Race, Nation and Culture*, 19: 3–4 (2013), 410–22, and Gervais, Thierry, 'Introduction', in Gervais (ed.), *The 'Public' Lives of Photographs* (Toronto: Ryerson Image Centre, 2016), pp. 1–13 (pp. 4–7).

13. Balázs, Béla in Erica Carter (ed.), *Béla Balázs: Early Film Theory: Visible Man and the Spirit of Film*, trans. Rodney Livingstone (New York: Berghahn, 2011), p. 144.

14. Balázs, *Early Film Theory*, pp. 37, 41, 144.

15. Carter, Erica, 'Introduction', in *Béla Balázs: Early Film Theory*, pp. xv–xlvi (p. xxvi).

16. Kracauer, Siegfried, *Theory of Film: The Redemption of Physical Reality* (New York: Oxford University Press, 1960), pp. 50–1.

17. Balázs, *Early Film Theory*, pp. 145, 42.

18. Ibid., p. 145.

19. On the bond between Soviet and Cuban films from these different eras and especially between Álvarez's and Dziga Vertov's work, see Chanan, Michael, *Cuban Cinema* (Minneapolis, MN: University of Minnesota Press, 2004), p. 227.

20. Balázs, *Early Film Theory*, p. 145.

21. Blümlinger, Christa, 'Procession and Projection: Notes on a Figure in the Work of Jean-Luc Godard', in Michael Temple, James S. Williams and Michael Witt (eds), *For Ever Godard* (London: Black Dog, 2004), pp. 178–87 (p. 179).

22. See Burton, Julianne, 'Part I. Revolutionary Cuban Cinema', *Jump Cut*, 19 (December 1978), 17–20, https://www.ejumpcut.org/archive/onlinessays/JC19folder/CubanFilmIntro.html (last accessed 15 January 2019).

23. Balázs, *Early Film Theory*, p. 145.

24. Blümlinger, 'Procession and Projection', p. 181.

25. Stewart, *Between Film and Screen*, p. 9.

26. On this 'dual' form of movement, see Blümlinger, 'Procession and Projection'. Álvarez's animation of Korda's photograph strengthens the bond between his filmmaking and Vertov's, whose *Man With a Movie Camera* (1929) inspects the transition from still photogrammes to moving images. See Blümlinger, 'Procession and Projection', pp. 181–2, for commentary on Vertov's rendering visible of 'the *défilement*, the passage of images'.

27. Chanan, *Cuban Cinema*, pp. 248–9.

28. Lefrère, Jean-Jacques, in Berrou and Lefrère, *Che: images*, pp. 170–81.

29. Freddy Alborta, author of this photograph, identifies these protagonists in the essay film made about the image by Leandro Katz, *El día que me quieras* (*The Day You'll Love Me*; 1997).

30. Alborta, Freddy, cited in Berrou and Lefrère, *Che: images*, p. 289 (translation mine).

31. Ibid., p. 289.

32. Berger, John, 'Image of Imperialism', in Geoff Dyer (ed.), *Understanding a Photograph* (London: Penguin, 2013), pp. 3–16 (pp. 4–5).

33. Lefrère in Berrou and Lefrère, *Che: images*, p. 176.

34. Barthes, *Camera Lucida*, p. 96.

35. Sutton, *Photography, Cinema, Memory*, p. 58.

36. Ibid., p. 7; Sutton draws on Didi-Huberman's description of the pose as photography's 'mother-temporality'.

37. Barthes, *Camera Lucida*, p. 78.

38. See Goldberg, *The Power of Photography*, p. 225.

39. This footage appears in several compilations in the Associated Press Archive, such as story no. 18261 (24 November 1995). It recurs in the documentary *Bolivia Siglo XX. Che: Vida y muertes* (Carlos D. Mesa Gilbert and Mario Espinoza Osorio, 2009).

40. Sturken, *Tangled Memories*, p. 90.

41. On final images and freeze-frames, see Daney, 'La dernière image' (discussed in Chapter 1).

42. Goldberg, *The Power of Photography*, p. 159.

43. Mestman, Mariano, 'The Last Sacred Image of the Latin American Revolution', *Journal of Latin American Cultural Studies*, 19: 1 (2010), 23–44 (37). Mestman also discusses the 're-signification' of photographs of the executed Guevara in the light of attempts in the late 1960s especially in Latin America 'to articulate the Church's pastoral mission with revolutionary practice' (29–30).

44. For discussion of the racial imagination articulated by Christian theology, see Carter, *Race: A Theological Account*.

45. Berger, 'Image of Imperialism', p. 5. On resonances between the iconic photograph and 'the historical and cultural Christ figure familiar in Western representation', see Mestman, 'The Last Sacred Image', p. 29.

46. Barthes, *Camera Lucida*, p. 82.

47. Mondzain, *Image, Icon, Economy*, pp. 202–3.

48. Ibid., p. 202.

49. Solanas, Fernando and Octavio Getino, 'Toward a Third Cinema', *Cinéaste*, 4: 3 (1970–1), 1–10 (10).

50. See, for example, Carlos Alonso's drawing 'Carne Argentina' (1970). For discussion of this artist's reworking of pictures from the laundry in Vallegrande, see Mestman, 'The Last Sacred Image', pp. 31–5.

51. Mestman, 'The Last Sacred Image', p. 38.

52. 'Ciné-tractez!' (guide pour réaliser un ciné-tract, 1968), reproduced in Raymond Bellour, Jean-Michel Frodon and Christine Van Assche (eds), *Chris Marker* (Paris: Cinémathèque française, 2018), pp. 274–5.

53. Cambre, Maria-Carolina, *The Semiotics of Che Guevara: Affective Gateways* (London: Bloomsbury, 2015), p. 149.

54. Guevara, Ernesto, 'Socialism and Man in Cuba' [1965], in David Deutschmann (ed.), *Che Guevara Reader* (Melbourne: Ocean Press, 2003), pp. 212–28 (pp. 213, 219).

55. Layerle, Sébastien, *Caméras en lutte en mai 68: 'par ailleurs le cinéma est une arme'* (Paris: Nouveau monde, 2008), p. 143 (my translation).
56. Balázs, *Early Film Theory*, p. 41.
57. Hariman and Lucaites, *No Caption Needed*, p. 6.
58. For helpful comments on Cieslewicz's reworking of a facial icon as 'the ground for *other* expressions', see Cambre, *The Semiotics of Che Guevara*, pp. 186–8.
59. On Godard and Miéville's use of video in *Six fois deux*, see Witt, Michael, 'On and Under Communication', in Tom Conley and T. Jefferson Kline (eds), *A Companion to Jean-Luc Godard* (Chichester; Malden, MA: Wiley-Blackwell, 2014), pp. 318–50 (pp. 324–5).
60. Witt, 'On and Under Communication', p. 326.
61. Ibid., p. 326.
62. See Prestholdt, *Icons of Dissent*, p. 21.
63. Deleuze, Gilles, 'Trois questions sur *Six fois deux*', *Cahiers du cinéma*, 271 (1976), 5–12.
64. Bergala, 'Le Pendule', p. 40.
65. Ibid., p. 41.
66. Ibid., p. 41.
67. Ibid., p. 42.
68. I return to Warhol's reappropriation of Monroe's iconic image in Chapter 5.
69. Gervais, 'Introduction', p. 4.
70. Grüner, Eduardo, 'A Question of *Details*, Che', trans. David Jacobson, in Leandro Katz et al., *The Ghosts of Ñancahuazú* (Buenos Aires: Viper's Tongue Books, 2010), pp. 195–202 (p. 195).
71. Bergala, 'Le pendule', pp. 40, 45.
72. Goldberg, *The Power of Photography*, p. 135.
73. Didi-Huberman, Georges, *Images in Spite of All: Four Photographs From Auschwitz*, trans. Shane B. Lillis (Chicago, London: University of Chicago Press, [2003] 2012), p. 120.
74. Ibid., p. 120.
75. Ibid., p. 123.
76. Ibid., p. 134.
77. For brief comments on Chaskel's role in the 'cinema of engagement' formed by short documentaries produced by the experimental film centre at the University of Chile and the 'Central Unica de Trabajadores de Chili', before Pinochet's coup forced him to leave the country, see Pick, Zuzana M., 'Cinéastes de l'Unité Populaire: où en-êtes vous?', *NS, NorthSouth*, 4: 8 (1979), pp. 136–71 (138–9) (my translation).
78. Balázs, *Early Film Theory*, p. 42.
79. Cambre, *The Semiotics of Che Guevara*, p. 149; Levinas, Emmanuel, *Totality and Infinity: An Essay on Exteriority*, trans. Alphonso Lingis (Pittsburgh, PA: Duquesne University Press, [1961] 1969), p. 51.
80. In remarks that problematically exclude women, Levinas criticises, for example, the notion of 'a humanity of interchangeable men': 'the substitution of men for one another, the primal disrespect, makes possible exploitation itself' (*Totality and Infinity*, p. 298).

81. *Totality and Infinity*, p. 253.
82. Critchley, Simon, 'Introduction', in Critchley and Robert Bernasconi (eds), *The Cambridge Companion to Levinas* (Cambridge: Cambridge University Press, 2002), pp. 1–32 (p. 13).
83. Levinas, *Totality and Infinity*, p. 43; Critchley, 'Introduction', p. 12.
84. Schultz, Edmund (ed.), *Die veränderte Welt. Eine Bilderfibel unserer Zeit*, introduction by Ernst Jünger (Breslau: Wilh. Gottl. Korn, 1933), for example, pp. 36–7.
85. Schultz (ed.), *Die veränderte Welt*, p. 35.
86. Balázs, *Early Film Theory*, p. 145.
87. On the connection between Guevara as 'exceptional individual' and the 'anonymous masses', see Grüner, 'A Question of *Details*, Che', p. 199.
88. Blümlinger, Christa, *Cinéma de seconde main: esthétique de remploi dans l'art du film et des nouveaux médias* (Paris: Klincksieck, [2009] 2013), p. 12.
89. Ghosh, *Global Icons*, pp. 7–8.
90. Ibid., p. 175.
91. Ibid., p. 175.
92. Ibid., p. 9.
93. Ibid., p. 274.
94. Ibid., p. 268.
95. Ibid., p. 268.
96. Ibid., p. 9.
97. Ibid., p. 273.
98. Cambre, *The Semiotics of Che Guevara*, pp. 183–4.
99. Deleuze, *The Movement Image*, p. 107.
100. Balázs cited in Deleuze, *The Movement Image*, p. 107.
101. Cambre, *The Semiotics of Che Guevara*, p. 156.

CHAPTER FIVE

Film Frame, Film Still, Star Portrait: The Marianne of '68

A sea of faces churns in the lower part of the image, chanting. They look like they are on a march, even if it has come to a standstill. She looms serenely and silently above this noisy, restless throng, looking straight ahead and brandishing a flag with a strong, straight arm. Her pose mirrors and magnifies the raised fist of the man carrying her, as if she is commanding the turbulent multitude. Like Korda's iconic snapshot of Guevara, on which the previous chapter focused, this photograph centres on a face in a crowd. But whereas Korda isolated Guevara, this picture, taken by the photojournalist Jean-Pierre Rey, incorporates the gesturing mass.[1] Much has been written about the gradual transformation of this image into a symbol of the protests in France that peaked in May and June 1968, and about the recasting of the woman riding the crowd as Marianne, 'figurehead of the Republic and icon of French womanhood', as Anna Kemp explains.[2] The fiftieth anniversary of the occupations, demonstrations and strikes by students and workers saw the publication of new research into this photograph and others that have become emblems of the uprising.[3] This occasion was also marked by fresh studies of cinema's involvement in what are often called, simply, 'the events of May '68'. Consideration of these two image repertoires, however, has remained largely distinct.

This chapter links them by examining how the 'Marianne of '68' fits into film history and highlighting connections between photography and cinema that scholarship on her iconicity has overlooked. In the same year as this picture began to appear in the press, its main protagonist, revealed two decades later to be British model, actor, filmmaker and disinherited aristocrat Caroline de Bendern, played roles in several films. One of the *ciné-tracts* incorporates another photograph of her at the same demonstration. Composed briskly from stills during May and June 1968 (as explained in Chapter 4), these shorts play an important role in this book since they exemplify how photographers and filmmakers collaborated to present current and future icons at a pivotal moment in the history of the iconisation of camera images. De Bendern also starred in three medium-length films directed by Serge Bard, the first of which, *Détruisez-vous* (*Destroy Yourselves*, 1968), prophesies the protests, and all of which belong to a loose grouping that later became known as the 'Zanzibar Productions'.[4] That both the *ciné-tracts* and the Zanzibar films in effect disappeared from view for several decades might seem to reinforce the conventional opposition, discussed at various junctures in this book, between the iconic photograph and the forgotten film. While Rey's picture became one of the two or three most prominent images of May 1968, the *ciné-tracts* only survive in part, and received little detailed scholarly attention until the past decade.[5] Some of the Zanzibar films, as cinema historian and critic Sally Shafto notes, have also 'disappeared, without a trace', while the rest were 'forgotten or overlooked' until the first decade of the new millennium.[6]

I aim further to complicate the traditional distinction between photography's unique capacity to produce icons and cinema's fleeting and forgettable images by teasing out connections between the 'Marianne of '68', stills created to promote films and de Bendern's screen performances. It was in response to this fleetingness or ephemerality, in Laura Mulvey's account, that 'the film industry produced, from the very earliest moments of fandom, a panoply of still images' which allowed fans to 'hold on to [cinema's] precious moments, images and, most particularly, its idols'.[7] I suggest that Rey's picture shares key features at different stages of its life with two kinds of photograph that enable such possession: the film still (distinct from the film frame or photogramme, to which I initially compare the famous image) and the star portrait. This chapter builds on my discussion in the previous one of Ghosh's account of crossovers between icon studies and star studies. I draw here particularly on Mulvey's commentary on the iconic status of the Hollywood star and the 'fusion' of 'energy' with 'stillness' in her performance.[8] My previous case studies have examined the filmic *afterlives* of images; this one argues, by contrast, that cinema *foreshadowed* Caroline (de Bendern)'s transformation into Marianne by casting her as a revolutionary whose performances of stasis and silence allude intermedially to photography and intertextually to pictures of established icons or stars in the making.

The 'Girls With the Flags'

Chapter 1 of this book traced the transformation of the 'Falling Soldier' in the first year of its life from a dynamic documentary montage component in *Vu*, *Time* and *Paris-soir* into an image singled out by *Life* and *Regards* for its symbolic power. The photograph on which this chapter focuses evolved in a similar way. Two months before picturing the militiaman defending the Spanish Republic, Capa photographed Parisian women, men and children raising their fists in celebration of the victory of the Front Populaire (Popular Front), another event that his work would help to define and whose memory would inspire those who took *en masse* to the streets of the same city with the same gesture thirty-two years later.[9] This crowd swelled to unite students and workers for the first time on 13 May 1968, when Rey encountered de Bendern in the place Edmond-Rostand. First to publish the picture that would become his most famous, according to Audrey Leblanc, was *Life* a week and a half later.[10] Leblanc's detailed and illuminating analysis of the image's life in the printed press (especially in France) has shown that its symbolic potential eluded its first set of editors, who were more likely to exploit its 'documentary value'.[11] No photograph, in fact, began to behave like an icon, according to Gunthert, until the following year. In his account, the revolt of the French students was one of the events whose imagery spurred the changed perception of photojournalism that produced the 'dynamic of iconisation'.[12] That Rey's snapshot is one of only three to be repeated in three consecutive special issues of *Life* in December 1968 and January 1969, which used nearly two hundred photographs to take stock of the 'perceived exceptional character' of the previous year's developments, demonstrates, for Gunthert, that this dynamic, 'which passes through the identification and reproduction of a canon, [was] not yet in place'.[13] The effort to vary images that Gunthert notices in these magazines also contributes to the 'cinematisation', to borrow Cortade's term, of Rey's photo and another reproduced in *Paris Match* of the same scene from a different angle, through consideration of which I seek to complement existing discussions of the future icon.[14]

Life's first presentation of the picture exemplifies the magazine's competition with cinema's dramatisation of motion and the expanding medium of television.[15] It appears in the middle of a dynamic double-page spread of recent photographs of the *quartier Latin* illustrating an article about the student action in France and other countries.[16] De Bendern's outstretched arm corresponds to those of members of the CRS (Compagnies Républicaines de Sécurité, a section of the police) brandishing truncheons and beating protestors and those of students hurling stones (rather than to fists raised in solidarity). Around the surging crowd that carries her, bodies amass, give chase, take flight and writhe wounded on the ground. The text accentuates the gestures of the performers in this 'vivid street theatre', pitting 'rock throwing bands' against the police who 'charged' and 'attacked without restraint' until 'workers and leftists rallied' and joined the students in 'raucous parades'. On beginning its public life, then, Rey's snapshot belonged to a series of images that pulsates with energy and depicts an unfolding event, anticipating Bergala's claim (paraphrased in Chapter 1) that 'stereotyped historical photos' 'curiously resemble a film frame'.[17]

The sense of movement conveyed by this array of still images persists in the photos, including the first appearance in the French press of the icon to be, tessellated across two pages of the 15–21 June issue of *Paris Match*.[18] Instead of the gestures of violence that bordered Rey's photo in *Life*, the feature in the French magazine, focusing on the demonstration of 13 May, surrounds this image with others of marchers. Just as *Vu* placed Capa's celebrated snapshot next to another 'falling soldier', foreshadowing what Cortade, discussing *Life*, describes as a 'photogramme effect', so too *Paris Match* assembles several versions of 'la jeune fille au drapeau' (the girl with the flag). Not only does the editor's 'iconographic choice', as Leblanc points out, underline what the article construes as a 'dangerous radicality', since the picture that dominates the display depicts a woman waving a black flag that both the article and caption point out is an anarchist symbol.[19] The nestling of Rey's image among a series of similar ones also heightens the impression, likewise created by the spread in *Life*, of a cinematic sequence unfolding. Although I have found no moving footage of de Bendern at this demonstration, the woman with the black banner caught the attention of film camera operators. Her image recurs from several angles in newsreels and rushes in the Gaumont Pathé Archive, where the crowd carrying her springs into action and, in some cases, erupts into chants.[20]

It was as the bearer of another such 'radical emblem' (to cite Leblanc) that de Bendern next featured in *Paris Match* just over a month later in a colour photograph that revealed for the first time that her flag – red and blue with a gold star – was that of the National Liberation Front of Vietnam.[21] Whereas the magazine previously assembled Rey's picture with other medium shots of young women, we can barely see de Bendern's face in Walter Carone's rarer, longer, high-angle shot, which recurs on the cover of this book. The point of the picture is the flag, as underlined by the caption in *Paris Match*, although, as Leblanc explains, this later issue draws attention to the 'coalition of the left' united by the demonstration of 13 May, 'no longer radical "groupuscules"'.[22] The crowd remains distant in two of the other three photos of the procession that make up the double-page spread, though we can still make out individuals. 'Within the iconography of May', according to Margaret Atack, where 'the collective and the individual are mutually reinforcing', prevalent 'aerial shots' avoid reducing the city to 'a blurred mass', like those of the impressionists, but are instead 'razor sharp in order precisely to render the pattern of multiplicity'.[23] 'Dizzying sharpness', as Steven Jacobs explains, is a defining characteristic of the (classical) film still, that is, as mentioned in Chapter 2, a photograph taken on a set, in contrast to the film frame, which is 'often blurred because the movie camera operates at a shutter speed that is not always fast enough to freeze movement'.[24] Like the earlier picture spreads that incorporate Rey's, the photographs that Carone's snapshot joins in *Paris Match* combine the film frame's dynamism and connection to a series of images with the film still's 'excess of detail'.[25] While the images selected by the magazine are full of motion, the layout associates the elevated figure and arm of de Bendern with those of Charles and Leopold Morice's bronze statue of Marianne (1883) in an adjacent snapshot of the place de la République.

The comparison with Marianne first became explicit, according to Gunthert, a year and a half later in a collage that assembles figures from Rey's photograph and Delacroix's painting 'La Liberté guidant le peuple' (1830).[26] As mentioned in Chapter 2, Gunthert likens 'the project of an incarnation of history by photography', which he distinguishes from 'the classical function of representation of the event', to historical painting in the nineteenth century.[27] The eye-catching illustration in the 10 October 1969 issue of *Life* not only 'binds [. . .] the recent events of May 68 to sources of revolutionary inspiration', in particular the popular revolt in Paris against Charles X in July 1830 which sparked the idea for the canvas.[28] This composite image also remakes a photomontage published on 24 September 1936 by *Regards* which in a similar way affirms the revolutionary validity of the Republican defence of Spain.[29] John Heartfield relocated the personification of Liberty to this war zone by sticking supporters of Republican troops cut from a newspaper photograph from July of that year onto a sepia reproduction of Delacroix's image, which thus constitutes another link between the first and last chapters of this book. But *Life*'s rapprochement of Rey's and Delacroix's pictures also anticipates the future iconicity of the photograph – how it will come to stand for May '68 – by mixing it with a painting that allegorises a historical event and, as the art historian Julian Bell recounts, became 'an icon of French nationalism'.[30] Leblanc also considers what the 'formal paralleling' of these two images reveals about photojournalism. In her account, their association illustrates the phenomenon of 'intericonicity', bolstering the notion that 'a "good" press picture is [. . .] an image that replays another'.[31]

As well as exemplifying the comparisons often made between photo-icons and paintings, *Life*'s photomontage plays on the dynamism that I have been arguing links Rey's photograph to cinema. Delacroix's scene, as the writer Italo Calvino points out, 'puts before the eyes of the observer the energy, movement and enthusiasm of the event'.[32] Calvino mentions in particular the 'movement of [Liberty's] arms and torso'.[33] Similarly, Didi-Huberman writes that 'the "body of Liberty" is not only a representation, it is also a gesture of antagonism [. . .]'.[34] 'We should recall', he continues in terms that loop back to my analysis of an antagonistic and protesting gesture in the 'Gestapo Informer', that 'Delacroix had taken the dynamic from the antique figures of nymphs that we call marching "Victories"'.[35] It is as if Liberty, striding over a barricade, is moving faster than her dress, which has slipped to her waist and billows around her hips and legs. What Calvino calls the 'proletarian masses', who 'for the first time' in 1830 'had taken to the streets *in person*' and 'been the decisive element in the change of regime', stream behind her.[36] The text beside *Life*'s reworking of the painting takes up the theme of motion, describing 'modern revolution', the subject of the ensuing two-part article, as a 'dramatic march'.[37] But Delacroix's canvas evokes an upwards thrust as much as a forwards charge, as if the event of revolution makes it necessary to reimagine the relationship between space and history, conventionally envisioned as an earthbound progression.[38] The pole of the *tricolore* raised by Liberty and the motley assortment of guns and swords that she and her followers brandish form parallel lines jabbing diagonally at the sky. Their movement upwards does not suggest a spiritual ascent, as animated in paintings of Mary's assumption, for example, but the secular rising up of those remaking history from below.[39] The cutting out and combining of protagonists from this painting and Rey's photograph by *Life* sustains this upsurge. The collagist positioned de Bendern's arm and the flagpole that extends it parallel to the tilting bodies of Liberty, the boy beside her and the pole, bayonetted rifle and pistol that they grip. These elements protrude upwards out of the mass of figures and stand out – the *tricolore* in vivid hues and the Vietnamese flag in monochrome – against the white background, evoking an upwards thrust.

The photomontage holds painterly motion in tension, however, with photographic stasis. Jacobs explains that the film frame and the film still offer different kinds of 'compromise between movement and standstill'.[40] Motion blur is typical of film frames, but rare in film stills, whose characteristic sharpness I mentioned earlier. 'Instead of the suggestion of a halted movement, which often marks the film frame', and makes the 'Falling Soldier' closely resemble one, 'the still', Jacobs observes, 'rather evokes a kind of frozen time.'[41] This is because the so-called 'stillmen' of cinema's classical era discovered that photographing actors posing between takes rather than moving during them produced superior results.[42] In a passage in her memoir which is worth quoting in full because it alludes to key themes of this chapter and which, written three decades after Rey took the crucial picture, surely owes a debt to commentary on its iconic power and art historical precedents, de Bendern recounts co-creating it by striking a pose:

> I waved [the Vietnamese flag] wildly, laughing, until suddenly, I realized that we were surrounded by photographers. Instinctively, my reflexes as a model were awakened: 'I have to steady myself.' That's when my body stiffened, my arm tightened, I became serious and then I let myself be trapped in the role. I realized the heavy symbolism of what I was carrying, it wasn't just any old thing. Then I thought about freedom, one of the dominant themes of the movement that I was taking part in. For a brief moment, I thought about the French Revolution, then about art reproductions of these events; representing people flourishing flags, like statues. Perhaps for a moment, I took myself for

one of them. And then, I felt a wave of emotion, my heart was beating furiously, as I froze in my pose, above the crowd.[43]

Whereas the earlier layouts I have discussed accentuate movement in Rey's photograph, tilting it towards a photogramme, *Life*'s reassembly 'balance[s] [its] narrative dynamics with iconic stillness', to borrow from Jacobs's account of the film still.[44] As the 'young girl with the flag' begins to turn into Marianne, the snapshot leans towards a film still rather than a film frame. As much as gesture, the collage emphasises pose by enlarging de Bendern's image and isolating it from other photographs, anticipating its future iterations. We need to turn from magazines to films to continue the untold story of the cinematic past of this future icon.

MODELLING REVOLUTION

In May or June 1968, around the same time that *Life* and *Paris Match* first published the image that would later become an icon of the uprising, another photograph of de Bendern found its way into a *ciné-tract*. Perhaps the director found this in one of the piles of snapshots that Marker, who involved photographers in the project, made available to would-be *tracteurs* because (as explained in Chapter 4) they offered a means of making films quickly and cheaply. The tracts may comprise of stills, but they often coax them into movement. Like the magazine issues from Spring and Summer 1968 discussed in the previous section of this chapter, the cinematic pamphlets arrange images of protesting students and striking workers into sequences that blur the boundary between the photograph and the film frame. However, the dynamisation of stills serves different purposes in the mainstream printed press and in the *ciné-tracts*, which, as Catherine Lupton explains, supplied 'counter-information'.[45] Informed by the Situationists' attack on the 'society of the spectacle', the short films aimed to redress gaps and inaccuracies in reporting by the established media and thus intervene in, rather than merely document, the events.

In the previous chapter I drew attention to the animation in several *ciné-tracts* of photographs of demonstrations and rallies, which highlights the energy and momentum of the revolutionary movement. The tract in which de Bendern appears, number 20, devotes more time to, and injects more pace into, gestures of violence. Atack evocatively likens these motions to dance: 'the violence of the street battles in the photographs and *Cinétracts* is a distanced, balletic violence of beautiful images: poised bodies, smoke, streetlights, flares, and dark shadows [. . .].'[46] Tract 20 adds to the photographic choreography by panning along menacing lines of CRS, confronting police and students in shot/reverse-shot patterns and zooming out from individual combatants to larger battles. The vision of de Bendern follows a rapid succession of photographs, animated by rostrum camera movements, of night-time clashes, perhaps on 10 May when demonstrators built barricades and the police responded with gas, bombs and beatings. Whereas contemporary issues of *Paris Match* and especially *Life*, which reproduces some of the same pictures, incorporate de Bendern into similarly dynamic sequences, her appearance in the film halts the spectacle of movement. I am interested in how this photo-cinematic performance of stillness prefigured her iconic future.

The relationship between stillness and iconicity receives attention in Mulvey's recent discussion of the performance of stars and our desire to hold on to their images which appear only momentarily on the cinema screen. Mulvey extends the icon's definition beyond the relation of resemblance to the referent that distinguished Peirce's iconic sign to take account of 'the heightened iconographic significance and iconophilia fundamental to the way Hollywood, and other mass cinemas, worked to generate star images'.[47] Iconic screen actors 'maintain a fundamental contradiction in balance: the fusion of energy with a stillness of display.'[48] That their performance, for Mulvey, relies on pose as much as gesture is 'reminiscent, figuratively, of the way that the illusion of movement is derived from still frames'.[49] Her remark that 'moments of almost invisible stillness, in which the body is displayed for the spectator's visual pleasure' have always formed part of female screen performance echoes her comments, three decades earlier, on the flattening of women stars by conventional close-ups into cut-outs or icons.[50] The idea of the woman as cut-out leads back to the collage of painted and photographic fragments six years earlier in *Life* that draws an analogy between current and future female icons. This photomontage shows that there is nothing inconsistent about the habitual display of 'the woman as icon, [. . .] for the gaze and enjoyment of men', as Mulvey puts it, and the woman as allegory.[51] As Ludivine Bantigny observes, 'even before women had the right to public speech and quite simply to democratic expression, it was them who incarnated political ideas – republic, justice, equality . . .'.[52] Mulvey's later text associates the pin-up, rather than the cut-out, with the icon. The pin-up exemplifies how still photographs played a crucial role in creating star images.[53] As Jacobs explains, 'the story of movie stills photography [. . .] started in the early 1910s, coinciding with the rise of the star system'.[54] Like stillmen, portrait photographers produced publicity stills depicting stars posing. The pin-up reinforces the iconic status of the star and, like the electronic or digital pause, enables the fan to 'possess' her 'elusive' image.[55]

De Bendern's performance in the *ciné-tract* is not (yet) that of a star. Although, as Sally Shafto notes, 'her image was already known thanks to the fashion magazines and the fact that she was "Miss Kodak"', she would not become the face of May until later.[56] It was particular publications marking anniversaries of the events, including special issues of magazines, as Leblanc has tracked, that turned her image into an icon, regularly accompanied from the late 1980s onwards by interviews with the 'Marianne'.[57] I suggest, however, that the *ciné-tract* foreshadowed this transformation of Rey's photograph into a portrait of a star. As a form of 'dissenting filmmaking' (to borrow Catherine Lupton's phrase), the tracts rejected the conventions of capitalist mass cinemas including Hollywood's star system, just as they dispensed with the bourgeois notion of the individual auteur, as mentioned in the previous chapter.[58] De Bendern participated anonymously in the tract, neither the protagonists nor the director of which are named. Like the film star in Mulvey's account, however, de Bendern delivers a performance that 'depends on pose' and of which photographs provide tangible souvenirs.[59] While the film animates the preceding snapshots of violence and injury, her entrance suspends and (implicitly) silences the action.

The still in which she appears, which lingers on the screen for three seconds, derives from an image by another photojournalist, Jacques Windenberger, of the demonstration on 13 May.[60] In contrast to the other versions of the scene that featured in the dynamic page spreads discussed above, Windenberger's portrait separates her from the moving crowd, framing her from the waist up raising the borrowed flag with which, due particularly to Rey's image, she would become inextricably linked. The shallow focus further isolates her in the foreground from the protest by rendering the background shadowy and indistinct. Photos of de Bendern at the march encourage a flexible notion of the pose, whose definition was broadened, as Penelope Rook has shown, by the magazine *Vu* in the late 1920s and early 1930s, which exhibited the 'confluence' of the new phenomenon of photojournalism with the fashion shoot.[61] As photographers increasingly abandoned the 'artificial' space of the studio to capture models 'on the move' through 'real' spaces, Rook explains, the boundary between reporting on an event and recording street fashion became blurred.[62] Among her examples are several photographs by André Kertész of modish female students used by *Vu* in 1933 to illustrate articles about life at the Sorbonne.[63] This merging of documentary and fashion photography persists in pictures of students, workers and revolutionaries uniting on 13 May 1968, including those of de Bendern, who cuts a stylish figure with her cropped blonde hair and striped jacket, and who modelled in the 1960s with the Catherine Harlé agency in Paris and with Stewart and Eileen Ford in New York.[64] Her work continues the 'merging' of 'revolutionary icons' and 'popular fashion' in this period that Prestholdt discusses with particular reference to Guevara, whose best-known portrait is the work of a fashion photographer.[65] De Bendern's memory of posing for photographers at the march further confuses the distinction between fashion and news imagery.

Ciné-tract 20 accentuates her stillness by cropping Windenberger's photograph into a close-up. As well as turning female stars (like Greta Garbo) into 2D icons, the close-up, according to Mulvey, 'has always provided a mechanism of delay, slowing cinema down into contemplation of the human face [. . .].'[66] This type of shot 'necessarily limits movement, not only due to the constricted space of the framing, but also due to the privileged lighting with which the star's face is usually enhanced'.[67] Part of the exclusionary pattern of idealising the white visage that links Hollywood and European film histories, De Bendern's magnified face stands out in luminous profile not only against its dark background but also against what Atack refers to (in the remark cited earlier) as 'distanced' action, which dominates the *ciné-tract*. While the film groups most protestors into medium or long shots, de Bendern is one of a handful singled out in close-ups at the beginning and end. A dissolve momentarily superimposes her portrait on a high angle long shot of a street strewn with overturned cars, as if she is surveying the aftermath of a battle. But the removal of her original setting and its emblematic prop (the flag), which – like Korda's extraction of Guevara from another crowd – concentrates attention on her face, turns her from an 'active participant' into a 'decorative addition', to borrow a distinction drawn by Rook.[68] Mulvey cites Mary Ann Doane's observation that traditional 'discourse' on the close-up 'seems to exemplify a desire to stop the film, to grab hold of something that can be taken away [. . .]'.[69] De Bendern's appearance in the *ciné-tract* fits this pattern. Not only is she the subject of a still image; the black leader to which it cuts, one of only two in the film, arrests the flow of pictures and the tract ends a few shots later. Doane's notion of a grabable image pre-empts Mulvey's comments on the pin-up as a precursor to electronic and digital means of 'hold[ing] on to' cinema's 'idols'.[70] The portrait of de Bendern in the *ciné-tract* anticipates her iconisation by associating her with revolution and coexisting as a 'take-away' image.[71]

'HER GESTURES ARE ORCHESTRATED AROUND MOMENTS OF POSE': MARILYN, CAROLINE AND MARIANNE

If the future 'Marianne of '68' made only a cameo appearance in the *ciné-tract*, she had recently played the leading role in another film.[72] Shot in Paris between March and May of that year, *Détruisez-vous* was the first of what would (after an aborted attempt to make a film on a trip to Tanzania) be dubbed the 'Zanzibar Productions', a set of films 'born', as Shafto explains, 'of the intellectual and revolutionary moment of May 68'.[73] Several of the members of the Zanzibar group, including Bard, Jackie Raynal and Alain

Jouffroy, who respectively directed, edited and acted in *Détruisez-vous*, also compiled *ciné-tracts*.[74] Raynal, for example, recounts shooting material for since-lost tracts with Philippe Garrel, another of the Zanzibar *cinéastes*, and Godard, one of their main inspirations. At least some of these filmic pamphlets comprised of moving images, rather than stills as stipulated in the rubric Marker titled 'Ciné-tractez!' The three films in which Bard cast de Bendern also avoid photographs. Stillness nevertheless assumes vital importance in these films and none more than *Détruisez-vous*. While photojournalism played a crucial role in the project overseen by Marker, Bard's own experimental cinema owes a greater debt, we will see, to the worlds of art and fashion. Another similarity between the Zanzibar films and the tracts produced by the collective organised by Marker is their dispensation with credits in a gesture that rejects the canonical concept of the auteur.[75] For this political and creative reason, the makers of and participants in what Shafto aptly describes as the Zanzibar group's 'renegade' cinema, like the *ciné-tracteurs*, embraced anonymity.[76] However, several features of *Détruisez-vous*, including prolonged static and silent poses held by de Bendern, suggest, in tension with this concern to anonymise, an underlying preoccupation with stardom and iconicity that would become more insistent in Bard's third film, *Fun and Games for Everyone* (1968).

In a book that exemplifies, for Shafto, how 'the work of memory of this period has blossomed' in the new millennium, Fabrice Gaignault places de Bendern in a group of '1960s muses' that includes stars such as Nico, Anita Pallenberg and Anna Karina.[77] He makes a rare connection between the long-neglected *Détruisez-vous* and the photo that elevated de Bendern too from a muse into an icon. In the film, Gaignault suggests, 'Caroline was executing the gesture that she would reproduce on 13 May on the barricades with the flag.'[78] He does not mean this literally; there are no flags or barricades in the film, whose shooting (as mentioned earlier) predates by a month or two the appearance in French streets of these tools for challenging the established order. *Détruisez-vous* imagines more murderous means of overthrowing the status quo, as underlined by its title and subtitle 'le fusil silencieux' (the silent gun), though the violence and destruction that it envisages are not of the apocalyptic kind that I have suggested is evoked by filmic references to other photo-icons and motionless iconic figures. Rather than a particular physical gesture, Gaignault seems to mean the gesture of revolution. The gestures that pre-empt de Bendern's future status as the iconic 'Marianne rouge' (red Marianne) typically take the form of words.[79] For example, her (unnamed) character fantasises with her (unnamed) friend (Juliet Berto) about blowing up the walls of a prison with bombs placed on the outside so that the 'freedom behind [them] pour[s] out onto the streets'. More often, though, she paraphrases what turn out to be the revolutionary theories of her (unnamed) lecturer and lover (Jouffroy): 'everything must explode: the ministries, the banks, everything that props up this society'.[80]

Just as important as verbal gestures for understanding how the film relates to the photo, I suggest, are silent poses. If a (revolutionary) gesture, for Gaignault, attaches Bard's muse to the future Marianne, so too does gesture's 'orchestrat[ion] around moments of pose', to paraphrase Mulvey's remark on Monroe's first dance (as Lorelei Lee) in *Gentlemen Prefer Blondes* (Howard Hawks, 1953).[81] Whereas Monroe pauses only momentarily in this number, protracted performances of stillness initiate and punctuate *Détruisez-vous*. I want to suggest that these scenes anticipate de Bendern's iconisation not only intermedially – by emulating photography – but also intertextually – by recalling Warhol's images of Hollywood icons and incipient stars. Gunthert situates the valorisation of photojournalistic icons from the late 1960s in the context of the circulation in the West of images of pop culture icons, 'portraits of celebrities, actors and actresses, pop singers, cartoon heroes, and so on'.[82] This connection supports my consideration of Warhol, who pioneered the artistic reappropriation of pop culture, as the missing link between Marianne, Marilyn and Caroline.

Perhaps the most famous celebrity image repurposed by Warhol – in abundant screen prints in the 1960s – is a publicity still for Monroe's film *Niagara* (Henry Hathaway, 1953). A moment during the dance in *Gentlemen Prefer Blondes*, especially when digitally arrested, reminds Mulvey of this promotional picture: 'Marilyn moved forward into close-up, throwing her head back and assuming the pose and expression of the essential Marilyn pin-up photograph'.[83] 'This paused image', Mulvey continues, 'seems to be almost exactly the same as the *Marilyns* that Andy Warhol made after her death [. . .].'[84] Mulvey describes these images as 'iconic', associating this term, as I do in this chapter, with a transition from gesture to pose.

But what does the American collector and creator of iconic images have to do with the transformation of a British model and actor into a French icon? De Bendern met Warhol and befriended several of his collaborators in 1967 during a year-long trip to New York to pursue her modelling career. Moving between 'the hippie milieu, the fashion world [. . .] and the underground scene', she got to know the painter and actor Susan Hoffmann who would become Viva, one of Warhol's 'superstars'.[85] De Bendern observed Warhol filming scenes with Viva for *Bike Boy* (1967) and *The Nude Restaurant* (1967).[86] In the same year that de Bendern watched Warhol's new and old films at the Factory, the legendary studio where he and his entourage worked, his *Chelsea Girls* (1966) appeared at the Cannes Film Festival and Henri Langlois curated a programme of his works at the Cinémathèque française in Paris.[87] We get a sense of the strong impression these avant-garde American imports made on Bard, Jouffroy, de Bendern and the painter Olivier Mosset, who acts in *Détruisez-vous*, *Ici et maintenant* (Bard, 1968) and *Fun and Games for Everyone*, from references scattered across this trilogy.[88] Not only does *Détruisez-vous*, as Shafto points out, rebuild the Factory: several times the film returns to a long attic full of people (including de Bendern, Bard and Mosset) standing or wandering around.[89] More significantly for my discussion of the relationship between photography and cinema, the film owes a debt to Warhol's experiments in portraiture.

Several of the scenes with de Bendern emulate what Warhol considered titling his 'Living Portrait Boxes' (1964–6).[90] Although these several hundred artworks are films, they were famously nicknamed 'Stillies', since he instructed their subjects not to move and his collaborators to keep the camera stationary during the nearly three minutes it took to shoot a 100-foot roll of film. In this sense the 'screen tests' refer, as screen media theorist and historian Brigitte Weingart has pointed out, to the history of the pose: 'while the film rolls on, the quality of the photographic medium of freezing the subject in front of the camera is delegated to the subject herself. This of course implies a nod to the media history of the static pose, most notably to the long times of exposure in early photography that required the sitter's extended immobility; but of course one may also think of the sitting for a painted portrait.'[91] This preoccupation with the still face links the screen tests to Warhol's paintings of Monroe (as well as to Mulvey's digital 'transform[ation]' of her '[. . .] into a pin-up').[92] Weingart distinguishes, however, between the Factory's 'silkscreen reproduction of circulating images of celebrities', which 'questions our relationship as viewers to those who already *are* public icons', and the screen tests, which 'focus on the process of *becoming* an image', which 'extends to the Not-yet and even the Not-even-wanting-to-be-stars'.[93] Mentioned in my earlier discussion of *ciné-tract* 20, the category 'Not-yet-star' pithily encapsulates how de Bendern's on-screen performance of poses in 1968 anticipates her transformation into an icon. Her extended mute confrontations with the camera in *Détruisez-vous* register something of Weingart's 'Not-even-wanting-to-be' a star, or the 'strain' of the 'production' and 'stewardship' of an iconic image that the art critic Hal Foster reads the silk screens of Monroe, Elizabeth Taylor and Natalie Wood as commenting on.[94] Similarly, in many of the screen tests, he suggests, 'the sheer duress of filmic iconicity [. . .] becomes the principal subject'.[95] Foster's observation that the 'Stillies' are about iconicity supports my reading of *Détruisez-vous* as marrying the theme of revolution with that of (in Weingart's phrase) '*becoming* an image'.

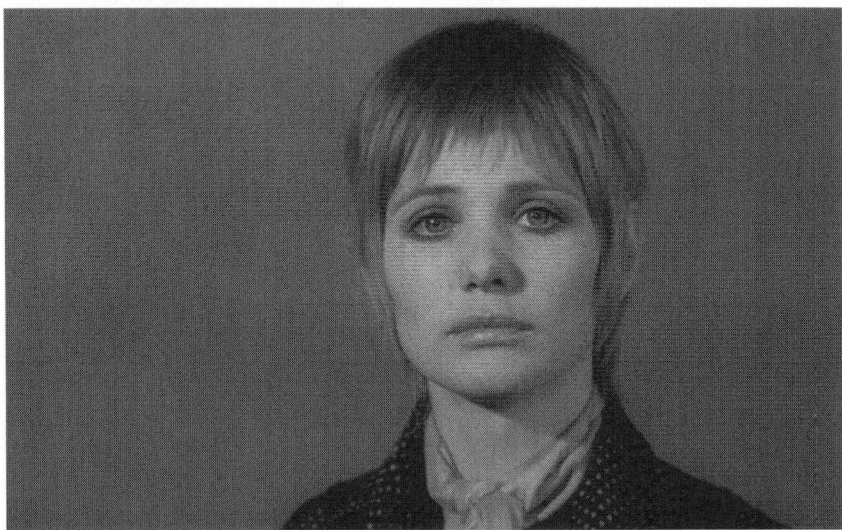

Figure 5.1 *Détruisez-vous* (*Destroy Yourselves*; dir. Serge Bard, France, 1968).

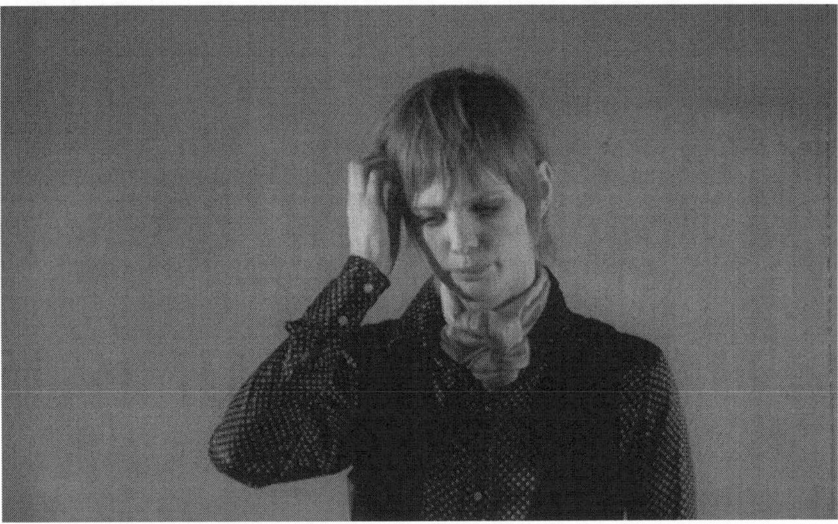

Figure 5.2 *Détruisez-vous.*

We sense de Bendern's awareness of 'becoming an image' during ten or so scenes spread through the film, each comprising one shot, throughout which she remains still and silent, staring at the immobile camera. The first example, which resembles one of the screen tests that stuck more closely to Warhol's rules (not all did) and leads us back to the previous chapter's comments on

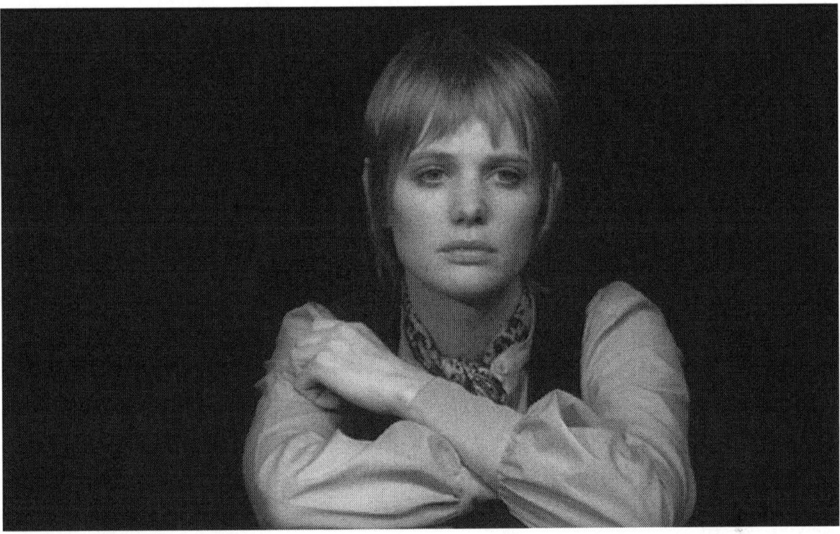

Figure 5.3 *Détruisez-vous.*

photogénie, is the opening shot (Figure 5.1), a black-and-white close-up which positions her face centre frame in front of a plain backdrop, and in which she barely moves even though it lasts over a minute.[96] This shot recurs just before the end of the film. In between there are all sorts of variations on it (as exemplified in figures 5.2 and 5.3), usually prefaced and succeeded by black leaders for emphasis. Often she sits or stands a bit further away in a medium shot. Sometimes she appears in colour or in an exterior setting. Occasionally Jouffroy, Mosset or Thierry Garrel keep her company. During one particularly gruelling five-minute take, Jouffroy's voice harangues her from off-screen, though she doesn't respond. Ranging in length from a few seconds to a few minutes, all these scenes display the riveting 'tension between movement and arrest' which, according to Weingart, the screen tests share with their 'predecessor' the *tableau vivant*, which combines elements of painting and theatre just as they combine elements of photography and film.[97] In one of the 'Stillies' in *Détruisez-vous*, Mosset underlines the homage that the film is paying to Warhol by re-enacting the pose, two fingers splayed across his lips, that the American assumes in the photograph on which he based a series of self-portraits in 1966, which have themselves, like his portraits of film stars, become iconic.[98]

Warhol thought of photographs as templates not only for painters but also for models. De Bendern's unflinching performances of stasis in *Détruisez-vous* recall his speculation that modelling is hard 'because you'd want to be like the photograph of you [. . .]. And so you start to copy the photograph.'[99] That she is wearing the same striped, tailored jacket in the 'Stillie' with Mosset as she would to the demonstration a month or so later compels my reading of these scenes as rehearsals for the 'shoot' that would turn her into Marianne. It is not only the skill in and stamina during posing de Bendern shows in the film but also the hip and glamorous clothes she wears while doing so – a camel trench coat, a black miniskirt, a silk neck scarf – that remind us of her career as a fashion model. Discussing links between the Zanzibar 'dandies' and the fashion world, Shafto remarks: 'Jackie, Caroline, Zouzou, Juliet, Audrey, Babette, Eve: they all seem to step out of the pages of a fashion magazine'.[100] The showcasing of fashion in *Détruisez-vous* complements its references to Warhol's explorations of stardom and iconicity. The subjects of some of the most famous screen tests bridged the worlds of fashion and film. This was the case with Edie Sedgwick, for example, whose wealthy background, as Sutton explains, 'placed her in a milieu between the screen test stars of the Factory and the unattainable stars of Hollywood' and would, like de Bendern's, become part of her identity as an icon.[101]

As important as stillness to the French film's anticipation of de Bendern's future iconicity is silence. Her long periods of muteness intensify the intermediality of her poses, their evocation of the soundless medium of photography.[102] Her silence also recalls that of the stars of the screen tests, which have no soundtrack. In a Deleuzian appreciation of two of Warhol's longer filmic portraits of Sedgwick from the same period, *Poor Little Rich Girl* (1965) and *Outer and Inner Space* (1965), Sutton comments on the affinity between silence and movie stardom: 'the images are returned to us as if from the silent cinema where stars were elevated to the status of gods, according to Dyer, and their becoming-star was one of total facialization'. Warhol's films about his 'superstar' reveal, Sutton goes on to argue, that it is a mistake 'to consider the silence of photography as an agent of *limitation* by absence. [. . .] [T]his silence instead is an agent of *liberation* by absence: liberation from its connection to movement in space.'[103] The relation between silence, stillness and liberation becomes vexed, however, in the poses de Bendern strikes for Bard, since these images of her unspeaking and unmoving reprise disempowering views of women as passive and inarticulate.

Détruisez-vous intermittently suppresses sound as a means of casting doubt on language, as underlined by de Bendern's retort to an insult from Jouffroy that his words are 'que du bruit' (mere noise). According to Philippe Azoury, 'while formulating revolutionary theory, [the film] also expresses an impatient desire to see language replaced by the resolute silence of opposition'. In keeping with its subtitle, it is 'a film shot in silence, taking aim against itself [. . .]'.[104] But the mutism it imposes on de Bendern when she is not repeating Jouffroy's lessons prefigures the difficulty that scholars like Khursheed Wadia would have 'find[ing] out what women had been thinking, saying and doing in May 1968'.[105] Wadia has stressed 'the extent to which women [have] been excluded' not only from written 'primary and secondary source commentaries, histories and interpretations' but also from photographic, televisual and poster images related to the uprising, in spite of their 'massive and unprecedented' participation.[106] She mentions Rey's enduring picture as an exception to this rule since it depicts a female form that is not 'unfocused, drowned in a sea of demonstrators or trivialised'.[107] The iconic photograph prioritises female participation in the events, apparently challenging prevalent reluctance at the time to view women as 'serious activists'.[108] Nevertheless, as suggested earlier, this picture of de Bendern imagining herself as a statue (as she puts it), perpetuates a tradition of idealising (and allegorising) mute women. The moments of silence and stillness that play such a significant role in de Bendern's performance in *Détruisez-vous* foreshadow the iconic image by sustaining the convention according to which the female film star exhibits her face and body for the viewer's pleasure.

CONCLUSION

Just as the repetition of the 'Marianne of '68' has helped to redress the marginalisation of women in written and visual material about the uprising to which Wadia draws attention, so too did the reappropriation by the Vancouver- and Paris-based artist Kathleen Ritter in 2013 of an image of its star. Ritter includes a black-and-white watercolour of the actor and activist in a series titled 'We Must Confront Vague Ideas With Clear Images', which recreates pictures drawn from eclectic media in the run-up to the revolt. Instead of the feted photograph, Ritter reproduces a frame from the endless, mesmerising close-up that opens and recurs near the end of *Détruisez-vous*. The 'curious concurrence between the documentary and the fictive' that Rittner notices in visuals from this period is not only a feature of her source; Bard's 'stillies' of de Bendern in this fiction film now call to mind the photojournalistic record of the mass protest of 13 May.[109] This chapter has explored how her roles as a revolutionary and her performances of muteness and immobility in *Détruisez-vous* and a *ciné-tract* pre-empt the evolution of Rey's photograph from an image that resembles a film frame into a portrait of a star. The films at once reduce her to a static, silent object of scopophilia and mobilise her within vocal demonstrations against the state and existing relations of power, establishing a tension that would persist in reappropriations of the photograph in the popular press that elevated her into an embodiment of the French Republic and an icon of dissent. The photojournalistic icon and the iconicity of the film star, then, can illuminate each other. But this photograph is not the only image of de Bendern that continues to circulate and mutate. Ritter's watercolour highlights the persistent power and iconic resonance of her screen performances. If the 'Marianne of '68' follows the template of Liberty's gestural rendering of emotion on Delacroix's dynamic canvas, she returns to painting via cinema as a face more ambiguously poised between movement and stillness.

Notes

1. For a fascinating recent discussion of the gesture of raising one's arms, see Didi-Huberman, Georges, 'Conflicts of Gesture, Conflicts of Images', *The Nordic Journal of Aesthetics*, 55–6 (2018), 8–22.
2. Kemp, Anna, 'Marianne d'aujourd'hui?: The Figure of the *Beurette* in Contemporary French Feminist Discourses', *Modern & Contemporary France*, 17: 1 (2009), 19–33 (25).
3. Leblanc and Versavel (eds), *Les Icônes de mai 68*, and 'Icônes de Mai 68', exhibition at the Bibliothèque nationale de France (17 April–26 August 2018).
4. The other two films in which Bard cast de Bendern are *Ici et maintenant* (Bard, 1968) and *Fun and Games for Everyone* (Bard, 1968). She also performed in the 3-minute *Un film porno* (Olivier Mosset, 1968), another work by members of the Zanzibar group.
5. For comments on the loss or marginalisation of much of the footage of May 1968 recorded by filmmakers, including some of the *ciné-tracts*, see Reader, Keith with Khursheed Wadia, *The May 1968 Events in France: Reproductions and Interpretations* (Basingstoke: Macmillan, 1993), p. 141.
6. Shafto, Sally, *Zanzibar: Les films Zanzibar et les dandys de mai 1968* (Paris: Éditions Paris Expérimental, 2007), pp. 173, 171.
7. Mulvey, *Death 24x a Second*, p. 161.
8. Ibid., p. 162.
9. On the mobilisation of the memory of 1936 in 1968, see Bantigny, Ludivine, '1968: le réel et son double: champs et hors-champs de l'événement', in Leblanc and Versavel (eds), *Les Icônes de mai 68*, pp. 33–47 (p. 41).
10. Leblanc, *Les Icônes de mai 68*, p. 76.
11. Leblanc, Audrey, 'De la photographie d'actualité à l'icône médiatique: "La jeune fille au drapeau" devient "la Marianne de 68"', https://clinoeil.hypotheses. org/448 (last accessed 1 September 2019) (translations from this text are mine).
12. Gunthert, 'Les Icônes du photojournalisme', pp. 19, 22.
13. Ibid., pp. 19, 22.
14. Cortade, *Le Cinéma de l'immobilité*, p. 219.
15. See Cortade, *Le Cinéma de l'immobilité*, p. 220.
16. 'Impact of Uprisings', *Life*, 64: 21 (24 May 1968), pp. 28–31 (31).
17. Bergala, 'Le pendule (la photo historique stéréotypée)', p. 44.
18. See Leblanc, *Les Icônes de mai 68*, p. 78; *Paris Match* (15–21 June 1968), pp. 60–1.
19. Leblanc, *Les Icônes de mai 68*, p. 78.
20. See 'Barricades élevées par les étudiants. Gaz lacrymogène. CRS en action', Gaumont Journal Actualité (15 May 1968); 'La France face à son drame', Pathé

Journal Actualité (29 May 1968); 'Homme des tempêtes', Pathé Journal Actualité (5 June 1968), all in Gaumont Pathé Archives.

21. Leblanc, *Les Icônes de mai 68*, p. 78; *Paris Match* (22–9 June 1968), 110–11.
22. Leblanc, 'De la photographie d'actualité à l'icône médiatique'.
23. Atack, Margaret, *May 68 in French Fiction and Film: Rethinking Society, Rethinking Representation* (Oxford: Oxford University Press, 1999), p. 4.
24. Jacobs, 'The History and Aesthetics of the Classical Film Still', 373, 380.
25. Ibid., p. 380.
26. See Gunthert, 'Les icônes du photojournalisme', p. 23; 'Revolution', *Life*, 67: 15 (10 October 1969), 100–12 (100–1).
27. Gunthert, 'Les icônes du photojournalisme', p. 23.
28. Ibid., p. 23.
29. Heartfield, John, 'La Liberté conduit le people d'Espagne', *Regards*, 141 (24 September 1936), 11.
30. Bell, Julian, *Mirror of the World: A New History of Art* (London: Thames & Hudson, 2010), p. 318.
31. Leblanc, *Les Icônes de mai 68*, p. 79. Leblanc borrows the concept of 'intericonicity' from Chéroux, Clément, *Diplopie. L'Image photographique à l'ère des médias globalisés: essai sur le 11 septembre 2001* (Cherbourg: Le Point du jour, 2009).
32. Calvino, Italo, 'A Novel Inside a Painting', *Collection of Sand: Essays*, trans. Martin McLaughlin (London: Penguin, [1983] 2013), pp. 51–8 (pp. 55, 53).
33. Ibid., p. 54.
34. Didi-Huberman, 'Conflicts of Gesture', p. 11.
35. Ibid., p. 14.
36. Calvino, 'A Novel Inside a Painting', p. 53.
37. 'Revolution', *Life* (10 October 1969), 101.
38. I am grateful to Chris Darke for his observations on this dimension of the image.
39. According to Edward Lucie-Smith, Delacroix was 'arguably' the French tradition's 'last great religious painter' (*A Concise History of French Painting* (London: Thames & Hudson, 1971), p. 199).
40. Jacobs, 'The History and Aesthetics of the Classical Film Still', 380.
41. Ibid., 381.
42. Ibid., 376.
43. de Bendern, Caroline, 'Caroline de Bendern Remembers . . .', extract from unpublished memoir [1998] in Shafto, *Zanzibar*, pp. 211–15 (p. 213).
44. Jacobs, 'The History and Aesthetics of the Classical Film Still', 380.
45. Lupton, Catherine, *Chris Marker: Memories of the Future* (London: Reaktion, 2005), p. 120.
46. Atack, *May 68 in French Fiction and Film*, p. 47.
47. Mulvey, *Death 24x a Second*, p. 162.
48. Ibid., p. 162.
49. Ibid., p. 162.
50. Ibid., pp. 162–3; Mulvey, 'Visual Pleasure and Narrative Cinema', *Screen*, 16: 3 (Autumn 1975), 6–18 (12).

51. Ibid., p. 13.
52. Bantigny, '1968: le réel et son double', p. 39 (my translation).
53. For a case study in the use of stills to publicise a star, see Marchant, Linda, 'Still Famous: Fixing the Star Image of Diana Dors in the Photography of Cornel Lucas', in Lucy Bolton and Julie Lobalzo Wright (eds), *Lasting Screen Stars: Images that Fade and Personas that Endure* (Palgrave Macmillan, 2016), pp. 261–76.
54. Jacobs, 'The History and Aesthetics of the Classical Film Still', 374.
55. Mulvey, *Death 24x a Second*, p. 161.
56. Shafto, *Zanzibar*, p. 223.
57. Leblanc, *Les Icônes de mai 68*, pp. 78–80.
58. Lupton, *Chris Marker*, p. 120.
59. Mulvey, *Death 24x a Second*, p. 162.
60. Windenberger's photo is reproduced in Leblanc and Versavel (eds), *Les Icônes de mai 68*, p. 127.
61. Rook, Penelope, 'Fashion Photography and Photojournalism: Posing the Body in *Vu*', *Fashion Theory*, 'Posing the Body', 21: 2 (2017), 131–56 (151).
62. Ibid., 135, 151.
63. Ibid., 143–5.
64. See Shafto, *Zanzibar*, p. 223.
65. Prestholdt, *Icons of Dissent*, p. 22.
66. Mulvey, *Death 24x a Second*, pp. 163–4.
67. Ibid., pp. 163–4.
68. Rook, 'Fashion Photography and Photojournalism', 136.
69. Doane, Mary Ann, 'The Close-Up: Scale and Detail in the Cinema', *differences: A Journal of Feminist Cultural Studies*, 14: 3 (Fall 2003), 89–111 (97).
70. Mulvey, *Death 24x a Second*, p. 161.
71. On the significance of de Bendern's beauty for the transformation of her image into an icon, see Bantigny, '1968: le réel et son double', p. 39.
72. The title of this subsection quotes Mulvey, *Death 24x a Second*, p. 172.
73. Shafto, *Zanzibar*, p. 173.
74. See Raynal, Jackie, 'The Zanzibar Group', in Shafto, *Zanzibar*, pp. 185–6.
75. See Shafto, *Zanzibar*, p. 176.
76. Ibid., p. 171.
77. Ibid., p. 173.
78. Gaignault, Fabrice, *Les Egéries sixties* (Paris: Fayard, 2006).
79. Ibid.
80. Since none of the characters in *Détruisez-vous* is named, I refer to them from here on by the name of the actors playing them, following the convention in writing on the film.
81. Mulvey, *Death 24x a Second*, p. 172.
82. Gunthert, 'Les icônes du photojournalisme', p. 28.
83. Mulvey, *Death 24x a Second*, p. 173.
84. Ibid., p. 173.
85. De Bendern, 'Caroline de Bendern Remembers . . .', p. 211.

86. Ibid., p. 212.

87. See Shafto, *Zanzibar*, pp. 223, 236 and Layerle, *Caméras en lutte en mai 68*, p. 192.

88. For more detail on and evidence of the interest in Warhol shared by de Bendern, Bard, Mosset and Jouffroy, see Shafto, *Zanzibar*, p. 193.

89. Shafto, *Zanzibar*, p. 193.

90. See Angell, Callie (ed.), *Andy Warhol Screen Tests: The Films of Andy Warhol: Catalogue Raisonné* (New York: Abrams/Whitney Museum of American Art, 2006), p. 14.

91. Weingart, Brigitte, '"That Screen Magnetism": Warhol's Glamour', *October*, 132 (Spring 2010), 43–70 (50).

92. Mulvey, *Death 24x a Second*, p. 167.

93. Weingart, '"That Screen Magnetism"', 46.

94. Foster, Hal, 'Test Subjects', *October*, 132 (Spring 2010), 30–42 (36–7).

95. Ibid., 40.

96. For remarks on the correlation between the close-up, stasis and *photogénie*, see Mulvey, *Death 24x a Second*, pp. 164, 166.

97. Weingart, '"That Screen Magnetism"', 50.

98. See Shafto, *Zanzibar*, p. 193. Mosset repeats this pose in *Ici et maintenant*.

99. Warhol, Andy, cited in Weingart, '"That Screen Magnetism"', 47.

100. Shafto, *Zanzibar*, p. 182.

101. Sutton, *Photography, Cinema, Memory*, p. 191. An example of an article about the 'Marianne of '68' that foregrounds de Bendern's aristocratic class background is Cojean, Annick, 'La Marianne de mai 1968: retour sur images', *Le Monde*, 21 August 1997, p. 8.

102. Weingart, '"That Screen Magnetism"', p. 50.

103. Sutton, *Photography, Cinema, Memory*, p. 193.

104. Azoury, Philippe, 'Notes on *Destroy Yourselves: The Silent Gun*', trans. Moira Tierney, in booklet accompanying Re:Voir DVD (2008), pp. 28–42 (p. 32).

105. Wadia, Khursheed, 'Women and the Events of May 1968', in Reader with Wadia, *The May 1968 Events in France*, pp. 148–66 (p. 148). See Shafto, *Zanzibar*, pp. 192–4, for a persuasive critique of the film's gender politics.

106. Wadia, 'Women and the Events of May 1968', pp. 148–50.

107. Ibid., pp. 149, 189.

108. Ibid., p. 154.

109. Ritter, Kathleen, description of the series 'We Must Confront Vague Ideas With Clear Images', http://kathleenritter.com/revolution/we-must-confront-description.html (last accessed 1 August 2019).

Protesting Women

At end of the 1960s, one of the most significant moments, as this book has discussed, in the history of iconic images, when the future 'Marianne of '68' began to circulate, so too did a series of arresting photographs of the singer Diana Ross. According to Nicole R. Fleetwood, author of an important recent contribution to the debate about icons, these portraits played a key role in Ross's transition from being one of the Supremes to the status of a celebrity icon. Fleetwood discusses gorgeous publicity images that use lighting and make-up to 'elevate' Ross's facial features 'with the intention of producing desire, envy, and idolization'.[1] The pictures 'exemplify [. . .] a mode of performance of *face* as an iconic form for modern celebrity'.[2] Like the celebrated image of de Bendern, which also resulted from a self-conscious and deliberate performance on the part of its subject, as discussed in the previous chapter, these images of Ross reinforce a view of photography as a privileged medium for the making of icons.

The form of these photographs and the styling of their subject owe a debt, however, as Fleetwood explains, to the culture of film. Ross's recording company, Motown, emulated the way Hollywood studios used to groom and publicise their stars.[3] Some of the photos that participated in her iconisation are by Harry Langdon, who '[took] many of his cues from cinema and celebrity portraiture of Hollywood's golden era'.[4] It was not only through stills reproduced in magazines or as posters that the movie industry had a bearing on Ross's iconisation. As Fleetwood notes, paraphrasing film theorist Richard Dyer, 'cinematic scale ("the big pictures") and aesthetics (Hollywood glamour lighting and familiar dramatic narrative) [were] the dominant lens for framing celebrity in twentieth-century culture'.[5] This is why Fleetwood's analysis of Ross's iconicity draws on one of Barthes's most famous essays on film, rather than his writings on photography. The 'performance of face', 'a quintessential feature of the celebrity as icon', derives from the culture of cinema, as Barthes's rumination in the late 1950s on Greta Garbo's visage reminds us.[6] In his 'fetishising' commentary on the 'snowy' make-up that enhances her beauty, Fleetwood argues, 'another important revelation about the power of the popular medium to deify emerges: that is, how whiteness serves as the chromatic default for the idealized face of the celebrity'.[7]

Although Fleetwood concentrates on iconic figures, rather than iconic photographs, her discussion of 'giving face' as a practice that forms (especially female) celebrity icons anticipates this book's insights in several ways. Her placement of eye-catching photos of Ross in a tradition of performance that stretches back to the early days of cinema foreshadows my discussion of the relation between the photojournalistic icon and film culture. In particular, Fleetwood's analysis of the influence of portraits of Hollywood stars on images of Ross parallels my reinterpretation of de Bendern's career as Marianne through the lens of her screen performances. *On Racial Icons* also prefigures my consideration of how cinema's incorporation and anticipation from the 1960s to the 1980s of iconic images of the Holocaust, Ho Dinh Van, Guevara and the uprising in France shed light on the affinity between the icon and the face. Like the countenance of Ross, rendered iconic in photographs that borrowed from the culture of cinema, those of Guevara and de Bendern emerged as icons between the two media, as we saw in Chapters 4 and 5. Fleetwood's recourse to writing on the filmed face also highlights the tendency to idealise whiteness discussed at several junctures in this book. 'One of the major effects of the black celebrity as racial icon', she argues, 'is a disruption of iconic whiteness through another staging of face.'[8]

Barthes's reflections on what Fleetwood calls 'iconic whiteness' also yield insights into the relation between still and moving images, another central concern of this book. He writes of Garbo in *Queen Christina* (Rouben Mamoulian, 1933), 'the make-up has the snowy thickness of a mask: it is not a painted face, but one set in plaster, protected by the surface of its colour, not by its lineaments.' This face, he goes on, is 'not drawn but sculpted'.[9] Although he is discussing a motion picture, his comparison of Garbo's iconic visage with inflexible substances implies that it is rigid and unmoving. In Barthes's account, the idealised face of the star suspends filmic movement. By contrast, just over a quarter of a century later, by which time stillness had become a popular theme in cinema studies, Deleuze described the face as polarised between 'a reflecting, immobile unity' and 'intensive expressive movements'.[10] The combination of the two 'constitutes the affect'.[11] Deleuze's analysis of the affect, whose primary examples are cinematic close-ups, reintroduced Peirce's concept of the icon to film studies. As discussed in Chapter 3, Deleuze defines affect as what is expressed by a face (or facial equivalent) and calls the set of the affect and the face 'icon'. The icon is thus 'the sign of the bipolar composition of the affection-image'.[12] Chapter 3 explored the relevance of Deleuze's philosophical approach to the icon, which draws inspiration from facial close-ups in *Persona*, to this fiction film's juxtaposition of Elisabet's expressive moving features with iconic historical images of an arrest and a protest performance of stasis. The following two chapters returned to the theme of facial stillness and movement, looking back first, like Deleuze, to Balázs's writing on the face and the crowd.[13] I suggested that Balázs's idea of cinema's distinctive capacity to render visible the expressive mobility that makes crowds resemble faces resonates freshly with films concerned with the late 1960s and the 1970s when transnational political movements embraced Guevara and other iconic figures. The final chapter considered how counter-cinematic close-ups of de Bendern's motionless visage pre-empted her own elevation into a revolutionary icon, reinforcing, like *Persona*, what Fleetwood terms whiteness as 'chromatic default'. While this case study turned to Mulvey's recent account of how the Hollywood star's performance combines energy and stasis, the notion of the crowd face returned around the same time, as we will see, in discussion of the iconography of contemporary protest movements.

By attending to the opposition between fixity and movement, and the interaction between photography and film, this book has tried to develop a new approach to iconic images. I have discussed reasons why writing on secular icons since the 1980s has paid more attention to photography than any other medium, in spite of their inherent intermediality. This is due particularly to photography's special capacity to capture moments that emblematise an event and to the circulation of photojournalistic images, especially before the digital era, in enduring material forms encountered in everyday life. By contrast, as Mulvey opens her book on still and moving images by noting, until the late twentieth century only a small range of professions had the means to slow down films for extended scrutiny; most people experienced cinema and television images as ephemeral.[14]

I have argued, nevertheless, that the iconic photograph needs understanding in the context of film. This argument has five main strands, the first of which looked back to this icon's paper origins. Before the photojournalistic icon became associated with stardom, the magazines that helped to create this genre of image maintained a dialogue with cinema and, in some cases, television.[15] Several of those studied in this book made early appearances in 'picture stories' which compete with cinema, unsettling the boundary between the photograph, the film still and the film frame or photogramme. Chapter 1 traced the 'Falling Soldier' through magazine and newspaper reports which juxtapose it with other images, including frames from the motion picture *The Spanish Earth*, in ways that spectacularise and animate the war in Spain. The 'Gestapo Informer' likewise began its public life beside an article which describes its abundant illustrations as belonging to a film, as we saw in Chapter 2. The spreads of photographs of marches and violent confrontations between protestors and police in which the 'Marianne of '68' initially recurred similarly recall the 'paper cinema' of interwar French weeklies while they vied for attention with TV. These cases shed light on the energy that often characterises iconic photographs of war and political contestation, including examples from different eras, even when they focus on a still body, as well as the impression of arrested movement that they produce when singled out from sequences of images and reframed as exceptional. While this 'freeze-frame effect' supported Bergala's attack on 'stereotyped historical photos' in the 1970s for illustrating the work of dominant ideology, I have also engaged with more recent studies, such as Michelle Yang's research on self-immolation, which detail the role of photojournalistic icons in attempts to change the status quo.

A second reason for locating iconic images from the middle decades of the twentieth century between photography and film is that they derived not only from cinema of the paper kind but also, more rarely but nonetheless significantly, from documentary, newsreel and TV footage. While iconic photographs are often more familiar than similar sequences of film or video, reinforcing the prevalent assumption that only photography can produce icons, this book has also highlighted the capacity of moving images to achieve this status. Reiterating the facial conception of the icon that film studies and iconic image studies inherited from art history and philosophy, my first and briefest example was the seven-second shot which lingers on Settela Steinbach, the girl watching from a boxcar bound for Auschwitz-Birkenau. This haunting moment has encapsulated a much longer event not only in documentary and essay films in cinemas and on television but also on paper.[16] Whereas magazine picture stories and movie reviews make the 'Falling Soldier', the 'Gestapo Informer' and the 'Marianne of '68' resemble images from a film, reproductions of frames of the 'Girl with the Headscarf' in books and artworks resemble photographs.[17] Stillness also pervades her encounter with the film camera operator (which prompts Lindeperg, as mentioned in the Introduction, to coin the term 'cine-photograph'), in contrast to Capa's, Cartier-Bresson's, Browne's and Rey's dynamic snapshots of different kinds of conflict and confrontation.

My main examples of iconic documentary sequences owe their status to repetition on television and in cinema newsreels and fiction, essay and experimental films, since there are equivalent photographs that reproduce better in print. Nevertheless, like the footage of Steinbach, these film and TV images derive their power from stasis as much as motion. In Chapter 3 I suggested that pieces of film contributed distinctively to the iconisation of Vietnamese self-immolators that began in 1963 by bearing witness to the unflinching, upright postures maintained by the burning protestors for long moments and thus accentuating their extraordinary strength and courage. Confirmation of the enduring stillness of a body, which photographs can't provide, also distinguishes moving images of the dead Guevara, as discussed in Chapter 4. This is particularly significant in the light of reports that stills of the open-eyed corpse failed to convince some viewers of Guevara's demise. The moving footage from

Vietnam and Bolivia demonstrates, I argued, that film has played more than the merely auxiliary role to iconic photographs to which several commentators have relegated it.

Not only has film provided a material support for iconic images; cinema has also played key roles in their dissemination and interpretation. A third proposal of this book is that the circulation of photographic icons and iconic news footage in fiction and documentary films from the 1960s to the early 1980s in Europe, North America and beyond amplified the disastrous connotations of the invasion of cinema by stillness. As explained in Chapters 1 and 3, the static forms that proliferated in films during the 1960s have inspired reflections by Bellour and Rust on death and apocalypticism which refer to multiple histories of political violence. The remakes of Capa's icon of the Spanish Civil War in *La Jetée* at the time of the Cuban missile crisis and in *Overlord* and *Gallipoli* in the aftermath of the war in Vietnam reinforce the connection between suspended or slowed motion and mass death. More problematically, the apocalyptic meanings acquired in a Pathé documentary, *Persona*, *Le Huitième Jour* and, to some extent, *In the Year of the Pig* by the iconic figures of Dinh Van and other Vietnamese Buddhists who unflinchingly immolated themselves risk distracting, I suggested, from their anti-imperialist politics. By contrast, *The Hour of the Furnaces* recruits still and moving post-mortem images of Guevara's body and especially his face to its critique of neo-colonial violence.

Cinema has not only incorporated photojournalistic icons into narrative and essayistic meditations on violence and disaster. Along with video, it has also served as a device for analysing and criticising them. A fourth claim developed in this book is that the iconic photograph played a significant role in the debate about still and moving images and the mass media that unfolded in film studies journals as well as in documentaries made for television, especially in France, in the 1970s and early 1980s. Like Jean-Louis Baudry's landmark essay in 1970 on the ideological effects of 'the projection operation (projection and screen)' that 'restores continuity of movement and the temporal dimension to the sequence of static images', Godard and Miéville's television programme *Photos et cie* mounts a critique of dominant imagery that plays on the relation between fixity and motion.[18] Among the photographs that the videographers mobilise by leafing through and oscillating between them are well-known pictures of Kim Phúc and Guevara, as discussed in Chapter 4. We encounter these icons amid the flood of photographs that the programme denounces for enriching magazines without helping victims of political violence.

The broadcast of the series to which *Photos et cie* belongs coincided, in the summer of 1976, with a succession of articles in *Cahiers du cinéma* which took up the investigation of photojournalism's relation to moving pictures. As we saw in Chapters 1 and 4, Bergala's contribution to this conversation indicts 'always-already-seen photos', including a number of the icons discussed in this book, as exemplary capitalist images. It does so by drawing analogies between these stills, whose conventional nature it underlines by linking them to freeze-frames, and Hollywood cinema's disavowal of the agency of 'the masses'. By contrast, the 'non cinematographic specificity' of the picture of Quang Duc's protest that filled the cover of the issue of the *Cahiers* in which Bergala's piece appeared took Bonitzer aback.[19] In the following issue, however, Bonitzer argues that the journal's analysis of this photo coheres with its recent emphasis on what we can't see in the cinema as a source of insight into the ideological problems it poses. This is because, he explains in terms that echo Baudry's intervention, 'cinema includes, even as it displaces, a reflection on photography'.[20] The study of historical photographs particularly can 'enrich' cinema, he insists. As well as *Photos et cie*, to which Bonitzer refers, Wehn-Damisch's *Photographie et société: d'après Gisèle Freund*, discussed in Chapter 1, illustrates this. Wehn-Damisch and Freund resume the discussion about stillness and motion by comparing the picture of Quang Duc and other photo-icons with similar pieces of film.

Godard and Miéville's programme and Bergala's essay anticipate more recent accounts of the icon as a commodity fetish. Ghosh writes, however: 'while in its hegemonic circulations as mass commodity an icon might well provide a glimpse into existing social relations, as volatilized signifier it alerts us to demands for social change'.[21] Unlike the French analysts of several decades before, Ghosh demonstrates the potential for icons (by which she means public figures, not photographs) to become catalysts, in certain circumstances, for collective action. Her account of popular uprisings stresses the dynamism of the encounter between the 'moving technology' of the icon and its devotees, as explored in Chapter 4. *No Power Without an Image* has highlighted ways in which iconic photographs and film sequences interrupt motion. But it has also suggested, fifthly, that cinema can provide unrivalled insights into their mobilisation of and by large gatherings of people. In a way that I didn't anticipate when embarking on research for the book, since iconic images from the twentieth century tend to single out individuals, the crowd has become one of its central protagonists, underlining the connection between the iconic and the popular. Deportees, monks, nuns, passers-by, mourners, students and workers collect *en masse* within or around the images on which I have focused. Although not about symbols held aloft by marchers, Chapter 2 revolved around a photograph of a protest, an image that is as memorable for details of the crowd in transit in the background as for its main protagonists. The following chapters explored connections between iconic image histories and the rise of protest and solidarity movements around the world in the 1960s, culminating in the uprisings of 1968. Onlookers also crowd around those protesting by immolation in the pictures from South Vietnam discussed in Chapter 3, including a photograph that recurred on banners brandished at subsequent demonstrations. Chapter 4 followed crowds to free copies of Guevara's Bolivian diary (in an ICAIC newsreel), around his corpse (in *The Hour of the Furnaces*) and on marches inspired by his example on multiple continents (in two 'film tracts' and *A Photo Travels Around the World*). The final chapter considered images of another figure borne along by marchers in May '68, who would later attain iconic status. As several of the documentary and essay films analysed in Chapters 4 and 5 suggest, cinema's capacity to assemble still and moving images makes it particularly good at exploring how photographs and crowds set each other in motion. I have also argued that theories of star performance in cinema studies can elucidate the relation between anonymous collectives of filmmakers and individual iconicity.

The iconic images examined in this book matter because they have shaped how people in different parts of the world remember forms of political violence and processes of contestation that erupted between 1936 and 1968. Studying their lives is also worthwhile because they shed light on the intertwined histories of photography, magazines, film and television during the twentieth century. What currency do they retain today? 'The icons of one generation or one audience', writes Perlmutter of photojournalistic images, 'are the enigmas, or at best, the shadows of another generation or audience.'[22] Yet some of the examples on which I have focused keep returning to prominence. In the past few years, for example, the 'Falling Soldier', the 'Gestapo Informer' and the 'Marianne of '68' (among other photo-icons) have filled the covers of new books devoted in whole or part to them. While I have been writing this monograph, Caroline de Bendern has reappeared particularly often and in a range of contexts. Not only was she the poster girl for events celebrating the fiftieth anniversary of May '68. She also cropped up, for instance, in *The Guardian* in 2017, explaining why she would be marching with a European Union flag.[23] A version of the 'Marianne' image recurred among the emblematic photos of feminist demonstrations in the 1960s and 1970s printed by the artist Lisa Rovner on coloured paper, titled 'I can't believe I'm still protesting this shit' and displayed in the 'Mademoiselle' collective show at the Centre régional d'art contemporain Occitanie, Sète (2018–19). Her iconic image gained fresh resonance during the second half of a decade which witnessed a global proliferation of protest movements and renewed upsurge of feminism. Her return to visibility has coincided with the viral spread of a handful of photojournalistic images of other young women demonstrating mainly, like the students and workers in France in 1968, against militarised states, including Jasmina Golubovska in Skopje, Macedonia (Ognen Teofilovski, 2015), Ieshia Evans in Baton Rouge, US (Jonathan Bachman, 2016), an unidentified protestor in Santiago, Chile (Carlos Vera, 2016) and Saffiyah Khan in Birmingham, UK (Joe Giddens, 2017).[24]

Like most of the images considered in this book, these four recent pictures evoke emotional responses because they place the expressive body in dramatic situations and 'are born in conflict or confusion', as Hariman and Lucaites observe of iconic photographs.[25] They are affecting because they show individual women fearlessly and without protection placing themselves in physical danger by confronting armoured police and an English Defence League supporter. In the thick of an anti-government demonstration, Golubovska is putting on scarlet lipstick using a riot shield as a mirror. The Chilean woman is staring up at a policeman's helmeted face during a rally commemorating Augusto Pinochet's victims. Wearing a long sundress, Evans is facing down state troopers in bulky riot gear as she revolts against the police killings of Philando Castile, Alton Sterling and other black Americans. Khan is also taking a stand against racism as she smilingly contests the street presence of a neo-fascist organisation.

The combination of dynamic protest with individual calmness and composure – which recurs in video footage of the acts of resistance by Evans and Khan – is familiar from a tradition of photojournalistic and filmic icons which similarly centre on single figures contesting abuses of power and ideologies that scapegoat. These include the burning Quang Duc and Dinh Van, the flag-waving de Bendern, the chrysanthemum-clutching and bayonet-facing Jan Rose Kasmir at an anti-war rally at the Pentagon (Marc Riboud, 1967) and the unidentified tank-stalling protestor in Tiananmen Square (Jeff Widener, 1989).[26] Like this older generation of images, their recent viral counterparts recall Mulvey's discussion of star performance (also cited in Chapter 5) as able 'to maintain a fundamental contradiction in balance: the fusion of energy with a stillness of display.'[27] Just as recent scholarship on war photography has referred to Mulvey's critique of the patriarchal form of mainstream cinema, so too her insights into (especially women's) screen performances of 'intensely controlled stillness' can enrich thinking about camera images of contestation.[28] Mulvey's account of the still images that have enabled fans to pore over favourite filmic moments also resonates with the viral photographs, which have likewise attracted admiration.

However, the images of Golubovska, Evans, Khan and the Chilean protestor have not (yet) become 'star' portraits in the same sense as the historical photographs and film sequences on which the preceding chapters have concentrated. The later pictures differ in this respect from another set of stills they bring to mind, video frames and photos of Neda Agha-Soltan, another young, female anti-government protestor. After Agha-Soltan's shooting during demonstrations provoked by Iran's presidential election in 2009, images of her face in life and, as Aleida Assmann and Corinna Assmann describe, 'defaced by streams of blood and death' multiplied on social media networks and marches.[29] Assmann and Assmann trace the transformation of her countenance in death into 'works of pop-art paintings' which bestow on it 'a "Warholian" iconicity that almost matches that of Che Guevara'.[30] The iconic image of Mohamed Bouazizi, the 26-year-old Tunisian whose self-immolation the following year sparked the protests that would build into the Arab Spring, similarly isolates his face. In contrast to the most prominent pictures of the sexagenarian Thich Quang Duc, which encompassed his burning body, the most widely disseminated of Bouazizi, which predates his protest, is a smiling portrait photograph.[31] As W. J. T. Mitchell anticipated in 2012, however, no single face defines the uprisings against authoritarian governments across North Africa and the Middle East in 2011. Mitchell draws a parallel between the 'antiiconic, nonsovereign image repertoire' insisted on by Tahrir Square and the iconography of the Occupy movement, which 'renounc[ed] the face and figure of the charismatic leader in favor of the face in and of the crowd, the assembled masses'.[32] As Mitchell notes, the Egyptian movement did this for 'partly tactical' reasons, to protect individuals from arrest and torture.

Since its early days, cinema has not only privileged the iconic face and figure of the star; it has also repeatedly examined 'the face in and of the crowd'. The photo-cinematic images of the expressive gestures of crowds and of their individual members discussed in this book, from Cartier-Bresson's pictures of Dessau in 1945 to Chaskel's pursuit of the 'Heroic Guerrilla' in 1981, become newly pertinent in the light of changes in the iconography of protest. Ghosh suggests that mass media photographs of Arundhati Roy framed by fellow activists 'inevitably render the "crowd" meaningful by hitching the indistinguishable many to a familiar, recognizable, and symbolically loaded star body'.[33] In contrast, the photographs of Golubovska, Evans, Khan and the Chilean woman downplay their distinction from associates assembled at the edges of, or just outside, the frame. Not only do these women, like Roy, give a face to collective efforts to challenge oppressive systems of power; they also derive power from the images that have had time to become 'stars', including the 'Marianne of '68', whose memory they revive and which they invest with fresh power in turn. This form of montage, to borrow a cinematic metaphor, can also empower the viewer, inviting her to bring knowledge of historical struggles to bear in forms of political resistance today. No power without an image.

Notes

1. Fleetwood, *The Racial Icon*, p. 58. Fleetwood underlines the particular significance of photographs of Ross by Harry Langdon and Victor Skrebneski.
2. Ibid., p. 58.
3. See Fleetwood, *The Racial Icon*, pp. 61–2.
4. Ibid., p. 63.
5. Ibid. See Dyer, Richard, *Heavenly Bodies: Film Stars and Society* (Basingstoke: Macmillan, 1987).
6. Fleetwood, *The Racial Icon*, p. 63.
7. Barthes, Roland, 'The Face of Garbo', in *Mythologies*, trans. Annette Lavers (London: Paladin, [1957] 1987), pp. 56–7 (p. 56); Fleetwood, *The Racial Icon*, p. 63.
8. Fleetwood, *The Racial Icon*, p. 63.
9. Barthes, 'The Face of Garbo', p. 56.
10. Deleuze, *The Movement Image*, p. 98. Deleuze draws in this passage on Henri Bergson's definition of the affect.
11. Ibid., p. 98.
12. Ibid., p. 108.
13. Ibid., pp. 106–7.
14. Mulvey, *Death 24x a Second*, p. 7.
15. My history of the emergence of the iconic photograph differs in this respect from Gunthert's, who dates the beginning of this process to the late 1960s ('Les icônes du photojournalisme').
16. Wagenaar, for example, writes of the images of Steinbach: 'despite their short duration they amount to a complete film documentary of the deportation of Jews somewhere in Europe, to the extermination camps of the National Socialist Third Reich' (*Settela*, p. 1).
17. See, for example, the reshaped portraits of this emblematic figure on the cover of Wagenaar's book and in Katarzyna Pollok's collage 'Porrajmos – Settela Steinbach' (2003), which is reproduced in Lindeperg's *La Voie des images* (p. 190).
18. Baudry, Jean-Louis, 'Ideological Effects of the Basic Cinematographic Apparatus' [1970], trans. Alan Williams, *Film Quarterly*, 28: 2 (1974–5), 39–47 (42).
19. Bonitzer, 'La Surimage', 29.
20. Ibid.
21. Ghosh, *Global Icons*, p. 105. On the photojournalistic icon as commodity, see also Perlmutter, *Photojournalism and Foreign Policy*, p. 13.
22. Perlmutter, *Photojournalism and Foreign Policy*, p. 10.
23. Abigail Frymann Rouch, 'Caroline de Bendern: "Leave Campaign Was Lies and Xenophobia"', *The Guardian*, 20 March 2017, https://www.theguardian.com/world/2017/mar/20/caroline-de-bendern-paris-1968-brexit-xenophobia (last accessed 1 August 2019).
24. On the relationship between viral and iconic images, see Cambre, *The Semiotics of Che Guevara*, pp. 146–8. Like my historical case studies, these four contemporary stills are the work of photojournalists. However, it is important to acknowledge

that, as Kathrin Fahlenbrach explains, 'the relevance of professional press pictures for social movements has diminished since [the 1960s] and activists use and distribute much more frequently photos by themselves or by amateurs' ('Images and Imagery of Protest', in Fahlenbrach, Martin Klimke and Joachim Scharloth (eds), *Protest Cultures: A Companion* (New York: Berghahn, 2016), pp. 243–58 (p. 246)). Opposition movements also circulate amateur video, such as the iconic mobile phone footage of Neda Agha-Soltan's death, which I mention later.

25. Hariman and Lucaites, *No Caption Needed*, pp. 35–6.
26. For discussion of the dense weave of historical associations evoked by the photograph of Evans, see Tierney, Matt, *Dismantlings: Words Against Machines in the American Long Seventies* (Ithaca, London: Cornell University Press, 2019), p. 165.
27. Mulvey, *Death 24x a Second*, p. 162. On the evolving relationship between still and moving images in the digital age, see Røssaak, Eivind, 'Algorithmic Culture: Beyond the Photo/Film Divide', in Røssaak (ed.), *Between Stillness and Motion*, pp. 187–203.
28. See, for example, Zarzycka, *Gendered Tropes*, p. xxiv; Mulvey, *Death 24x a Second*, p. 162.
29. Assmann, Aleida and Corrina Assmann, 'Neda – the Career of a Global Icon', in Aleida Assmann and Sebastian Conrad (eds), *Memory in a Global Age: Discourses, Practices and Trajectories* (Basingstoke: Palgrave Macmillan, 2010), pp. 225–42 (p. 235).
30. Ibid., p. 235.
31. See Halverson, Jeffry R., Scott W. Ruston and Angela Trethewey, 'Mediated Martyrs of the Arab Spring: New Media, Civil Religion, and Narrative in Tunisia and Egypt', *Journal of Communication*, 63 (2013), 312–32 (317). Halverson, Ruston and Trethewey explain how the privileging of this photograph perpetuates long-standing North African traditions of the 'living martyr'.
32. Mitchell, W. J. T., 'Image, Space, Revolution: The Arts of Occupation', *Critical Inquiry*, 39 (Autumn 2012), 8–32 (9).
33. Ghosh, *Global Icons*, p. 271.

Bibliography

Ahmed, Sara, *Queer Phenomenology: Orientations, Objects, Others* (Durham, NC: Duke University Press, 2006).

Alexander, Jeffrey C., Dominik Bartmański and Bernhard Giesen (eds), *Iconic Power: Materiality and Meaning in Social Life* (New York: Palgrave Macmillan, 2012).

Always Audrey: Six Iconic Photographers. One Legendary Star (Woodbridge: ACC Art Books, 2019).

Angell, Callie (ed.), *Andy Warhol Screen Tests: The Films of Andy Warhol: Catalogue Raisonné* (New York: Abrams/Whitney Museum of American Art, 2006).

Assmann, Aleida and Corrina Assmann, 'Neda – the Career of a Global Icon', in Aleida Assmann and Sebastian Conrad (eds), *Memory in a Global Age: Discourses, Practices and Trajectories* (Basingstoke: Palgrave Macmillan, 2010), pp. 225–42.

Atack, Margaret, *May 68 in French Fiction and Film: Rethinking Society, Rethinking Representation* (Oxford: Oxford University Press, 1999).

Azoury, Philippe, 'Notes on *Destroy Yourselves: The Silent Gun*', trans. Moira Tierney, in booklet accompanying the Re:Voir DVD of *Détruisez-vous* (2008), pp. 28–42.

Baert, Barbara, 'Nymph: The Reproduction of a Phantom. A Contribution to the Study of Aby Warburg (1866–1929)', in Shigetoshi Osano and Milosz Wozny (eds), *Between East and West: Reproductions in Art. Proceedings of the 2013 CIHA Colloquium in Naruto, Japan, January 15–18, 2013* (Cracow: Irsa, 2015), pp. 167–90.

Bailey, George A. and Lawrence W. Lichty, 'Rough Justice on a Saigon Street: A Gatekeeper Study of NBC's Tet Execution Film', *Journalism Quarterly*, 49: 2 (1972), 221–9, 238.

Balázs, Béla, *Béla Balázs: Early Film Theory: Visible Man and the Spirit of Film*, Erica Carter (ed.), trans. Rodney Livingstone (New York: Berghahn, 2011).

Bantigny, Ludivine, '1968: le réel et son double: champs et hors-champs de l'événement', in Audrey Leblanc and Dominique Versavel (eds), *Les Icônes de mai 68: les images ont une histoire* (Bibliothèque nationale de France, 2018), pp. 33–47.

Baqué, Dominique (ed.), *Les Documents de la modernité: anthologie de textes sur la photographie de 1919 à 1939* (Nîmes: Jacqueline Chambon, 1993).

Barthes, Roland, 'Rhetoric of the Image' [1964] in *Image Music Text*, essays selected and translated by Stephen Heath (London: Fontana Press, 1977), pp. 32–51.

—— 'The Face of Garbo', in *Mythologies*, trans. Annette Lavers (London: Paladin, [1957] 1987), pp. 56–7.

—— 'The Third Meaning' [1970], in *Image Music Text*, essays selected and translated by Stephen Heath (London: Fontana Press, 1977), pp. 52–68.

—— *Camera Lucida*, trans. Richard Howard (London: Vintage [1980] 2000).

Bataille, Georges, 'Mouth' [1930], in *Visions of Excess: Selected Writings, 1927–1939*, trans. Allan Stoekl (Minneapolis: University of Minnesota Press, 1985), pp. 59–60.

Bathrick, David, 'Introduction: Seeing Against the Grain: Re-Visualizing the Holocaust', in Bathrick, Brad Prager and Michael D. Richardson (eds), *Visualizing the Holocaust: Documents, Aesthetics, Memory* (Rochester, NY: Camden House, 2008), pp. 1–18.

Baudry, Jean-Louis, 'Ideological Effects of the Basic Cinematographic Apparatus' [1970], trans. Alan Williams, *Film Quarterly*, 28: 2 (1974–5), 39–47.

Beaumont-Maillet, Laure, 'Robert Capa: une vie de passions', in Beaumont-Maillet (ed.), *Capa connu et inconnu* (Paris: Bibliothèque Nationale de France, 2004), pp. 11–35.

Bell, Julian, *Mirror of the World: A New History of Art* (London: Thames & Hudson, 2010).

Bellour, Raymond, *Between-the-Images*, trans. Allyn Hardyck (Zürich/Dijon: JRP/Ringier/Les Presses du réel, [1990] 2012).

—— 'Concerning "the Photographic"', trans. Chris Darke, in Karen Beckman and Jean Ma (eds), *Still Moving: Between Cinema and Photography* (Durham, NC: Duke University Press, 2008), pp. 253–76.

Bentin, Doug, 'Mondo Barnum', in Gary D. Rhodes and John Parris Springer (eds), *Docufictions: Essays on the Intersection of Documentary and Fictional Filmmaking* (Jefferson, NC; London: McFarland & Co., 2006), pp. 144–53.

Bergala, Alain and Jean-Jacques Henry, introduction to dossier, 'Photographies', *Cahiers du cinéma*, 268–9 (1976), 39.

Bergala, Alain, 'Le pendule (la photo historique stéréotypée)', *Cahiers du cinéma*, 268–9 (1976), 40–6.

Berger, John, 'Image of Imperialism', in Geoff Dyer (ed.), *Understanding a Photograph* (London: Penguin, 2013), pp. 3–16.

Bergman, Ingmar, *Bergman on Bergman*, trans. Paul Britten Austin (New York: Da Capo Press, 1993).

—— *Images: My Life in Film*, trans. Marianne Ruth (New York: Arcade Publishing, 1994).

Berrou, Jean-Hughes and Jean-Jacques Lefrère, *Che: images* (Paris: Fayard, 2003).

Biggs, Michael, 'Self-Immolation in Context, 1963–2012', *Revue d'Études Tibétaines*, 25 (December 2012), 143–50.

Bingham, Adam, 'Apocalypse Now: Images of The End in the Cinema of Ingmar Bergman', in Virginie Selavy (ed.), *The End: An Electric Sheep Anthology* (London: Strange Attractor Press, 2011), pp. 236–50.

Blaylock, Sara, 'Bringing the War Home to the United States and East Germany: *In the Year of the Pig* and *Pilots in Pajamas*', *Cinema Journal*, 56: 4 (Summer 2017), 26–50.

Blocker, Jane, *What the Body Cost: Desire, History, and Performance* (Minneapolis, MN; London: University of Minnesota Press, 2004).

Blümlinger, Christa, 'Procession and Projection: Notes on a Figure in the Work of Jean-Luc Godard', in Michael Temple, James S. Williams and Michael Witt (eds), *For Ever Godard* (London: Black Dog, 2004), pp. 178–87.

—— *Cinéma de seconde main: esthétique de remploi dans l'art du film et des nouveaux médias* (Paris: Klincksieck, [2009] 2013).

Bonitzer, Pascal, 'La Surimage', *Cahiers du cinéma*, 270 (1976), 29–34.

Boyd, William, *Sweet Caress* (London, New York: Bloomsbury, 2015).

Brink, Cornelia, 'Secular Icons: Looking at Photographs from the Nazi Concentration Camps', *History and Memory*, 12: 1 (2000), 135–50.

Browne, Malcolm, *The New Face of War: A Report on a Communist Guerrilla Campaign* (London: Cassell, 1965).

Buck-Morss, Susan, 'Visual Empire', *diacritics*, 37: 2–3 (2007), 171–98.

Burton, Julianne, 'Part I. Revolutionary Cuban Cinema', *Jump Cut*, 19 (December 1978), 17–20, https://www.ejumpcut.org/archive/onlinessays/JC19folder/CubanFilmIntro.html (last accessed 15 January 2019).

Calvino, Italo, 'A Novel Inside a Painting', *Collection of Sand: Essays*, trans. Martin McLaughlin (London: Penguin, [1983] 2013), pp. 51–8.

Cambre, Maria-Carolina, *The Semiotics of Che Guevara: Affective Gateways* (London: Bloomsbury, 2015).

Campany, David (ed.), *The Cinematic (Documents of Contemporary Arts)* (London: Whitechapel, 2007).

Campany, David, *Photography and Cinema* (London: Reaktion, 2008).

Campbell, Neil and Alfredo Cramerotti (eds), *Photocinema: The Creative Edges of Photography and Film* (Bristol: Intellect, 2013).

Capa, Robert and Gerda Taro, *Death in the Making* (New York: Covici-Friede, 1938).

Capa, Robert, *Images of War* (London: Paul Hamlyn, 1964).

—— *Slightly Out of Focus* (New York: Henry Holt & Co., 1947).

Carter, Erica, 'Introduction', in Carter (ed.), *Béla Balázs: Early Film Theory: Visible Man and the Spirit of Film*, trans. Rodney Livingstone (New York: Berghahn, 2011), pp. xv–xlvi.

Carter, J. Kameron, *Race: A Theological Account* (Oxford: Oxford University Press, 2008).

Cartier-Bresson, Henri, foreword to *The Decisive Moment* (Göttingen: Steidl, 2014).

Cavell, Stanley, 'The Fact of Television', in William Rothman (ed.), *Cavell on Film* (New York: State University of New York Press, [1982] 2005), pp. 59–85.

Chanan, Michael (ed.), *Santiago Álvarez*, BFI Dossier no. 2 (London: British Film Institute, 1980).

Chanan, Michael, *Cuban Cinema* (Minneapolis, MN: University of Minnesota Press, 2004).

Chéroux, Clément, *Diplopie. L'Image photographique à l'ère des médias globalisés: essai sur le 11 septembre 2001* (Cherbourg: Le Point du jour, 2009).

Cojean, Annick, 'La Marianne de mai 1968: retour sur images', *Le Monde*, 21 August 1997, p. 8.

Convert, Pascal, 'Médée l'algérienne', *Art Press*, 286 (January 2003), 19–22.

—— 'Images passages', http://www.pascalconvert.fr/histoire/lamento/lamento.html (last accessed 1 April 2020), revised version of an article in *Art Press*, 'Images et religions du livre', 25 (2004), 90–5.

Cooper, Sarah, *Chris Marker* (Manchester: Manchester University Press, 2008).

Correll, Barbara, 'Rem(a)inders of G(l)ory: Monuments and Bodies in "Glory" and "In the Year of the Pig"', *Cultural Critique*, 19 (Autumn 1991), 141–77.

Cortade, Ludovic, *Le Cinéma de l'immobilité* (Paris: Publications de la Sorbonne, 2008).

Critchley, Simon, 'Introduction', in Critchley and Robert Bernasconi (eds), *The Cambridge Companion to Levinas* (Cambridge: Cambridge University Press, 2002), pp. 1–32.

Daney, Serge, 'La dernière image', in Raymond Bellour, Catherine David and Christine Van Assche (eds), *Passages de l'image* (Paris: Éditions du Centre Pompidou, 1990), pp. 57–60.

De Antonio, Emile, interview by Bernard Eisenschitz and Jean Narboni, *Cahiers du cinéma*, 214 (July/August 1969), 43–56.

De Baecque, Antoine, *Les Cahiers du cinéma: histoire d'une revue, Volume II, Cinéma, tours détours 1959–1981* (Paris: Cahiers du cinéma, 1991).

De Bendern, Caroline, 'Caroline de Bendern Remembers . . .', extract from unpublished memoir [1998] in Sally Shafto, *Zanzibar: Les films Zanzibar et les dandys de mai 1968* (Paris: Éditions Paris Expérimental, 2007), pp. 211–15.

De Roux, François, 'Le Retour', *France Illustration*, 3 (20 October 1945), 69–70.

De Saint-Exupéry, Antoine, 'Sergent, pourquoi acceptes-tu de mourir?', *Paris-soir*, 5.115 (28 June 1937), 1, 5.

Debray, Régis, 'La belle mort', in *L'Œil naïf* (Paris: Seuil, 1994), pp. 146–53.

Deleuze, Gilles, 'Trois questions sur *Six fois deux*', *Cahiers du cinéma*, 271 (1976), 5–12.

—— *Cinema 1: The Movement Image*, trans. Hugh Tomlinson and Barbara Habberjam (London: Athlone Press, [1983] 1986).

Delluc, Louis, 'The Crowd' [1918], trans. Richard Abel in Abel (ed.), *French Film Theory and Criticism: A History/Anthology, 1907–1939*, vol. 1, 1907–1929 (Princeton, NJ: Princeton University Press, 1988), pp. 159–64.

—— *Photogénie* (Paris: Brunoff, 1920).

Denby, David, 'Boys at War', *New York* (31 August 1981), p. 52.

Denoyelle, Françoise, 'De l'errance à l'épopée lyrique: naissance d'un mythe', in Beaumont-Maillet, Laure (ed.), *Capa connu et inconnu* (Paris: Bibliothèque Nationale de France, 2004), pp. 49–65.

Didi-Huberman, Georges, *Images in Spite of All: Four Photographs From Auschwitz*, trans. Shane B. Lillis (Chicago, London: University of Chicago Press, [2003] 2012).

—— *The Surviving Image. Phantoms of Time and Time of Phantoms: Aby Warburg's History of Art*, trans. Harvey Mendelsohn (University Park, PA: Penn State University Press, [2002] 2016).

—— 'Conflicts of Gesture, Conflicts of Images', *The Nordic Journal of Aesthetics*, 55–6 (2018), 8–22.

—— *Ninfa dolorosa: essai sur la mémoire d'un geste* (Paris: Gallimard, 2019).

Doane, Mary Ann, 'The Close-Up: Scale and Detail in the Cinema', *differences: A Journal of Feminist Cultural Studies*, 14: 3 (Fall 2003), 89–111.

Donaldson, Day Blakely (ed.), *The Self-Immolators* (2013), http://thespeaker.co/wp-content/uploads/2013/06/The-Self-Immolators.pdf (last accessed 10 July 2018).

Dubois, Philippe, '*La Jetée* ou le cinématogramme de la conscience', in Dubois (ed.), *Recherches sur Chris Marker, Théorème 6* (Paris: Presses Sorbonne Nouvelle: 2002), pp. 8–45.

Dyer, Richard, *Heavenly Bodies: Film Stars and Society* (Basingstoke: Macmillan, 1987).

Eco, Umberto, 'Critique of the Image' (1970), in Burgin, Victor (ed.), *Thinking Photography*, (London, Basingstoke: Macmillan, 1982), pp. 32–8.

Fahlenbrach, Kathrin, 'Images and Imagery of Protest', in Fahlenbrach, Martin Klimke and Joachim Scharloth (eds), *Protest Cultures: A Companion* (New York: Berghahn, 2016), pp. 243–58.

Farinotti, Luisella, Barbara Grespi and Barbara Le Maître (eds), 'Overlapping Images: Between Cinema and Photography', *Cinéma&cie*, xv: 25 (Fall 2015).

ffrench, Patrick, 'The Memory of the Image in Chris Marker's *La Jetée*', *French Studies*, 59: 1 (2005), 31–7.

Fierke, Karin M., *Political Self-Sacrifice: Agency, Body and Emotion in International Relations* (Cambridge, New York: Cambridge University Press, 2013).

Fleetwood, Nicole R., *On Racial Icons: Blackness and the Public Imagination* (New Brunswick, New Jersey, London: Rutgers University Press, 2015).

Fontcuberta, Joan, 'Archive Noise', artist's statement, www.fontcuberta.com (last accessed 2 August 2018).

Fortes, Susana, *Waiting for Robert Capa*, trans. Adriana V. López (London: HarperPress, 2012).

Foster, Hal, 'Test Subjects', *October*, 132 (Spring 2010), 30–42.

Franklin, H. Bruce, *Vietnam and Other American Fantasies* (Amherst, MA: University of Massachusetts Press, 2000).

Freund, Gisèle, *Photographie et société* (Paris: Points, [1974] 2017).

Frizot, Michel and Cedric de Veigy, *Vu: The Story of a Magazine*, trans. Ruth Sharman (London: Thames and Hudson, 2009).

Frizot, Michel, 'D'imprévisibles regards: les géométries subjectives d'Henri Cartier-Bresson', *L'Homme photographique* (Paris: Hazan, 2018), pp. 393–423.

Gaignault, Fabrice, *Les Egéries sixties* (Paris: Fayard, 2006).

Garanger, Marc, *Femmes algériennes 1960* (Paris: Contrejour, 1982).

Gervais, Thierry, '"The Little Paper Cinema": The Transformations of Illustration in *Belle Époque* Periodicals', in Laurent Guido and Olivier Lugon (eds), *Between Still and Moving Images* (Eastleigh: John Libbey, 2012), pp. 147–64.

—— 'Introduction', in Gervais (ed.), *The 'Public' Lives of Photographs* (Toronto: Ryerson Image Centre, 2016), pp. 1–13.

Ghosh, Bishnupriya, *Global Icons: Apertures to the Popular* (Durham, NC: Duke University Press, 2011).

Goldberg, Vicki, *The Power of Photography: How Photographs Changed Our Lives* (New York, NY: Abbeville Press, 1991).

Gorrara, Claire, 'Fashion and the *Femmes Tondues*: Lee Miller, *Vogue* and Representing Liberation France', *French Cultural Studies*, 29: 4 (2018), 330–44.

Gough, Kathleen M., 'Between the Image and Anthropology: Theatrical Lessons from Aby Warburg's "Nympha"', *The Drama Review*, 56: 3 (2012), 114–130.

Guevara, Ernesto, 'Socialism and Man in Cuba' [1965], in David Deutschmann (ed.), *Che Guevara Reader* (Melbourne: Ocean Press, 2003), pp. 212–28.

Grüner, Eduardo, 'A Question of *Details*, Che', trans. David Jacobson, in Leandro Katz et al., *The Ghosts of Ñancahuazú* (Buenos Aires: Viper's Tongue Books, 2010), pp. 195–202.

Guido, Laurent and Olivier Lugon, 'Introduction', in Guido and Lugon (eds), *Between Still and Moving Images* (Eastleigh: John Libbey, 2012), pp. 1–5.

Gunning, Tom, 'The "Arrested" Instant: Between Stillness and Motion', in Laurent Guido and Olivier Lugon (eds), *Between Still and Moving Images* (Eastleigh: John Libbey, 2012), pp. 23–31.

Gunthert, André, 'Les icônes du photojournalisme: de l'information à la pop culture', in Audrey Leblanc and Dominique Versavel (eds), *Les Icônes de mai 68: les images ont une histoire* (Bibliothèque Nationale de France, 2018), pp. 19–31.

Hägele, Ulrich, 'War is Over! Pour une iconographie des fins de guerres', *Revue des Sciences Sociales*, 'Nouvelles figures de la guerre', 35 (2006), 62–75.

Hagopian, Patrick, 'Vietnam War Photography as a Locus of Memory', in Annette Kuhn and Kirsten Emiko McAllister (eds), *Locating Memory: Photographic Acts* (New York, Oxford: Berghahn, 2006), pp. 201–22.

Halverson, Jeffry R., Scott W. Ruston and Angela Trethewey, 'Mediated Martyrs of the Arab Spring: New Media, Civil Religion, and Narrative in Tunisia and Egypt', *Journal of Communication*, 63 (2013), 312–32.

Hanrot, Juliette, *La Madone de Bentalha: histoire d'une photographie* (Paris: Armand Colin, 2012).

Hariman, Robert and John Louis Lucaites, *No Caption Needed: Iconic Photographs, Public Culture and Liberal Democracy* (Chicago, London: University of Chicago Press, 2007).

Heartfield, John, 'La Liberté conduit le people d'Espagne', *Regards*, 141 (24 September 1936), 11.

Henri Cartier-Bresson: Scrapbook. Photographies 1932–1946 (Steidl: Göttingen, 2006).

Hicks, Jeremy, Libby Saxton and Guy Westwell, 'Rising Flags, Falling Soldiers: Film, Icons and Political Violence', *Screen*, 57: 3 (2016), 336–70.

Jacobs, Steven, 'The History and Aesthetics of the Classical Film Still', *History of Photography*, 34: 4 (2010), 373–86.

Jacques, Vincent, 'Images floues, frontières troubles: la pratique photographique de Chris Marker', in Vincent Jacques (ed.), *Chris.Marker.Photographie* (Ivry-sur-Seine: Créaphis Éditions, 2018), pp. 85–105.

Jeong, Seung-hoon, *Cinematic Interfaces: Film Theory after New Media* (New York: Routledge, 2013).

Johnson, Christopher, *Metaphor, Memory and Aby Warburg's Atlas of Images* (Ithaca, NY: Cornell University Press, 2012).

Kemp, Anna, 'Marianne d'aujourd'hui?: The Figure of the *Beurette* in Contemporary French Feminist Discourses', *Modern & Contemporary France*, 17: 1 (2009), 19–33.

Kemp, Martin, 'Che', *Christ to Coke: How Image Becomes Icon* (Oxford, New York: Oxford University Press, 2012), pp. 167–96.

Kin Gagnon, Monika, 'The Christian Pavilion at Expo 67: Notes from Charles Gagnon's Archive', in Rhona Richman Kenneally and Johanne Sloan (eds), *Expo 67: Not Just a Souvenir* (Toronto: University of Toronto Press, 2010), pp. 143–60.

Kirstein, Lincoln, 'Henri Cartier-Bresson: Documentary Humanist', in *The Photographs of Henri Cartier-Bresson* (New York: The Museum of Modern Art, 1947), pp. 7–11.

—— 'Artist With a Camera', *New York Times*, 2 February 1947, 12.

Kracauer, Siegfried, *Theory of Film: The Redemption of Physical Reality* (New York: Oxford University Press, 1960).

Krauss, Rosalind, '". . . And Then Turn Away?": An Essay on James Coleman', *October*, 81 (Summer 1997), 5–33.

Kuhn, Annette and Guy Westwell, *Oxford Dictionary of Film Studies* (Oxford: Oxford University Press, 2012).

Latour, Bruno and Peter Weibel (eds), *Iconoclash: Beyond the Image Wars in Science, Religion and Art* (London: MIT Press, 2002).

Lavoie, Vincent, *L'Affaire Capa: le procès d'une icône* (Paris: Textuel, 2017).

Layerle, Sébastien, *Caméras en lutte en mai 68: 'par ailleurs le cinéma est une arme'* (Paris: Nouveau monde, 2008).

Leblanc, Audrey, 'De la photographie d'actualité à l'icône médiatique: "La jeune fille au drapeau" devient "la Marianne de 68"', https://clinoeil.hypotheses.org/448 (last accessed 1 September 2019).

Lebrun, Bernard and Michel Lefebvre, *Robert Capa: The Paris Years 1933–1954*, trans. Nicholas Elliot (New York: Abrams, 2012).

Leenaerts, Danielle, *Petite histoire du magazine 'Vu' (1928–1940): entre photographie d'information et photographie d'art* (Brussels, New York: Peter Lang, 2010).

Lessing, Gotthold Ephraim, *Laocoon: An Essay on the Limits of Painting and Poetry*, trans. E. C. Beasley (London: Rugby printed, 1853).

Levinas, Emmanuel, *Totality and Infinity: An Essay on Exteriority*, trans. Alphonso Lingis (Pittsburgh, PA: Duquesne University Press, [1961] 1969).

Lindeperg, Sylvie, *Les Écrans de l'ombre: la seconde guerre mondiale dans le cinéma français* (Paris: CNRS, 1997).

—— 'Fabrication et destin d'une icône', in *La Voie des images: quatre histoires de tournage au printemps-été 1944* (Paris: Verdier, 2013), pp. 83–93.

Liveley, Genevieve, 'Orpheus and Eurydice', in Vanda Zajko and Helena Hoyle (eds), *A Handbook to the Reception of Classical Mythology* (Malden, MA: Wiley Blackwell, 2017), pp. 287–98.

Lucie-Smith, Edward, *A Concise History of French Painting* (London: Thames & Hudson, 1971).

Lupton, Catherine, *Chris Marker: Memories of the Future* (London: Reaktion, 2005).

Marchant, Linda, 'Still Famous: Fixing the Star Image of Diana Dors in the Photography of Cornel Lucas', in Lucy Bolton and Julie Lobalzo Wright (eds), *Lasting Screen Stars: Images that Fade and Personas that Endure* (Palgrave Macmillan, 2016), pp. 261–76.

Maynard, Patrick, 'The Secular Icon: Photography and the Functions of Images', *The Journal of Aesthetics and Art Criticism*, 42: 2 (Winter 1983), 155–69.

Mestman, Mariano, 'The Last Sacred Image of the Latin American Revolution', *Journal of Latin American Cultural Studies*, 19: 1 (2010), 23–44.

Metz, Christian, 'Photography and Fetish', *October*, 34 (1985), 81–90.

Michaels, Lloyd, 'Bergman and the Necessary Illusion: An Introduction to *Persona*', in Michaels (ed.), *Ingmar Bergman's 'Persona'* (Cambridge: Cambridge University Press, 2000), pp. 1–23.

Michaud, Philippe-Alain, *Aby Warburg and the Image in Motion*, trans. Sophie Hawkes (New York: Zone Books, 2007).

Miedema, Gary, *For Canada's Sake: Public Religion, Centennial Celebrations, and the Re-making of Canada in the 1960s* (Montreal, Kingston: McGill-Queen University Press, 2006).

Mieszkowski, Jan, *Watching War* (Stanford, CA: Stanford University Press, 2012).

Mitchell, W. J. T., *Iconology: Image, Text, Ideology* (Chicago, London: University of Chicago Press, 1986).

—— 'Image, Space, Revolution: The Arts of Occupation', *Critical Inquiry*, 39 (Autumn 2012), 8–32.

Mondzain, Marie-José, *Image, Icon, Economy: The Byzantine Origins of the Contemporary Imaginary*, trans. Rico Franses (Stanford, CA; Stanford University Press, [1996] 2005).

—— *Homo spectator* (Paris: Bayard, 2007).

Moore, Alison M., 'History, Memory and Trauma in Photography of the *Tondues*: Visuality of the Vichy Past Through the Silent Image of Women', *Gender and History*, 17: 3 (2005), 657–81.

Morvan, Jean-David, Séverine Tréfouël and Sylvain Savoia, *Cartier-Bresson, Allemagne 1945* (Charleroi: Dupuis, 2016).

Moss, Georg Donelson, *Vietnam: An American Ordeal* (Englewood Cliffs, NJ: Prentice Hall, 1990).

Mulvey, Laura, 'Visual Pleasure and Narrative Cinema', *Screen*, 16: 3 (Autumn 1975), 6–18.

—— *Death 24x a Second: Stillness and the Moving Image* (London: Reaktion, 2006).

Nicéphore, *Discours contre les iconoclastes*, translated, presented and with notes by Marie-José Mondzain (Paris: Klincksieck, 1990).

Nikephoros, 'Extracts from the *Antirrhetics*', trans. Vassiliki Dimitropoulou, in Marie-José Mondzain, *Image, Icon, Economy: The Byzantine Origins of the Contemporary Imaginary*, trans. Rico Franses (Stanford, CA; Stanford University Press, [1996] 2005), pp. 233–45.

Ohlin, Peter, 'The Holocaust in Ingmar Bergman's *Persona*: The Instability of Imagery', *Scandinavian Studies*, 77: 2 (Summer 2005), 241–74.

Peirce, Charles Sanders, 'On the Algebra of Logic: A Contribution to the Philosophy of Notation' [1885], in Nathan Houser and Christian Kloesel (eds), *The Essential Peirce: Selected Philosophical Writings*, vol. 1 (1867–93) (Bloomington: Indiana University Press, 1992), pp. 225–8.

Perlmutter, David D., *Photojournalism and Foreign Policy: Icons of Outrage in International Crises* (Westport, CT; London: Praeger, 1998).

The Photographs of Henri Cartier-Bresson (New York: The Museum of Modern Art, 1947).

Pick, Zuzana M., 'Cinéastes de l'Unité Populaire: où en-êtes vous?', *NS, NorthSouth*, 4: 8 (1979), pp. 136–71.

Pollock, Griselda and Max Silverman, 'Introduction', in Pollock and Silverman (eds), *Concentrationary Cinema: Aesthetics as Political Resistance in Alain Resnais's 'Night and Fog'* (New York, Oxford: Berghahn, 2011), pp. 1–54 (pp. 8–13).

Prestholdt, Jeremy, *Icons of Dissent: The Global Resonance of Che, Marley, Tupac and Bin Laden* (London: C. Hurst & Co., 2019).

Raskin, Richard, *A Child at Gunpoint: A Case Study in the Life of a Photo* (Aarhus: Aarhus University Press, 2004).

Reader, Keith with Khursheed Wadia, *The May 1968 Events in France: Reproductions and Interpretations* (Basingstoke: Macmillan, 1993).

Reynolds, Siân, 'Camera Culture and Gender in Paris in the 1930s: Stills and Movies', *Nottingham French Studies*, 31: 2 (1992), 39–51.

Rook, Penelope, 'Fashion Photography and Photojournalism: Posing the Body in *Vu*', *Fashion Theory*, 'Posing the Body', 21: 2 (2017), 131–56.

Røssaak, Eivind, 'The Still/Moving Field: An Introduction', in Eivind Røssaak (ed.), *Between Stillness and Motion: Film, Photography, Algorithms* (Amsterdam: Amsterdam University Press, 2011), pp. 11–24.

—— 'Algorithmic Culture: Beyond the Photo/Film Divide', in Røssaak (ed.), *Between Stillness and Motion: Film, Photography, Algorithms* (Amsterdam: Amsterdam University Press, 2011), pp. 187–203.

Roth, Philip, *American Pastoral* (London: Jonathan Cape, 1997).

Rouch, Abigail Frymann, 'Caroline de Bendern: "Leave Campaign Was Lies and Xenophobia"', *The Guardian*, 20 March 2017, https://www.theguardian.com/world/2017/mar/20/caroline-de-bendern-paris-1968-brexit-xenophobia (last accessed 1 August 2019).

Rousseau, Frédéric, *L'Enfant juif de Varsovie: histoire d'une photographie* (Paris: Seuil, 2009).

Russell, Catherine, 'Archival Apocalypse: Found Footage as Ethnography', in *Experimental Ethnography: The Work of Film in the Age of Video* (Durham, NC; London: Duke University Press, 1999), pp. 238–72.

Rust, Amy, 'Hitting the "Vérité Jackpot": The Ecstatic Profits of Freeze-Framed Violence', *Cinema Journal*, 50: 4 (Summer 2011), 48–72.

Salomon, Kim, 'The Anti-Vietnam War Movement in Sweden', in Christopher Goscha and Maurice Vaïsse (eds), *La Guerre du Vietnam et l'Europe, 1963–1973* (Brussels: Bruylant, 2003), pp. 327–38.

Schaeffer, Jean-Marie, *L'Image précaire du dispositif photographique* (Paris: Seuil, 1987).

Schoenberner, Gerhard, *The Yellow Star*, trans. Susan Sweet (London: Corgi, 1969).

Schultz, Edmund (ed.), *Die veränderte Welt. Eine Bilderfibel unserer Zeit*, introduction by Ernst Jünger (Breslau: Wilh. Gottl. Korn, 1933).

Sealy, Mark, 'Human Rights, Human Wrongs', http://www.thephotographersgallery.org.uk/images/Mark_Sealy_HRHW_essay_54d4be1c76ea8.pdf (last accessed 4 July 2016).

Shafto, Sally, *Zanzibar: Les films Zanzibar et les dandys de mai 1968* (Paris: Éditions Paris Expérimental, 2007).

Silverman, Kaja, *The Acoustic Mirror: The Female Voice in Psychoanalysis and Cinema* (Bloomington: Indiana University Press, 1988).

—— *The Miracle of Analogy, or the History of Photography, Part 1* (Stanford, CA: Stanford University Press, 2015).

Skow, Lisa M. and George N. Dionisopoulos, 'A Struggle to Contextualize Photographic Images: American Print Media and the "Burning Monk"', *Communication Quarterly*, 45: 4 (1997), 393–409.

Sliwinski, Sharon, 'Air War and Dream: Photographing the London Blitz', *American Imago*, 68: 3 (Fall 2011), 489–516.

Sobchack, Vivian, 'The Violent Dance: A Personal Memoir of Death in the Movies', *Journal of Popular Film*, 3: 1 (Winter 1974), 2–14.

Solanas, Fernando and Octavio Getino, 'Toward a Third Cinema', *Cinéaste*, 4: 3 (1970–1), 1–10.

Sontag, Susan, *Styles of Radical Will* (London: Secker & Warburg, 1969).

—— 'Photography', *The New York Review of Books*, 20: 16 (18 October 1973), 59–63.

—— *Regarding the Pain of Others* (London: Penguin, 2003).

Stallabrass, Julian, 'Memory and Icons: Photography in the War on Terror', *New Left Review*, 105: 1 (May–June 2017), 29–50.

Steve McCurry: The Iconic Photographs (London: Phaidon Press, 2012).

Stewart, Garrett, *Between Film and Screen: Modernism's Photo Synthesis* (Chicago, London: University of Chicago Press, 1999).

Sturken, Marita, *Tangled Memories: The Vietnam War, the AIDS Epidemic and the Politics of Remembering* (Berkeley, London: University of California Press, 1997).

Sutton, Damian, *Photography, Cinema, Memory: The Crystal Image of Time* (Minneapolis, MN; London: University of Minnesota Press, 2009).

De Thézy, Marie, *La Photographie humaniste, 1930–1960: histoire d'un mouvement en France* (Paris: Contrejour, 1992).

Tierney, Matt, *Dismantlings: Words Against Machines in the American Long Seventies* (Ithaca, London: Cornell University Press, 2019).

Tobing Rony, Fatimah, *The Third Eye: Race, Cinema and the Ethnographic Spectacle* (Durham, NC; London: Duke University Press, 1996).

Tode, Thomas, 'Une larme sur la joue du temps: *Le Retour* d'Henri Cartier-Bresson', trans. Clara Bloch, *1895*, 74 (2014), 12–37.

—— 'Henri- Cartier-Bresson: la liberté, le mouvement et l'instant', trans. Clara Bloch, in Jean-David Morvan, Séverine Tréfouël and Sylvain Savoia, *Cartier-Bresson, Allemagne 1945* (Charleroi: Dupuis, 2016), pp. 119–41.

Toubiana, Serge, et al., *L'Image d'après: le cinéma dans l'imaginaire de la photographie* (Göttingen: Steidl, Paris: Cinémathèque française, 2007).

Vestberg, Nina Lager, 'Robert Doisneau and the Making of a Universal Cliché', *History of Photography*, 35: 2 (2011), 157–65.

Vidal, Belén, *Figuring the Past: Period Film and the Mannerist Aesthetic* (Amsterdam: Amsterdam University Press, 2012).

Wadia, Khursheed, 'Women and the Events of May 1968', in Keith Reader with Khursheed Wadia, *The May 1968 Events in France: Reproductions and Interpretations* (Basingstoke: Macmillan, 1993), pp. 148–66.

Wagenaar, Aad, *Settela*, trans. Janna Eliot (Nottingham: Five Leaves, 2005).

Wall, Jeff, 'Photography and Liquid Intelligence' [1989], in *Jeff Wall: Selected Essays and Interviews* (New York: Museum of Modern Art, 2007), pp. 109–10.

Warburg, Aby, 'Dürer and Italian Antiquity', in *The Renewal of Pagan Antiquity: Contributions to the Cultural History of the European Renaissance*, trans. David Britt (Los Angeles, CA: Getty Research Institute for the History of Art and the Humanities, [1932] 1999), pp. 553–8.

Webster, Frank, *The New Photography: Responsibility in Visual Communication* (London: John Calder, 1980).

Weingart, Brigitte, '"That Screen Magnetism": Warhol's Glamour', *October*, 132 (Spring 2010), 43–70.

Westwell, Guy, 'One Image Begets Another: A Comparative Analysis of Flag-Raising on Iwo Jima and Ground Zero Spirit', *Journal of War and Culture Studies*, 1: 3 (2008), 325–40.

—— 'Accidental Napalm Attack and Hegemonic Visions of America's War in Vietnam', *Critical Studies in Media Communication*, xxviii: v (2011), 407–23.

—— *War Cinema: Hollywood on the Front Line* (London: Wallflower, 2006).

Whelan, Richard, *This Is War! Robert Capa at Work* (New York/Göttingen: International Center of Photography/Steidl, 2007).

Williams, Rowan, *Lost Icons: Reflections on Cultural Bereavement* (London, New York: T&T Clark/Continuum, 2000).

Wilson, Emma, 'Material Remains: *Night and Fog*', *October*, 112 (2005), 89–110.

Wilson, Kristi M., '*Ecce Homo Novus*: Snapshots, the "New Man" and Iconic Montage in the Work of Santiago Alvarez', in *Social Identities: Journal for the Study of Race, Nation and Culture*, 19: 3–4 (2013), 410–22.

Witt, Michael, 'On and Under Communication', in Tom Conley and T. Jefferson Kline (eds), *A Companion to Jean-Luc Godard* (Chichester; Malden, MA: Wiley-Blackwell, 2014), pp. 318–50.

Woldt, Isabella, 'Ur-Words of the Affective Language of Gestures: The Hermeneutics of Body Movement in Aby Warburg', *Interfaces: Image, Texte, Language*, 40 (2018), https://preo.u-bourgogne.fr/interfaces/index.php?id=605 (last accessed 5 August 2019).

Wollaston, Isabel, 'The Absent, the Partial and the Iconic in Archival Photographs of the Holocaust', *Jewish Culture and History*, 12: 3 (Winter 2010), 439–62.

Wollen, Peter, *Signs and Meaning in the Cinema* (Bloomington: Indiana University Press [1969] 1972).

—— 'Fire and Ice' [1984], in David Campany (ed.), *The Cinematic (Documents of Contemporary Arts)* (London: Whitechapel, 2007), pp. 108–13.

Wurmser, André, 'Lettre ouverte à Pyrrhus non-interventionniste', *Regards*, 183 (14 July 1937), 21.

Yang, Michelle Murray, 'Still Burning: Self-Immolation as Photographic Protest', *Quarterly Journal of Speech*, 97: 1 (2011), 1–25.

Zarzycka, Marta, *Gendered Tropes in War Photography: Mothers, Mourners, Soldiers* (London: Routledge, 2016).

Zelizer, Barbie, *About to Die: How News Images Move the Public* (New York: Oxford University Press, 2010).

NEWSPAPER AND MAGAZINE ARTICLES AND PAMPHLETS WITHOUT AUTHORIAL ATTRIBUTION

'A Great War Reporter and His Last Battle', *Life*, 36: 23 (7 June 1954), 27–33 (29).

'Ciné-tractez!' (guide pour réaliser un ciné-tract, 1968), reproduced in Bellour, Raymond, Jean-Michel Frodon and Christine Van Assche (eds), *Chris Marker* (Paris: Cinémathèque française, 2018), pp. 274–5.

'Death in Spain', *Life*, 3: 2 (12 July 1937), 19–25.

'Impact of Uprisings', *Life*, 64: 21 (24 May 1968), 28–31.

'La Guerre Civile en Espagne', *Vu*, 445 (23 September 1936), 1106–8.

'Revolution', *Life*, 67: 15 (10 October 1969), 100–12.

'The Year in Pictures', *Life*, 73: 25 (29 December 1972), 54.

Paris Match (15–21 June 1968), 60–1.

Paris Match (22–9 June 1968), 110–11.

Time, xxviii: 14 (5 Oct 1936), 20.

Filmography

Aufschub (Harun Farocki; *Respite*, 2007)
Battleship Potemkin (Sergei Eisenstein, 1925)
Bike Boy (Andy Warhol, 1967)
Bonnie and Clyde (Arthur Penn, 1967)
Butch Cassidy and the Sundance Kid (George Roy Hill, 1969)
Chelsea Girls (Andy Warhol, 1966)
Ciné-tracts (anonymous, 1968)
Day of Wrath (Carl Theodor Dreyer, 1943)
Détruisez-vous (*Destroy Yourselves*; Serge Bard, 1968)
El día que me quieras (*The Day You'll Love Me*; Leandro Katz, 1997)
En homage à Nicéphore Niépce (*In Homage to Nicéphore Niépce*, Pathé 'Magazine', 1966)
Entranced Earth (Glauber Rocha, 1967)
The Exorcist (William Friedkin, 1973)
Un film porno (Olivier Mosset, 1968)
Una foto recorre el mundo (*A Photo Travels Around the World*; Pedro Chaskel, 1981)
Fun and Games for Everyone (Serge Bard, 1968)
Fury (Fritz Lang, 1936)
Le Gai Savoir (*Joy of Learning*; Jean-Luc Godard, 1969)
Gallipoli (Peter Weir, 1981)
Gentlemen Prefer Blondes (Howard Hawks, 1953)
The Haunting (Robert Wise, 1963)
Histoire(s) du cinéma (Jean-Luc Godard, 1988–98)
La hora de los hornos (*The Hour of the Furnaces*; Fernando Solanas and Octavio Getino, 1968)
Le Huitième Jour (*The Eighth Day*; Charles Gagnon, 1967)
Ici et maintenant (Serge Bard, 1968)
In the Year of the Pig (Emile de Antonio, 1968)
La Jetée (*The Pier*; Chris Marker, 1962)
LBJ (Santiago Álvarez, 1968)
Level Five (Chris Marker, 1995)
Loin de Vietnam (*Far from Vietnam*; anthology film, 1967)
Man With a Movie Camera (Dziga Vertov, 1929)
Mondo Cane 2 (Gualtiero Jacopetti and Francesco Prosperi, 1963)
Mother (Vsevolod Pudovkin, 1926)
Niagara (Henry Hathaway, 1953)
Night of the Living Dead (George A. Romero, 1968)
Now! (Santiago Álvarez, 1965)
The Nude Restaurant (Andy Warhol, 1967)
Nuit et brouillard (*Night and Fog*; Alain Resnais, 1956)

Outer and Inner Space (Andy Warhol, 1965)
Overlord (Stuart Cooper, 1975)
Persona (Ingmar Bergman, 1966)
Photographie et société: d'après Gisèle Freund (*Photography and Society: According to Gisèle Freund*; Teri Wehn-Damisch, 1983)
Platoon (Oliver Stone, 1986)
Poor Little Rich Girl (Andy Warhol, 1965)
Professione: reporter (*The Passenger*; Michelangelo Antonioni, 1975)
Queen Christina (Rouben Mamoulian, 1933)
La Rabbia (*Anger*; Pier Paolo Pasolini, 1963)
Le Retour (*The Return*; Henri Cartier-Bresson, 1945)
Robert Capa: In Love and War (Anne Makepeace, 2003)
Les quatre cents coups (*The 400 Blows*; François Truffaut, 1959)
The Seventh Seal (Ingmar Bergman, 1957)
Six fois deux (Sur et sous la communication) (*Six Times Two [On and Under Communication]*), episode 3a, *Photos et cie* (*Photos and Co*) (Jean-Luc Godard and Anne-Marie Miéville, 1976)
The Spanish Earth (Joris Ivens, 1937)
A Test of Violence (Stuart Cooper, 1969)
Tropic Thunder (Ben Stiller, 2008)
Verdun, visions d'histoire (*Verdun, Visions of History*; Léon Poirier, 1928)
Victoire de la vie (*Return to Life*; Henri Cartier-Bresson, 1938)
The Vietnam War (Ken Burns and Lynn Novick, 2017)

CINEMA NEWSREELS

'Barricades élevées par les étudiants. Gaz lacrymogène. CRS en action', Gaumont Journal Actualité (15 May 1968)
'Homage to Che' (6 November 1967), *Noticieros: les actualités cubaines 1960–1970* (INA, 2017)
'Homme des tempêtes', Pathé Journal Actualité (5 June 1968)
'La France face à son drame', Pathé Journal Actualité (29 May 1968)
'Problèmes au Vietnam', Pathé Journal Actualité (1963)
'Publication in Cuba of Che's Diary' (5 July 1968), *Noticieros: les actualités cubaines 1960–1970* (INA, 2017)
'Suicide d'un bonze à Saigon', Pathé Journal Actualité (1963)

Printed and bound by CPI Group (UK) Ltd, Croydon, CR0 4YY

18/03/2025

01834131-0001

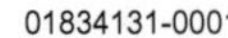